Palgrave European Film and Media Studies

Series Editors
Ib Bondebjerg
University of Copenhagen
Copenhagen, Denmark

Andrew Higson
University of York
York, UK

Mette Hjort
Hong Kong Baptist University
Hong Kong, Hong Kong

Palgrave European Film and Media Studies is dedicated to historical and contemporary studies of film and media in a European context and to the study of the role of film and media in European societies and cultures. The series invite research done in both humanities and social sciences and invite scholars working with the role of film and other media in relation to the development of a European society, culture and identity. Books in the series can deal with both media content and media genres, with national and transnational aspects of film and media policy, with the sociology of media as institutions and with audiences and reception, and the impact of film and media on everyday life, culture and society. The series encourage books working with European integration or themes cutting across nation states in Europe and books working with Europe in a more global perspective. The series especially invite publications with a comparative, European perspective based on research outside a traditional nation state perspective. In an era of increased European integration and globalization there is a need to move away from the single nation study focus and the single discipline study of Europe.

More information about this series at
http://www.palgrave.com/gp/series/14704

James Harvey
Editor

Nationalism in Contemporary Western European Cinema

palgrave
macmillan

Editor
James Harvey
Independent Scholar
London, UK

Palgrave European Film and Media Studies
ISBN 978-3-319-73666-2   ISBN 978-3-319-73667-9   (eBook)
https://doi.org/10.1007/978-3-319-73667-9

Library of Congress Control Number: 2018942558

© The Editor(s) (if applicable) and The Author(s) 2018
This work is subject to copyright. All rights are solely and exclusively licensed by the Publisher, whether the whole or part of the material is concerned, specifically the rights of translation, reprinting, reuse of illustrations, recitation, broadcasting, reproduction on microfilms or in any other physical way, and transmission or information storage and retrieval, electronic adaptation, computer software, or by similar or dissimilar methodology now known or hereafter developed.
The use of general descriptive names, registered names, trademarks, service marks, etc. in this publication does not imply, even in the absence of a specific statement, that such names are exempt from the relevant protective laws and regulations and therefore free for general use. The publisher, the authors and the editors are safe to assume that the advice and information in this book are believed to be true and accurate at the date of publication. Neither the publisher nor the authors or the editors give a warranty, express or implied, with respect to the material contained herein or for any errors or omissions that may have been made. The publisher remains neutral with regard to jurisdictional claims in published maps and institutional affiliations.

Cover illustration: Colin McPherson / Alamy Stock Photo

Printed on acid-free paper

This Palgrave Macmillan imprint is published by the registered company Springer International Publishing AG part of Springer Nature.
The registered company address is: Gewerbestrasse 11, 6330 Cham, Switzerland

ACKNOWLEDGEMENTS

This collection came to fruition through a deeply held, shared desire, amongst contributors and others, to explore the ways cinema today is engaging with a new ideological climate and the changing face of national identity. I would like to thank the people at Palgrave Macmillan for their commitment to the project. I thank the series editors at Palgrave European Film and Media Studies. I would like to especially thank Andrew Higson for his support and guidance in the early stages of this collection. For their input at various stages in this collection, I would also like to thank Marco Abel, Tiago de Luca, Kevin Flanagan, Tina Kendall, Josip Kesic, Gozde Naiboglu, Martin O'Shaugnessy, Richard Rushton, Jeremi Szaniawski, Ruth Wodack and Sarah Wright.

CONTENTS

1 Introduction: On the Visual Cultures of the New
Nationalisms   1
James Harvey

2 The 'Liberal Left' Response to Twenty-First Century
Nationalism: *Le Week-end* (2013) and *I, Daniel Blake*
(2016)   17
John White

3 From *Down Terrace* to *High-Rise*: The 'Unreal Estate'
Cinema of Ben Wheatley   43
William Brown

4 Approaches to Othered Identities and Spaces in French
Cinema   63
Şirin Fulya Erensoy

5 Documenting the *Charlie Hebdo* Tragedy   85
Hugo Frey

viii CONTENTS

6 Diasporic Belgian Cinema: Transnational and Transcultural
Approaches to Molenbeek and Matonge in *Black* 97
Jamie Steele

7 The Freedom to Make Racial Jokes: Satires on Nationalism
and Multicultural Comedies in Dutch Cinema 125
Peter Verstraten

8 Building Bridges: Fatih Akin and the Cinema of
Intercultural Dialogue 145
Owen Evans

9 "*Kapitalismus tötet*": Liquid National Identities in the
Cinema of the Berlin School 169
Anna Batori

10 Resistance Against Itself: Austrian Cinema's Responses
to the Far-Right 191
Nikhil Sathe

11 Frivolity and Place Branding in Martínez Lázaro's
'Nationalist Comedies' 215
Alfredo Martínez-Expósito

12 After the Crisis: Europe and Nationhood in Twenty-First-
Century Portuguese Cinema 235
Mariana Liz

Index 257

Notes on Contributors

Anna Batori is a Lecturer in Film Studies at the Babeş-Bolyai University (Cluj-Napoca, Romania) with an MA in Film Studies (Eötvös Loránd University, 2012) and a PhD in Film Studies (University of Glasgow, 2017). Her recent book, *Space and Place in Romanian and Hungarian Cinema* (2018), is published by Palgrave Macmillan. She writes and teaches on European and world cinema, modern film theory and digitised narrative techniques.

William Brown is a Senior Lecturer in Film at the University of Roehampton, London. He is the author of *Non-Cinema: Global Digital Filmmaking and the Multitude* (Bloomsbury, 2018) and *Supercinema: Film-Philosophy for the Digital Age* (Berghahn, 2013). He is the co-author, with Dina Iordanova and Leshu Torchin, of *Moving People, Moving Images: Cinema and Trafficking in the New Europe* (College Gate Press, 2010) and the co-editor, with David Martin-Jones, of *Deleuze and Film* (Edinburgh University Press, 2012). He is also the director of various zero-budget films, including *En Attendant Godard* (2009), *Selfie* (2014), *Circle/Line* (2016) and *The Benefit of Doubt* (2017).

Şirin Fulya Erensoy is an Assistant Professor at Istanbul Kültür University in the Film and Television Department. She has completed her PhD dissertation in Cinema and Media Research at Bahçeşehir University in January 2017. She lectures and writes on film history, film genres, film editing and documentary film. Furthermore, Şirin works as a producer and advisor for independent productions.

Owen Evans is Professor of Film in the Media Department at Edge Hill University. He has published on GDR literature, German film and European Cinema. His monographs have looked at GDR author Günter de Bruyn, and German literary autobiography, and his articles and chapters comprise studies of *The Lives of Others, Sophie Scholl: The Last Days, Kontroll*, the work of Humphrey Jennings and European Film Festivals. He is co-founding editor of the international journals *Studies in European Cinema* and *The Journal of European Popular Culture*, and co-founding director of the European Cinema Research Forum (ECRF). His current research also includes explorations of the field of arts, health and wellbeing, alongside his ongoing interest in European cinema.

Hugo Frey is a cultural and political historian whose research work focuses on twentieth-century France and Francophone Europe with a special emphasis on the politics of visual culture. He has published over 40 substantial outputs in this field including *Louis Malle* (Manchester University Press 2004), *Nationalism and the Cinema in France* (Berghahn Books 2014) and is co-author of *The Graphic Novel: An Introduction* (Cambridge University Press, 2015).

James Harvey has published widely on the politics and aesthetics of film and visual culture. He is the author of *Jacques Rancière and the Politics of Art Cinema* (Edinburgh University Press, 2018).

Mariana Liz completed a PhD at King's College London in 2012. She is the author of *Euro-Visions* (2016), editor of *Portugal's Global Cinema* (2017) and co-editor of *The Europeanness of European Cinema* (2015). She has published on contemporary European cinema and Portuguese film in Studies in *European Cinema and the Journal of Romance Studies*, among others. She is currently a postdoctoral fellow at the Institute of Social Sciences, University of Lisbon, in Portugal, where she conducts research on European cities, cinema and tourism.

Alfredo Martinez-Expósito is Head of the School of Languages and Linguistics at the University of Melbourne. His research focuses on homosexuality in Spanish literature and film and auteurism in Spanish film. He is the co-editor (with Santiago Fouz-Hernández) of *Live Flesh: The Male Body in Contemporary Spanish Cinema* (2007).

Nikhil Sathe is an Associate Professor of German at Ohio University, where he regularly directs the university's Spring Semester Study Abroad Program in Salzburg, Austria. His research focuses on Austrian Cinema and Postwar German and Austrian Literature. Recent publications have examined films by Ulrich Seidl, Erwin Wagenhofer, Florian Flicker, Anja Salomonowitz, Arash Riahi, Umut Dağ and Sudabeh Mortezai.

Jamie Steele is currently Lecturer in Film and Screen Studies at Bath Spa University. Steele has published articles in the context of national and transnational cinema, regional and local filmmaking, and film as business. He is currently completing his first monograph (under contract with Edinburgh University Press) on contemporary francophone Belgian cinema with a particular focus on the following filmmakers: the Dardenne brothers, Bouli Lanners, Olivier Masset-Depasse, Joachim Lafosse and Lucas Belvaux.

Peter Verstraten is Assistant Professor Film and Literary Studies at Leiden University. His books include *Screening Cowboys* (1999), *Celluloid Echoes* (2004, in Dutch), *Film Narratology* (2009, translation of the second print of *Handboek filmnarratologie*) and *Humour and Irony in Dutch Post-war Fiction Film* (2016). With two directors of photography, he co-edited *Shooting Time: Cinematographers on Cinematography* (2012).

John White is a Senior Lecturer in Film Studies at Anglia Ruskin University. He is a co-editor of *The Routledge Encyclopedia of Films* (2015) and author of *Westerns* (Routledge 2011) and *European Art Cinema* (Routledge 2017). He has contributed chapters to books being published by Edinburgh University Press in their ReFocus series on Budd Boetticher, Delmer Daves and Fred Zinnemann. He is currently working on a new book with the working title *The Contemporary Western: An American Genre Post-9/11*.

LIST OF FIGURES

Fig. 6.1	The brief pause on the canal after the 'Back to Black' sequence, a border between Molenbeek and Brussels' centre	111
Fig. 6.2	Marwan escapes from the historic centre with the stolen handbag beneath the Palais de Justice	114
Fig. 9.1	Nina's objectified position in *Ghost*	184
Fig. 9.2	Nina's mirror image in *Ghost*	185
Fig. 10.1	*Zur Lage*: Jörg Haider appearing in an icon-like image	201
Fig. 12.1	Empty, abandoned and destroyed locations mark the initial sequence of *Saint George*	244
Fig. 12.2	Jorge being physically and visually oppressed in *Saint George*	245
Fig. 12.3	Rosa as seen by the narrator in *O Pátio das Cantigas*	251

CHAPTER 1

Introduction: On the Visual Cultures of the New Nationalisms

James Harvey

In June 2016, when 52% of the British electorate voted to leave the European Union, it became clear that Benedict Anderson's notion of nations as 'imagined communities' (1984) was as relevant as ever. The transnational promise of fluid borders and comingling cultures was being forced out of the geopolitical landscape by a rejuvenated nostalgia for a singular, native identity. Since the millennium, signs of such nostalgia have pierced the seamlessness of an economically open and socially mobile Western Europe. This is peculiar: have not Western European governments defined themselves in terms of fluid diversity for decades? As events from recent years have shown, ideals of openness have struggled to cope with mounting right-wing populism. The European electorate's taste for organised far-right parties has intensified in recent years, exemplified by the rise of Lega Nord in Italy, Partij voor de Vrijheid in the Netherlands and the FPO in Austria. Terror attacks in Belgium and France have been opportunistically mobilised for political leverage by Vlaams Belang in Belgium and Front National in France. Such electoral shifts have been

---

J. Harvey (✉)
Independent Scholar, London, UK

© The Author(s) 2018   1
J. Harvey (ed.), *Nationalism in Contemporary Western European Cinema*, Palgrave European Film and Media Studies,
https://doi.org/10.1007/978-3-319-73667-9_1

accompanied by a surge in hate crimes across Western Europe, frequently involving attacks against places of worship and aimed at cultural and ethnic minorities. While some of the effects of these new nationalisms are clear, the cultural response to these contemporary developments is in urgent need of address.

In these times of mounting tensions and increasing hostilities to difference, understanding the ways in which cultural artefacts and artistic texts respond will provide a vital perspective on the contemporary moment. This collection brings together analyses of case studies from across Western Europe to explore the way individual nations are being figured in and through films today. Broaching a breadth of questions regarding identity and indigeneity, borders and hybridity, dissent, heritage, nation-branding and patriotism, contributors to *Nationalism in Contemporary Western European Cinema* are engaged in addressing the persistent cultural tendencies of the century past—but in ways that reflect the uneasy moment of the early twenty-first century. To begin, then: what has changed?

The Return of the National

The title of this book is dense by necessity. Each of the terms—contemporary, Western European, even cinema—are equally important to understanding what is at stake in the visual culture of today's nationalist formations.

By contemporary, we recognise that one cannot remain contented by the contemporariness of post-Enlightenment modernity, nor even postmodernity. Nor is the moment in which we find ourselves containable in the contemporary described by Peter Osborne: 'first, structurally, as *idea, problem, fiction* and *task*; and second, historically, in its most recent guise as *the time of the globally transnational*' (Osborne 2013: 15). There have been some profound changes on the political scene in recent years that—while perhaps not yet causing any radical change in the order of global capitalism—have at least introduced novel challenges. These challenges cross the social, cultural and economic realms.

First, the attacks on the World Trade Centre on 11 September 2001 and the global 'war on terror' that ensued. The state of perpetual war that followed initiated a new era of global securitisation. Borders, previously permeated for the free and inventive mobility of labour and capital, rehardened. Ruth Wodack has demonstrated how such 'border politics' have been co-opted as effective strategies by right-wing populist parties

(Wodack 2018: 412). Such border politics have of course been part of the mainstream for some time, now. Their contemporariness can be measured in relation to the new wave of xenophobia, especially in the form of Islamophobia. As Liz Fekete has demonstrated, nativist scapegoating of minorities—specifically Muslims—preceded twenty-first century anti-terror legislation. Citing as exemplary the German and French governments' institutionally racist treatment of Muslim communities, formerly populist rhetoric became mainstream in the 1990s (Fekete 2009: 10). However, it is impossible to understate quite how much the institutional racism of border politics intensified throughout the early twenty-first century. It is emblematised famously, for instance, by ever-increasing surveillance and information-sharing, Donald Trump's 'travel ban' and the lack of official opposition to such discriminatory policies.

The second challenge regards the market crash of 2008, which threw Western economies into disarray, destroyed the livelihoods of millions of people and, in some cases, collapsed the economies of many formerly comfortable nation states. In his study of the revival of nationalism across Europe, Geoffrey Hosking identifies the anachronism of national economies in the globalised free-market economy as the principle reason for the rise of populist ethno-nationalism. As such, Hosking defines these new nationalisms as 'a challenge to us to find new ways of reconciling global markets, nation-states and democracy' (Hosking 2016: 220). Wolfgang Streeck has offered some vital thoughts towards the way these three realms interact. The economic crisis produced a sharp decline in 'the political manageability of democratic capitalism' (Streeck 2011: 24) with the resultant effect that 'democracy is as much at risk as the economy' (ibid.: 25). Widespread austerity policies and the continued accumulation of wealth by a tiny minority have cemented the fact that 'economic power seems today to have become political power, while citizens appear to be almost entirely stripped of their democratic defences' (ibid.: 29). This politico-economic reality seems to provide a crucial determining factor in the populist backlash against the status quo. Elsewhere, Streeck has addressed the mechanisms of how said populism has taken its nationalist form:

> [N]eoliberal globalization was far from actually delivering the prosperity for all that it had promised…Instead of trickle-down there was the most vulgar sort of trickle-up: growing income inequality between individuals, families, regions and, in the Eurozone, nations…'Global governance' didn't help, nor did the national democratic state that had become uncoupled from the

capitalist economy for the sake of globalization. To make sure that this did not become a threat to the Brave New World of neoliberal capitalism, sophisticated methods were required to secure popular consent and disorganize would-be resisters. In fact, the techniques developed for this purpose initially proved impressively effective. (Streeck 2017: 7)

Streeck accounts both for the (temporary) re-stabilisation of precarious global neoliberal economies and the resurgence of populist nationalism through sophisticated methods: lies. The emergence of the so-called 'post-factual' age—emblematised by Donald Trump in the US and the Brexit campaign in the UK. An emergent distaste for experts paved the way for a new consensus led by anti-globalist personalities. Streeck is critical of the 'moral denunciation' (ibid.: 12) directed at those supporting this position, ironically ventriloquising the retortive battle cries of ethno-nationalism. While Streeck is correct to problematise those that dismiss the contemporary opposition to globalism as ethno-nationalistic, the stunning breadth of his argument itself neglects the important ethnocentric dimension of today's populist nationalisms. The very post-truth strategies he associates with mainstream media and governmental rhetoric revolves above all around the non-native: the foreigner becomes the point of interest as much—perhaps even more so—for cultural and aesthetic reasons as she does for her socio-economic status.

The resurgent visibility of ethno-nationalism in the public sphere has also fed into the public response to the third challenge. As state and non-state forms of terror escalated across the Middle East, mass migrations of people seeking refuge tested the infrastructure of European states. One of the primary motivations for the slim majority that voted to 'leave' the European Union in the UK's EU referendum of 2016 regarded the rehoming of refugees. Angela Merkel's subsequent demand for all EU member states to 'do their part' involved the proposed introduction of quotas to ensure a fair spread of refugees across Europe. As Rainer Bauböck has explained though, most states are happy to ignore this plea 'as long as moral blame is the only consequence of non-cooperation' (Bauböck 2017: 6). The far-right's recent achievement of permeating the Central European political establishment has fed into much of the West's contemptuous official response to rehoming refugees. And since the official line has been largely apathetic and often hostile, those previously on the fringes of political discourse have penetrated the mainstream across Western Europe too. The margins have altered and hate campaigns led by the likes of Britain

First, Pim Fortuyn in the Netherlands and AfD in Germany have been given unprecedented mainstream exposure as a result.

Consequently, the inability of the centrist political establishment to forge an effective way of coping with these three pivotal threats has thrown into question what Osborne called 'the time of the globally transnational' (Osborne 2013: 15). The contemporary today involves the re-introduction of an earlier, mainstream political binary: between a pluralistic social democracy and conservative nationalism. It is the latter that has quickly made ground in recent years and provides the core concern for contributors here. It is our intention to unpack the localised representations of—and disputes with—nationalism, at the level of cinema.

By Western European, we recognise the distinct geopolitical character of these changes. For nearly seventy years, this geographic area has been commonly viewed as the most socially stable and coherent democratic arena in the world. That moral codes established at the end of the Second World War could be deemed dispensable by the very culture that lived and breathed such horror, is surely no less than a shocking, tragic failure of humanity. It is a failure to learn the lessons of history. It is a failure to adapt to the inevitable comingling of vastly different social and cultural realities. It is a failure to understand cultural identity as, in Stuart Hall's words, 'a matter of "becoming" as well as of "being"' (Hall 1990: 225). And, insofar as social change involves cultural hybridity, it is a failure to care for and about our world and its people. As right-wing populism reaches sophisticated levels of organisation across Western Europe, purposeful resistance to well-documented historical experience begins to mimic other past tragedies, whereby a people consent to what is bad for them. One might be reminded of some words by Walter Benjamin:

> Mankind, which in Homer's time was an object of contemplation for the Olympian gods, now is one for itself. Its self-alienation has reached such a degree that it can experience its own destruction as an aesthetic pleasure of the first order. This is the situation of politics which Fascism is rendering aesthetic. (Benjamin 1968: 242)

As Benjamin expressed so effectively, when this failure unfolds in the social arena, it also registers as an aesthetic phenomenon. It is this intersection between aesthetics and politics that preoccupies the contributors herein. While Benjamin's essay, 'The Work of Art in the Age of Mechanical Reproduction', explored the democratic potential of cinema against

6   J. HARVEY

Fascism over seventy years ago, it is still no clearer to what extent cinema provides an effective tool of resistance to the cultural essentialism of nationalism generally. Contributors to this collection are concerned with considering how today's nationalisms are being negotiated aesthetically as much as thematically. As such, each of the following chapters should be read as an attempt to engage with the way cinema itself is adapting to the current moment. In order to better understand the novelty of the present situation, the rest of this introduction briefly brings together some well-known writing on nationalism with more recent discussions of its disparate visual cultures.

Thinking Nationalism Today

Benedict Anderson's seminal text from 1983, *Imagined Communities*, is one of the most widely cited works to broach formations of nationalism. Anderson deals with several scholarly landmarks throughout, including Eric Hobsbawm's *The Age of Revolution: Europe 1789–1848* (1962), Ernest Gellner's *Thought and Change* (1964) and Tom Nairn's *The Break-up of Britain* (1977). Unlike Anderson, these authors share the tendency to frame nation as a uniquely imaginary social invention—fabrication rather than creation (Anderson 1983: 6). For Anderson though, the imagined is *the only* form of belonging to a community. While Anderson's book provided a revisionary historical engagement with imaginary community formation, Etienne Balibar and Immanuel Wallerstein's collection of essays, *Race, Nation, Class: Ambiguous Identities* (1991), is an inquiry into the philosophical underpinnings of nation. While accepting implicitly Hobsbawm's, Gellner's and Anderson's position on national identity as imagined, both also place an emphasis on the material forms of national collectivisation, which is referred to by both as a 'people'. For Wallerstein, a national people is a proactive state construction, built to defend against the threat of 'internal disintegration or external aggression':

> Any group who sees advantage in using the state's legal powers to advance its interests against groups outside the state or in any subregion of the state has an interest in promoting nationalist sentiment as a legitimation of its claims. States furthermore have an interest in administrative uniformity that increases the efficacy of their policies. Nationalism is the expression, the promoter and the consequence of such state-level uniformities. (Balibar and Wallerstein 1991: 81–82)

Wallerstein aligns nationalism entirely to the concept of state sovereignty. Nationalism is expressed by, and shared through, what he calls 'administrative uniformity'—that is, homogeneity reinforced through, for and because of a system of government that takes an interest in it. Nation states rely upon the sharing of collective sentiment on belonging and distinction. Thus, even objects—like flags—can function as an index of benign state officialdom, but also of aggressive neo-fascism. This is expressed in Paul Gilroy's *There Ain't No Black in the Union Jack* (1987). For Gilroy, nationalism cannot be understood through the mechanisms of state alone. To do so would obscure several key questions, such as:

> Under what conditions is national identity able to displace or dominate the equally 'lived and formed' identities which are based on age, gender, region, neighbourhood or ethnicity? How has it come to be expressed in racially exclusive forms? What happens when 'social identities' become expressed in conflicting political organisations and movements and when they appeal to the authority of nature and biology to rationalise the relations of domination and subordination which exist between them? (Gilroy 1987: 52)

Gilroy's attention to the many constituent layers of national identity introduces the vital role of cultural politics, which accompanies the divergent allegiances of peoples to nations. Gilroy's use of 'displace' is revealing—nationalism affects the idea each individual has of his or her own identity and, somehow, establishes itself as primary in the individual and collective psyche. The inquisitive quality of Gilroy's prose, here, conjures up something of the essentially fictive nature of national identity, which is a theme Balibar builds on in fruitful ways:

> It is fictive ethnicity which makes it possible for the expression of a pre-existing unity to be seen in the state, and continually to measure the state against its 'historic mission' in the service of the nation and as consequence, to idealize politics. By constituting the people as a fictively ethnic unity against the background of a universalistic representation which attributes to each individual one – and only one – ethnic identity and which thus divides up the whole of humanity between different ethnic groups corresponding potentially to so many nations, national ideology does much more than justify the strategies employed by the state to control populations. (Balibar and Wallerstein 1991: 96)

8   J. HARVEY

Fictive ethnicity is the root of each person's identification with the nation and their sense of *feeling at home* in their respective nation. Once fictive ethnicity is established, and human beings divided accordingly, a fertile ground will always exist for the flourishing of ethnic nationalism and the xenophobia that accompanies it. Both Balibar and Wallerstein are concerned with foregrounding the primacy of a 'people' as a concept somewhat outside race, nation and class, but pivotal to explaining the mechanisms of nationalism. A people is formed through, in and after nationalism; those that make up the people are products, symbols and models for national identity. But as Ernesto Laclau so expertly explained in *On Populist Reason* (Laclau 2005), while subscribing to a popular identity (such as nationality), a people is an empty construct that relies upon the crystallisation of a number of demands, thus bringing a number of particulars together towards a shared commitment.[1] The demands of the new nationalisms are directed towards a shared national identity; the dialogues initiated through film spectatorship are emblematic of this formation. Therefore, if we are to understand the relationship between cinema and nationalism, we must engage with its capacity both to represent and construct a people. Insofar as this construction is essentially *empty*, the potential exists for an alternative anti-national narrative, too—one that mimics the progressive populisms that have arisen in response to the new nationalisms. Contributors to this collection are engaged in exploring these diverse forms through the relationships initiated between screen and spectator, the aesthetic forms through which this peopling occurs, and the strategies used by films to frame a dialogue.

A Visual Culture of Nationalism

Theorising the nation in cinema today requires a dialectical approach—one that considers both traditional conceptions of national cinema and the now commonplace notion of transnational cinema. While both are still integral to this study, neither alone provides a sufficient account of the relationship between the new nationalisms and contemporary cinema.

In his article, 'The Concept of National Cinema', Andrew Higson identifies two methods of defining any one national cinema. It is, he claims, a choice between (1) comparing and contrasting between distinct

---

[1] See in particular, 'The people and the discursive construction of emptiness' (Laclau 2005: 68–128).

INTRODUCTION: ON THE VISUAL CULTURES OF THE NEW NATIONALISMS   9

national cinemas in order to 'establish varying degrees of otherness'; or alternatively, (2) 'exploring the cinema of a nation in relation to other already existing economies and cultures of that nation state' (Higson 1989: 38). Higson claims that the many diverse subjectivities that make up a national people undermine the credibility of national cinema studies, which too often constrains too tightly an all-encompassing vision of national identity. Higson's way of conceiving national identity formed in and through film culture is identical to Balibar's: everyone fits into a nation, everyone can only have one nationality, people and nations can be distinguished thusly. The suggestion is, therefore, that a fictively ethnic notion of film spectators and filmmakers is disingenuously conceived; an attempt is made to frame as homogeneous a vastly heterogeneous variety of film cultures, aesthetics and histories. Higson would come to update this view, framing the argument in terms of the transnational. In so doing, he disagrees with John Hill's (1992) and Paul Willemen's (1994) arguments for cultural specificity in film analysis, arguing that cultures themselves cannot be sufficiently understood in terms of national specificity (2006: 22). The transnational becomes, then, a commonplace way of contesting national cinema studies.

On many levels, this is reasonable. Breaching national borders is an everyday activity in free-market global capitalism, so it makes perfect sense to fold-in to any consideration of national and cultural identity in film a concern for the points of intersection between two or more different national identities. Moreover, the transnational has also taken on a more visible presence in the industrial, social and textual economies of cinema (be that through narratives of migration or international conflict, international co-productions, or increased access to foreign productions through more open distribution platforms). National specificity has even been roundly dismissed by some who have made claims like, '[t]he study of national cinemas must then transform into transnational film studies' (Lu 1997: 25).

However, a comment of this sort loses credibility when national identity has returned so forcefully to the fore. Will Higbee and Song Hwee Lim offer the more moderate assertion, claiming that transnational cinema studies must maintain 'a critical, discursive stance towards the question of the transnational...alert to the challenges and potentialities that greet each transnational trajectory' (2010: 18). Despite the varying tones of each argument, though, we might still challenge them wholesale, questioning the purpose and historicity of such claims. The transnational remains (to some extent, at least) an idealist category that neglects the persistence of nation as one of the primary identitarian categories—perhaps, even, the most. If not unthinkable, it remains almost entirely impracticable to operate in contemporary reality without a determined national identity. While offering a broader, more fluid conception for textual contexts, then, one's undeniable inclination to hold fast to nationality continues to cloud the cosmopolitan ethos of the transnational scholar. At a time when nationalism has penetrated the mainstream, it is vital to retain a critical perspective on the transnational, attentive to the way borders persist as well as break. To understand the way cinema reflects and refracts the nationalisms of today, contributors to this collection attend to the persistence of the national frame, incorporating traditional national and recent transnational discourses alongside the emerging politico-aesthetic trends.

Since little work currently exists on the aesthetics of contemporary nationalism, we stand at the cutting edge of research into these emerging trends. Some notable contributions to this inquiry can be taken from the January 2011 issue of *e-Flux journal*, edited by Paul Chan and Sven Lütticken. Chan and Lütticken open their dossier with some revealing comments on the 'global speculative economy' that compromises art's ability to function as either social or economic value. At first, this seems like something of a tangent detracting from the point at hand. However, in so doing, they are able to draw attention to the critical potential of artworks universally, irrespective of both site of reception and conception, and the stylistic movement into which it fits. Since art 'does not explicitly express and affirm the values that embody the country…one should affirm and exacerbate art's problematic status, its essential undecidability'. Doing so 'holds the promise of a more productive politicization of contemporary art above and beyond any projects on "aesthetics and politics" or "art and activism"' (Chan and Lütticken 2011). The idea that today's artworks inherently problematise the category of nation thus grants contemporary art privileged access to socially disruptive activity. Contemporary artworks are responsive to the era of new nationalisms, revealing points of potential antagonism with the current political climate through their in-between status—produced and consumed both inside and outside the system. The impetuous quality of today's artists resembles closely the Platonic conception of the poets: not fitting and thereby immorally compromising the order of the republic. Chan and Lütticken's solution, then, is close to Jacques Rancière's contention that artistic fictions provide 'simultaneously a locus of public activity and the exhibition-space for "fantasies",

INTRODUCTION: ON THE VISUAL CULTURES OF THE NEW NATIONALISMS   11

disturb[ing] the clear partition of identities, activities, and spaces' (Rancière 2004: 13). Exacerbating art's 'problematic status' might, therefore, disrupt contemporary nationalist fantasies, disturb the clear partition delineating one fictive ethnicity from another, and, in Rancière's terms, redistribute the sensible arrangement of bodies belonging to falsely homogeneous national orders. Central to this task is the need to question essentialising definitions of culture. In his solo contribution to the issue, Lütticken develops this argument:

> While art is being disparaged, the term culture has met with a more positive fate, being intimately connected to that other fetish, 'national identity'...In a reversal of Carl Andre's dictum that 'art is what we do' and 'culture is what is done to us', the contemporary populist imagination regards art as what is done to us while culture is what we do, or rather: what we simply are. Strictly speaking, this means that culture would need to be defined without having recourse to art at all. In fact, it is usually not that art as such is opposed to culture, only contemporary art: the good art lies in the safe and idealized past, in the golden age. (Lütticken 2011)

In many senses, there is nothing new about the claim that culturally acceptable, nationally authorised, 'good' art regards an idealised past. It concerns the immobilising effects of a nostalgia reflex, regressively injuring our chances of progress while providing comforting reassurance that a mythical, earlier time once existed. This sensation is encapsulated in Benjamin's comments on Paul Klee's *Angelus Novus* (1920): the angel of history is caught in the spectacle of a past catastrophe. While wreckage piles up, 'the angel would like to stay...But a storm is blowing from Paradise; it has got caught in his wings with such violence that the angel can no longer close them' (Benjamin 1968: 258). Benjamin locates in Klee's painting a clear allegory, describing history as a phenomenon that is experienced as a spectacle, mourned passively rather than engaged with in the present. This sensation is echoed by Higson in his discussion of the British heritage film. As a genre, these films regularly promote a determined aesthetic style with the effect of prohibiting the way we conceive the past, 'refusing the possibility of a dialogue or a confrontation with the present' (Higson 1993: 100). Phil Powrie has located a similar nostalgic penchant for rural communities in the French cinema of the 1980s, resisting post-colonial narratives through classical pastoral imagery (Powrie 1997: 13–27). More recently, *Good Bye, Lenin!* (Wolfgang Becker 2003) and *The Lives of Others* (Florian von Donnersmarck 2006) have been criticised for their brand of *Ostalgie*: nostalgically, sometimes romantically, revisiting and revising past eras and ideologies (as discussed by Anna Batori in Chap. 9). Moreover, the success and critical acclaim of these films suggests more than a transparent form of statist propaganda that short-circuits upon delivery. Often, these works are viewed to be the very best of a national cultural industry, which is demonstrative of the ease with which such narratives gain credibility.

The idealisation of the past routinely frames itself through clearly discernible formal strategies pitched at the mainstream. This relationship between style and resistance has a strong presence throughout art history. For instance, while the aforementioned example of *Angelus Novus* provided Benjamin with a crucial philosophical thesis on a figurative level, there is also an important formal distinction to be made. As a cutting-edge work of modernism, *Angelus Novus* is, in Lütticken's terms, 'opposed to culture'. As well as being an evocative metaphor for the hazards of nostalgia, the painting's status as a work of the *avant garde* embodies a disruptive potential. Klee's modernism (let alone his eventually untenable position as a German Jew) is antagonistic to the German cultural identity of the era. With this in mind, does resistance to the new nationalisms require a new *avant garde*? Or could the clarity of the classical narrative form be more accessible to a public and, therefore, more resistant to processes of fictive ethnicisation? Do discernible formal strategies cross social and historical particularities? Is there a preferred nationalist mode of expression? Can we trace a shared film language of either preaching, representing or disrupting the new nationalist narrative? We hope this collection can offer material towards answering these questions.

Approaches

The first two chapters approach such questions in the context of contemporary British cinema. In Chap. 2, John White considers the differing class commentaries offered in *Le Week-end* (Roger Michell 2013) and *I, Daniel Blake* (Ken Loach 2016). Employing the term, 'liberal left', White investigates the bourgeois liberalism of the former in relation to Loach's insistent socialism. He turns to Chantal Mouffe's theories of pluralist democracy in order to dissect the contrasting positions each film offers regarding the contemporary British subject. In Chap. 3, William Brown explores the significance of real estate in the films of Ben Wheatley.

Property is seen to condition class in Wheatley's films. Their use of chaotic events and surreal imagery present a confrontational resistance to enduring social hierarchies, which, Brown argues, feed into the Brexit rhetoric of 'taking back control' of one's nation. The following two chapters explore French national identity through its minority cultures. In Chap. 4, Şirin Fulya Erensoy analyses two films set in the Parisian *banlieues*—*Dheepan* (Jacques Audiard 2015) and *Fatima* (Philippe Faucon 2016). Continuing Brown's concern for the relationship between space and society, Erensoy explores how today's multicultural Europe tests the republican ideal French national identity. Hugo Frey's chapter closely analyses Daniel and Emanuel Leconte's documentary on the attack on the Charlie Hebdo offices. Frey's conviction that *L'Humour à Mort* (2015) is a work of contemporary French nationalism dwells on the affective dimensions of documentary film and its historical ability to divide viewers, provoking strong emotional responses.

In Chap. 6, Jamie Steele considers Adil El Arbi and Bilall Fallah's *Black* (2015) against the backdrop of recent terrorist activities in contemporary Belgium. Steele engages with debates framing *Black* as a radical film, exploring the extent to which it reinforces the separation between excluded groups. In Chap. 7, Peter Verstraten turns to contemporary Dutch comedies, broaching the topic of 'racial jokes'. Acknowledging notions of tolerance in the Netherland's today, Verstraten considers the uses of so-called 'progressive racism' as a disavowal of white privilege. The following two chapters engage with two of the twenty-first century's major European auteurs: Fatih Akin and Christian Petzold. Owen Evans explores a number of films by Akin—a filmmaker often credited with labels such as 'multicultural', 'cosmopolitan' and 'transnational'. Refining our understanding of the sorts of communities forged in these films, Evans instead proposes the notion of 'the intercultural' as a way of understanding the ultimately optimistic outlook in diverse societies. In Chap. 9, Anna Batori broaches the question of nostalgia in Petzold's films. Drawing on the considerable theoretical inquiries on *Ostalgie* and *Westalgie*, Batori re-evaluates Petzold's images of national identity in the current climate.

Nikhil Sathe's study confronts directly acts of neo-fascism in Austria. Tracing the link between the post-war Freedom Party's xenophobic rhetoric and the contemporary social climate, Sathe turns to several twenty-first century documentaries and reconstruction narratives. The dark and darkly comic tones and styles of each of the films delineates something of the shared aesthetic strategies of contemporary nationalism. Greatly differing in tone, Martínez Lázaro's *Spanish Affair* franchise (2014, 2015) is the subject of Alfredo Martínez-Expósito's chapter. The highest grossing Spanish film of all time in Spain, *Spanish Affair* and its sequel is considered in relation to the practice of 'nation branding'. Viewed against the backdrop of today's post-ETA and territorially disputed Spain, these supposedly clichéd films, Martínez-Expósito argues, are highly loaded with socio-political motivation. Finally, exploring the effects of the financial crash on contemporary Portuguese society, Mariana Liz approaches some narratives that deal directly with a crisis that has been as personal and social as it has been fiscal. Liz explores the resultant reconsideration of national identity staged in the art film, *Saint George* (Marco Martins 2016), and the popular success of Leonel Vieira's *O Pátio das Cantigas* (2015).

It is our hope that the sum of these many parts amounts to a critical overview of some of the aesthetic forms taken by the new nationalisms. Such a task expects to provide no answers. Rather, we hope to provide some essential ground upon which to build a decisive account of the disparate visual cultures that circulate as a result of, and in response to, the reconfiguration of Western European national identities in the twenty-first century.

Bibliography

Anderson, Benedict. 1983. *Imagined Communities*. London and New York: Verso.

Balibar, Etienne and Wallerstein, Immanuel. 1991. *Race, Nation, Class: Ambiguous Identities*. Trans. Chris Turner. London and New York: Verso.

Bauböck, Rainer. 2017. Europe's Commitments and Failures in the Refugee Crisis. *European Political Science*, https://link.springer.com/article/10.1057/s41304-017-0120-0. Accessed 12th January 2018.

Benjamin, Walter. 1968. *Illuminations*. Trans. H. Zohn. New York: Random House.

Chan, Paul and Lütticken, Sven. 2011. Idiot Wind: An Introduction. *E-flux Journal*, 22. http://www.e-flux.com/journal/22/67701/idiot-wind-an-introduction/. Accessed 13th October 2017.

Fekete, Liz. 2009. *A Suitable Enemy: Racism, Migration and Islamophobia in Europe*. London and New York: Pluto Press.

Gellner, Ernest. 1964. *Thought and Change*. London: Weidenfeld and Nicolson Ltd.

Gilroy, Paul. 1987. *There Ain't No Black in the Union Jack*. London: Unwin Hyman Ltd.

Hall, Stuart. 1990. Cultural Identity and Diaspora. In *Identity: Community, Culture, Difference,* ed. Jonathan Rutherford, 222–237. London: Laurence and Wishart.

Higbee, Will and Lim, Song Hwee. 2010. Concepts of Transnational Cinema: Towards a Critical Transnationalism in Film Studies, *Transnational Cinemas,* 1 (1): 7–21.

Higson, Andrew. 1993. Representing the National Past: Nostalgia and Pastiche in the Heritage Film. In *British Cinema and Thatcherism: Fires Were Started,* ed. Lester D. Friedman. London: UCL Press.

Higson, Andrew. 1989. The Concept of National Cinema. *Screen,* 30 (4): 36–47.

Higson, Andrew. 2006. The Limiting Imagination of National Cinema. In *Transnational Cinema: The Film Reader,* ed. Elizabeth Ezra and Terry Rowden, 15-25. New York: Routledge.

Hill, John. 1992. The Issue of National Cinema and British Film Production. In *New Questions of British Cinema,* ed. Duncan Petrie. London: BFI.

Hobsbawm, Eric. 1962. *The Age of Revolution: Europe 1789–1848.* London: Weidenfeld and Nicolson Ltd.

Hosking, Geoffrey. 2016. Why has Nationalism Revived in Europe? The Symbolic Attractions and Fiscal Capabilities of the Nation-state. *Nations and Nationalism,* 22 (2), 210–221.

Laclau, Ernesto. 2005. *On Populist Reason.* London and New York: Verso.

Lu, Sheldon Hsiao-peng. 1997. *Transnational Chinese Cinemas: Identity, Nationhood, Gender.* Honolulu: University of Hawaii Press.

Lütticken, Sven. 2011. A Heteronomous Hobby: Report from the Netherlands. *E-flux Journal,* 22. http://www.e-flux.com/journal/22/67753/a-heterono-mous-hobby-report-from-the-netherlands/. Accessed 13th October 2017.

Nairn, Tom. 1977. *The Break-Up of Britain.* London: NLB.

Osborne, Peter. 2013. *Anywhere or Not at All: Philosophy of Contemporary Art.* London and New York: Verso.

Powrie, Phil. 1997. *French Cinema in the 1980s: Nostalgia and the Crisis of Masculinity.* Oxford: Clarendon Press.

Rancière, Jacques. 2004. *The Politics of Aesthetics.* London and New York: Continuum.

Streeck, Wolfgang. 2011. The Crisis of Democratic Capitalism. *New Left Review,* 71, September–October 2011, 5–29.

Streeck, Wolfgang. 2017. The Return of the Repressed. Trans. R. Livingstone. *New Left Review,* 104, March–April 2017, 5–18.

Willemen, Paul. 1994. *Looks and Frictions: Essays in Cultural Studies and Film Theory.* London and Bloomington: Indiana University Press.

Wodack, Ruth. 2018. Discourses about Nationalism. In *The Routledge Handbook of Critical Discourse Studies,* ed. John Flowerdew and John E. Richardson, 403–420. Abingdon and New York: Routledge.

CHAPTER 2

The 'Liberal Left' Response to Twenty-First Century Nationalism: *Le Week-end* (2013) and *I, Daniel Blake* (2016)

John White

With the rejuvenation of nationalism across Europe during the past decade, the process of European integration would seem to have reached a crisis point. There has been a general trend towards strengthening borders, as a 'protection' against both terrorism and refugee migration. This has brought with it an intensification of political debate. It is within this atmosphere, and within contexts not of its choosing, that the 'liberal left' has been forced to respond to growing, media-expressed fears, constructed or real, and an accompanying resurgence of interest in right-wing politics (Adler 2016; Raffaello 2016). Nick Pearce, Professor of Public Policy at the University of Bath, has argued in the *New Statesman* that, '[t]he liberal left cannot retreat to the comforts of moral outrage and political protest. The new times demand a progressive engagement with the politics of identity and belonging, as well as renewed radicalism on economic policy and social protection' (Pearce 2016). Given this situation, how have British filmmakers (challengingly characterised by Ken Loach, in accepting

---

J. White (✉)
Anglia Ruskin University, Cambridge, UK
e-mail: John.White2@anglia.ac.uk

© The Author(s) 2018

J. Harvey (ed.), *Nationalism in Contemporary Western European Cinema*, Palgrave European Film and Media Studies,
https://doi.org/10.1007/978-3-319-73667-9_2

an award for *I, Daniel Blake* at the British Academy Film Awards, as being 'with the people' and against 'the rich and the powerful, the wealthy and the privileged' [Loach 2017]) responded to conservative voices of protectionism and an increasing confidence within right-wing European groups? What has been British cinema's response to Pearce's call for 'a progressive engagement with the politics of identity and belonging'? What are the possibilities for UK filmmakers necessarily needing to place their work within the current European political context? This chapter will attempt to consider these questions through an examination of two films: *Le Weekend* (Roger Michell 2013) and *I, Daniel Blake* (Ken Loach 2016).

There has certainly already been what might be characterised as a broad 'liberal left' response within British cinema to the intensification of nationalist discourses. A film such as *Mr Turner* (Mike Leigh 2014), for example, might be seen as exploring Britain and Britishness from a cultural perspective that embraces Europe; and *Pride* (Matthew Warchus 2014), as a further example, seems to aim to take its audience towards ideology-driven reflection on the politics of post-war Britain. In documentaries, radical voices have been heard in films such as *London: The Modern Babylon* (Julien Temple 2012), *The Stuart Hall Project* (John Akomfrah 2013) and *The Spirit of '45* (Loach 2013).[1] But, the term 'liberal left', as employed by Pearce and as found in use within the wider UK media, is clearly intensely problematic in its yoking together of the liberal and socialist traditions. Not only that, but definitions of both 'liberalism' and 'socialism' are themselves highly contested and open to multiple interpretations. Michael Freeden sets out a basic position with regards to 'liberalism':

> Classical liberalism revolved around individual liberty…human independence, and the rule of Law, and it importantly restricted what states and governments were entitled to do to individuals. Social liberalism…explored the conditions for individual development and growth, sustained by networks of mutual assistance and interdependence. From that branch of liberalism arose the modern welfare state. (Freeden 2015: 2)

---

[1] Frequently, as with these examples, the starting point might be seen as an attempted reclamation of history, a determined shaping of the socio-historical contexts within which it is suggested the contemporary political landscape needs to be viewed. *Le Week-end* considers the present through the lens of the political activism of the 1960s. *I, Daniel Blake* sees the contemporary situation through the lens of a post-war, consensually agreed, welfare state.

The origins of liberalism have frequently been viewed as grounded within the capitalist economy. 'Liberalism is… seen as the ideology of capitalism,' says Andrew Vincent, for example. He characterises this as 'the Marxist and more general socialist reading of liberalism' (1995: 24–25). On the other hand, although a particularly important early work for liberalism, John Locke's *Second Treatise of Government* (1689) does emphasise the importance of private property [2] and the rule of law; it also asserts that individuals are free and government can only be administered with the consent of the people.[3] Vincent says the idea that people had natural rights, which came from Locke, 'eventually developed into the socialist movements of the later nineteenth century' (1995: 43). So, here we have an apparent link between liberalism and the left. Turning to socialism, attempting to identify some commonality at the heart of this ideology while also admitting that the left takes 'many forms' (2005: 2), Michael Newman suggests:

> [T]he most fundamental characteristic of socialism is its commitment to the creation of an egalitarian society…In particular, socialists have maintained that, under capitalism, vast privileges and opportunities are derived from the hereditary ownership of capital and wealth at one end of the social scale, while a cycle of deprivation limits opportunities and influence at the other end. (2005: 2–3)

'Socialism,' says Andrew Heywood, 'arose as a reaction against the social and economic conditions generated in Europe by the growth of industrial capitalism'. Heywood goes on to say: 'Although socialism and liberalism have common roots in the Enlightenment, and share a faith in principles such as reason and progress, socialism emerged as a critique of liberal market society' (2007: 100). Clearly, there are shared roots but also stark differences contained within the binary nature of the phrase 'liberal left'. One difficulty centres on the concept of property ownership, which

---

[2] 'Political power, then, I take to be the right of making laws with penalties of death, and consequently all less penalties, for the regulating and preserving of property' (Wootton 1993: 262). In his introduction to this book, Wootton makes it clear that for Locke 'although the world was given to all men in common, men can by labour appropriate private property without having to obtain the consent of their fellow commoners' (1993: 81).

[3] 'that which begins and actually constitutes any political society is nothing but the consent of any number of freemen capable of a majority to unite and incorporate into such a society' (1993: 311).

is considered fundamental to classical liberalism but which is also a core tenet of capitalism. Within socialism itself a further tension exists around the question of whether an egalitarian society can be achieved via reforming the in-place system, or whether it is necessary to overthrow capitalism and replace it with something else. Forms of both liberalism and socialism focus considerable attention on the relationship of the rights of the individual to the achievement of the common good for the collective society. Through his use of the term 'liberal left', Pearce is suggesting any response to increased conservatism must depend on some version of liberalism and/or socialism, but basic ideological differences would seem to mitigate against the achievement of a united oppositional voice.

Contemporary films, whether *Le Week-end* and *I, Daniel Blake* or any others, exist in relation to this briefly sketched history of ideas. They also, of course, take their place within the specifics of the current political context and in relation to contemporary debates around the nature of society. Some time ago, but with continuing relevance to the contemporary situation, Eric Hobsbawm pointed out in *Nations and Nationalism since 1780: Programme, Myth, Reality* that individual nations and, therefore, concepts of nationalism have been profoundly challenged by the increasing pace and intensity of globalisation in recent decades. Nation states are no longer the self-contained units of power they might once have been. Within a militarily volatile global context, small nation states are vulnerable to, either, outright invasion, or, regional destabilisation. And, within the context of an increasingly transnational world economy, even more powerful states find themselves dependent on 'a global economy over which they have no control and which determines their internal affairs' (1990: 184). The rise in nationalism across Europe has occurred, therefore, within a context in which nation states are less able to express independence and increasingly pushed towards acceptance of economic interdependence. As Hobsbawm expresses it: '"The nation" today is visibly in the process of losing an important part of its old functions, namely that of constituting a territorially bounded "national economy"' (1990: 181).

However, despite this relative decline of the nation, Chantal Mouffe has counselled against believing that 'collective identities which always entail a we/they discrimination' can be erased (Mouffe 2005: 5). For her, these identities continue to 'play a central part in politics' (Mouffe 2005: 5–6). In the face of nationalism, her concern is with 'liberal rationalism' and its belief that reason is able to eradicate the 'archaic "passions"' of 'collective identities' (Mouffe 2005: 6). For Mouffe, the 'task of democratic politics' is not to overcome people's commitment to group identification by achieving some sort of consensus but to construct these identifications in a way that 'energizes the democratic confrontation' (ibid.).

In the past decade in Europe, a complex range of socio-political tensions have resulted from (a) massive transnational migrations that have taken place in the wake of a variety of military interventions and a world market recession described by the International Monetary Fund as the worst since the Second World War (IMF 2009: xii),[4] and (b) increasing economic uncertainty and frailty on the part of nation states faced with globalisation. With the theoretical and political contexts outlined here in mind, this chapter will consider *Le Week-end* and *I, Daniel Blake* as representing different possible 'liberal left' responses to resurgent nationalism. These films have been chosen for the distinctive ways in which they position themselves in relation to ideological debate. In some ways, the difference between the two films might be seen to centre on their acceptance, or rejection, through their filmic practice of Mouffe's idea that 'the conflictual nature of politics constitutes the necessary starting point for envisaging the aims of democratic politics' (Mouffe 2005: 13–14).

CULTURE AND IDENTITY

Le Week-end takes the audience to the Continent, and specifically to a city, Paris, that might be seen to embody the cultural heart of Europe. The film views 'us' as close to, part of, integrated with (rather than, distant or detached from) Europe, and raises the ghost of a past of youthful vigour and revolutionary ideas. This past belongs to our central characters, Nick (Jim Broadbent) and his wife, Meg (Lindsay Duncan), but is also seen as belonging to a whole generation. A friend of Nick's from their days at Cambridge University, Morgan (Jeff Goldblum), who the couple meet unexpectedly in Paris, says: 'We were the spark – the 60s and 70s lit the fuse'. There is a comfortable, middle-class socialism expressed in *Le Week-end* that views itself as having left the youthful energetic vibrancy of politics 'on the streets' behind. 'I'm still an anarchist of the Left, I suppose,'

---

[4] 'global activity is projected to contract by 1.3 percent in 2009. This represents the deepest post-World War II recession by far. Moreover, the downturn is truly global: output per capita is projected to decline in countries representing three-quarters of the global economy' (International Monetary Fund 2009: xii).

says Nick in such a way that the phrase 'I suppose' sums up all his political lethargy and uncertainty. By contrast, *I, Daniel Blake* provides a representation of the current state of the UK and a challenging engagement with politics that is guaranteed to polarise critical responses. This film could be seen as attempting to reclaim a very particular form of British nationalism centred around the successful post-war creation of welfare state institutions. Freeden's approach to politics, given above, might link this moment of social change to liberalism, but for Loach, as evidenced by his documentary *The Spirit of '45*, this period is clearly viewed as existing in relation to socialism.[5]

In a period supposedly built around identity politics, both films in their different ways return us to a strong recognition of the continuing divisions of class in society and push us towards contemplation of the position of class politics within contemporary society. *Le Week-end* may be focused on the plight of the middle classes, while *I, Daniel Blake* looks at the struggles of the working class, but both place 'class' centre stage. There are ways in which these films might be seen to explore further key divisions in society, such as gender, ethnicity and sexuality, but what comes through most strongly is the class base given to both films. In considering these films we are, therefore, taken back to a foundational perspective that might be seen as critical for the left if it is to achieve genuine populist engagement with contemporary conservative political impulses. Taking up Pierre Bourdieu's concept of class as 'an aprioristic identity', Deidre O'Neill considers that this issue of class has taken on very particular nuances in recent decades. According to O'Neill:

> we are born into a class position we feel powerless to change not least because we often do not attempt to change it considering it to be natural. This state of affairs has intensified over the last thirty years as the collective historical knowledge and instances of social and political resistance of the working class are ignored or marginalised. (2016: 119)

On this basis, O'Neill takes issue with Ernesto Laclau when he sees contemporary society as offering 'a proliferation of subject positions, all of which contribute to the diluting of antagonisms and militate against

---

[5] It should be recognised that in positioning themselves in this way in relation to relatively recent historical periods, both films run the risk of doing nothing more than championing nostalgia for a (believed to be) now lost, (British) past.

classed identity' (2016: 119). She suggests Laclau 'fails to consider the ways in which consciousness is formed and shaped through the daily experience of poverty, unemployment and marginalisation' and concludes that '[w]hat may have declined is class-consciousness, but not consciousness shaped by class' (2016: 120).

Le Week-end and *I, Daniel Blake* slot neatly into two historically important strands of the British cinematic tradition. *Le Week-end* takes a largely theatrical approach to filmmaking. It employs a small cast, being essentially a 'two-hander' built around the relationship between Nick and his wife, Meg, and owes much to a strongly literary script provided by Hanif Kureishi. *I, Daniel Blake*, on the other hand, positions itself within the field of British social realist filmmaking. As a fiction it relies on condensing an array of real life experience into its 100 minutes running time. Its fundamental aim is to produce a series of scenes that each take realism as their keynote style. *Le Week-end* is written and filmed with a middle-class, art-house audience in mind, the sort of spectators who might also be theatregoers. The characters are recognisably from this same sector of the population and will be easily identified by the audience. *I, Daniel Blake* is, by contrast, as has been said, focused on the experiences of the working class. It still played to what would have been largely middle-class audiences in art-houses but it was written with the aim of moving beyond this to communicate with a wider population of 'ordinary' people. Whether it could ever have achieved this to any serious extent within the context of UK cinema exhibition remains doubtful.[6]

The locations employed by the filmmakers reflect the very different films with which we are dealing. Although *Le Week-end* technically opens in a tunnel we quickly find ourselves on board a Eurostar train to Paris. Inside a well-lit carriage, there is a man pouring champagne, a woman

[6] In its opening weekend in October 2013 *Le Week-end* took £324,000 and played in 124 cinemas (Gant 2013). It never played in more than 127 cinemas and by its sixth weekend on the circuit it was down to less than 20 cinemas ('Le Week-end'. Box Office Mojo). In its opening weekend in October 2016 *I, Daniel Blake* took more than £400,000 from 94 cinemas (Gant 2016). By its third week this film had moved out to 273 cinemas and had taken more than £2 million, making it the biggest ever opening in the UK for one of Loach's films. In its sixth week *I, Daniel Blake* was still playing at more than 120 cinemas, although figures dropped off after that date ('I, Daniel Blake.' Box Office Mojo). *Le Week-end* did almost as much business in cinemas in the USA as it did in the UK. *I, Daniel Blake* did almost a third more business in France than it did in the UK. In the first instance, having Jeff Goldblum in the cast was presumably a factor and, in the second instance, winning the Palme d'Or at the Cannes Film Festival will have had an impact.

laughing, a man on his mobile phone, a woman flicking through a magazine, someone else reading a broadsheet newspaper. This is an experience an educated, middle-class elite may be likely to recognise, as they will when the couple arrive in the Gare du Nord. Paris itself is immediately (seemingly instinctively, but actually through a long-standing, media-induced, learnt response) associated by the audience with art and architecture, fine food and wine, all that is 'best' in cultural experiences. By contrast, the opening to *I, Daniel Blake* first of all confronts the audience with a blank, black screen and the sound of an interview for a benefits assessment taking place and then with a tight close-up of a balding man in late middle-age with a shaved head answering questions for this assessment. Behind the man is a blank wall so that there is nothing to distract the audience from the questions being asked and the answers being given. Moments later when we move outside we watch our central character, Dan (Dave Johns), walking through a very ordinary looking housing estate. It is a grey and dismal late autumn day with bare trees and leaves on the ground. Eventually, if Dan's accent had not already made this clear to us, we find we are in Newcastle. The focus of each film is clear from the outset: one is going to investigate the experience of an ageing, middle-class couple, while the other will follow the experience of an ageing, working-class man.

While the locations for *I, Daniel Blake* alternate between a Job Centre, a variety of working-class flats and a range of generally bland urban spaces in Newcastle, Nick and Meg move between their upmarket hotel room, an array of Parisian cultural highlights, and a penthouse in a well-to-do apartment block. Along the way little, if anything, of the social divisions existing within Paris are allowed to intrude. We are comfortably placed and contained within the theme-park bubble of central Paris. The working class and the underclass have been erased. By contrast, Loach very deliberately places bit-part characters in the empty spaces of shots that show Dan walking through urban locations—a man in a wheelchair passing Dan on a ramp walkway, a man with a crutch standing on the corner as Dan enters Newcastle's Central Arcade. When Dan has to wait around in town before he can use the computers in the library Loach positions him standing next to a shop window advertising high-class, expensive jewellery and featuring the image of a glamorous model. He follows this by showing him walking past a sign advertising 'The Pearl' with the catch-line, 'offices at the heart of the city.' This is a building in Newcastle that Loach will know pitches itself on its website as 'a rejuvenated city centre icon delivering new offices for entrepreneurial businesses.' The clash between Dan's experience and the world around him is made clear, and by the use of extras within shots (as described above), Loach further makes it clear Dan's experience is not unique. Loach's ultimate use of extras comes when he takes his audience to a food bank. Dan and Katie (Hayley Squires), the young mother from London he has befriended, along with Katie's children, join a lengthy queue that snakes around the corner from the hall where food is distributed. Again, the point is clear: the experiences of Dan and Katie as they struggle to make ends meet while on benefits is far from unique (Hutchinson 2015). Of course, the genres of these two films are entirely different—one is written as a social realist drama, the other as a comedy—and so, we might expect different uses to be made of set and location. Even so, the stark difference remains and is a defining aspect of our engagement with each film.

This is not to deny that Kureishi and Michell's comedy sets out to explore challenging issues. Despite the feel-good requirements of the comedy genre it has a seriousness that some have found difficult to deal with.[7] However, what we are interested in in this chapter is not so much intellectual depth but the range of choices being made by the makers of these films in relation to the current socio-political context of the period in Europe and the UK. Beyond this, our interest is in what effect these choices might be said to have on the audience; and, in particular, how potential meanings and understandings being conveyed to the audience by these filmmakers might be said to sit in relation to political forces at work during a period of resurgent nationalism.

In fact, *Le Week-end* is undeniably an extremely rich text, containing a range of approaches aimed at provoking thought and engagement. In a film exploring the struggle to keep a relationship alive after 30 years of marriage, the Sacré-Cœur, for example, is not simply a cinematographically interesting tourist hotspot for the couple to visit. The Roman Catholic basilica acts as a reminder of the linkage of the institution of marriage to the Church. Further, when Nick kisses Meg and receives tut-tuts of moral censure from others we are reminded of the Church's attitudes towards sex and the expression of passionate love. Similarly, the Cimetière du Montparnasse works not only to highlight themes of old age and death but, as he stands amongst the graves of his heroes, also reiterates our cen-

---

[7] 'the kind of gentle melancholy comedy after which you leave the cinema not sure quite how depressed you are supposed to be feeling' (Bradshaw 2013).

26   J. WHITE

tral character's failure to achieve his potential. Beyond this, the location links to the ancient Greek idea of Mount Parnassus, perhaps in particular its association with Dionysus and concepts of liberating the individual from social constraints. When later we find Nick and Meg in the Musée Rodin, the film activates a further series of references. As Meg dismisses Nick's idea for writing 'the ultimate Cambridge novel' by asking if he has 'any less tired ideas' the sculpted head of Rodin's mistress and muse, Camille Claudel, is in the left foreground of the shot. The theme of couples who in their anguished relationships lurch between intensities of love and detestation is further underpinned and amplified. Claudel's most famous work, *The Age of Maturity* (bronze, 1902), might offer ways of commenting on Meg and Nick's relationship, and there are a range of other works by the same sculptor that might be seen as relevant.[8] All of this is without beginning to consider significant works by Rodin himself such as *Le Penseur/The Thinker* (bronze, 1904), *Le Baiser/The Kiss* (marble, 1887), and *Le Porte de l'Enfer/The Gates of Hell* (bronze, 1880–1917), that might come into the purview of potential cultural references triggered by the filmmakers. There is, then, no denying the depth of the allusions at work in *Le Week-end*. From the outset, the filmmakers aim to produce something that is full of cultural connotations. In the first scene on the Eurostar train, Meg is reading *The Elegance of the Hedgehog*, a novel by Muriel Barbery. This is set in Paris, contains clear class distinctions, and considers the emptiness of life and of bourgeoisie existence in particular. It is full of a very obvious interest in literature and philosophy, and driven by an effort to define what it is that makes life worth living. In other words, it is motivated by the same things as Kureishi's script and Michell's resulting film. The characters in *Le Week-end*, Morgan (Jeff Goldblum), Meg and, in particular, Nick, each feel their lives to be pointless and restlessly search for something to give meaning to existence.

There are also much lighter references throughout *Le Week-end*, in particular to films from the French New Wave. Most famously the dance from Jean-Luc Godard's *Bande à part* (1964) is first of all shown on the television in Nick and Meg's hotel room and then the film closes with the couple along with Morgan performing their version of the routine in a small café. Broadbent as Nick and, even more so, Duncan as Meg often seem to be paralleling the roles, performances and dress of couples in New

---

[8] For example, *L'Implorante/The Implorer* (1898–1905), *La Valse/The Waltz* (1889–1905), *La Vague/The Wave* (1897–1903).

Wave films, perhaps in particular Jean-Paul Belmondo as Michel and Jean Seberg as Patricia in *À bout de soufflé/Breathless* (Godard 1960). The period of the French New Wave effectively reminds the audience of the central couple's youth and the freedom they felt as those younger people, while the irony of an ageing couple being identified with the young people who populated the original films further amplifies themes of ageing and moving towards death.[9] In a further homage to the way in which French New Wave films liberated the camera and created the familiarity of the Parisian backdrop, Nick and Meg are shown careering around Paris in a taxi when they first arrive in the city. They are also shown arriving at the hotel they have booked only to find it is not as they remember it 30 years ago. Rather than 'Hotel Audran' the sign over the front of the building in Montmartre now reads 'HOT L AUDRAN', a reference to one of the iconic, sexually attractive, female stars from the New Wave, Stéphane Audran. What we notice is that even with these at first sight 'light' references there are more serious underlying themes. As suggested above, photographing a couple in late middle-age as if they are Seberg and Belmondo, and showing them attempting to youthfully freewheel around Paris, in fact intensifies the focus on their age. Audran's name also recalls the bourgeois women she frequently played and, as already noted with reference to *The Elegance of the Hedgehog*, the pointlessness of middle-class existence is a further crucial idea for the film. Audran acted in Luis Buñuel's surrealist film *Le Charme discret de la bourgeoisie / The Discreet Charm of the Bourgeoisie* (1972), and *Le Week-end*, while it does not approach the task in quite the same way, would seem like Buñuel to be interested in dissecting the self-congratulatory veneer of middle-class existence.

When our couple cannot decide where to eat, it is amusing to hear them coming up with a list of stock phrases—'too empty', 'too modern', 'too touristy', 'too expensive'—but it is a comfortable and gentle form of humour that plays on the fact that members of the middle-class audience who have been to Paris may well have done something similar. However, here again there are further potential connotations. We see Nick and Meg outside a restaurant with the name, 'Restaurant Le Dur'. (Is there a sexual pun at work here?) The way in which the shot is framed means the name does not appear in full on the screen but it is the Restaurant Le Durer in Montmartre. The filmmakers give us the first part of the title of a poetry collection ('Le Dur') by Paul Éluard, *Le dur désir de durer /The Hard*

---

[9] There is a whole study to be written about bodies in relation to this film.

28   J. WHITE

Desire to Endure (1946), along with (if we know the actual restaurant) the final word of the title ('durer'). *Le Week-end* is very much about enduring, 'carrying on' in the sense of continuing but it is also about desire and love, a key focus for Éluard. Are Kureishi and Michell elevating the love of Nick and Meg to place it on a par with 'great' love affairs of history and culture? (Another possible eating place Nick and Meg consider is the Restaurant Josephine!) Or, are Kureishi and Michell gently mocking the seriousness with which Nick, in particular, approaches all of this? Certainly, Éluard famously both with his first long-term partner, Gala, and his second, Nusch, attempted to approach sexual relationships with a sense of freedom and openness. It is in the Cimetière du Montparnasse near Samuel Beckett's grave that Nick announces: 'As Beckett says, "Do we mean 'love' when we say 'love'?"' Meg's response to this tautology is, 'That's stupid.' And Nick's reply, 'I think, he means there's more to love than loving and being loved.' Critics have debated the meaning of this phrase taken from the radio play, *Words and Music* (1962). Beckett definitely elevates 'love' to a pinnacle of importance in this play: another line suggests, 'Love is of all the passions the most powerful passion.' He seems to suggest love comes close to being an expression of that which is most deeply redolent of the human experience: 'Is love the word? Is soul the word? Do we mean love when we say love? Soul when we say soul?' As always for Beckett the struggle is with the inadequacy of words to explain and, most surely, to communicate the human experience. We might also note that Meg's response ('that's stupid') echoes Patricia's retort to Michel in *À bout de souffle* when he considers the choice between grief and nothing (as posed by William Faulkner in *The Wild Palms* [1939]) and says he would opt for nothingness (Sterritt 1999: 53). Whatever we might take from all of these possible references, it is clear there are deep questions being asked within this 'comedy'.

In *I, Daniel Blake* there is nothing like the level of highbrow cultural references to be identified in *Le Week-end*. However, there are certain recurring themes that may be relevant to this discussion. There is, for example, a continuing interest in the value of education for the working class. Early in the film Katie tells Dan that she has plans to 'go back to me books.' She has been studying with the Open University, an institution set up by a Labour government in 1969 with the aim of widening access to

THE 'LIBERAL LEFT' RESPONSE TO TWENTY-FIRST CENTURY... 29

higher education.[10] Following the same theme of ordinary people attempting to educate themselves, Dan spends time in a library trying to fill in the necessary form to appeal against the loss of his social security benefits. Public libraries have always been associated with a social agenda of enabling working people to access knowledge and the library we see is both heavily used and a place designed to enable people to access new futures.[11] As Dan enters the library the camera holds in shot a poster advertising 'Books on Tyne – The Newcastle Book Festival.' Beneath the title of the festival there is the slogan 'Turn a new page' and beneath this 'Newcastle Libraries' and 'Newcastle City Council'. The attention given to this poster and these seemingly small parts of the mise en scène is further emphasised when we reflect that in the previous scene the chance to use product placement has been starkly refused. 'China' (Kema Sikazwe), a young black neighbour of Dan's, takes a drink from a plastic bottle of something that looks like coke but there is no label on the bottle. The drink has been deliberately placed in a clear, unmarked bottle. The use of the bottle as a prop is so apparent and so highlighted as to make the absence of any company labelling obvious. We would seem to have a deliberately flagged up comment on the film industry and its implication in commercial practices.

Loach, in his early 80s, and screenwriter, Paul Laverty, in his early 60s, also seem to be interested in the cultural interests of younger people. On the wall in China's flat there is a poster showing an image of the grey industrial city imagined by Travis Stewart, working as Machinedrum, for his album *Vapor City* (2013). Is the referencing of more recent elements of 'youth' (Stewart is now 35) culture a crazy position for older filmmakers to take; or, does it show an awareness that older aspects of cultural experience, like the Open University and the public library tradition, need

---

[10] The extent to which working-class people were actually given increased opportunities to take degrees via the Open University is much debated and disputed (see, for example, Taylor and Steele 2011). However, it is certainly the case that widening working-class participation was the origin of the concept. Taylor and Steele's book states, for example: 'in March 1963, a Labour Party study group under Lord Taylor presented a report about the continuing exclusion from higher education of lower-income groups. They 'proposed an experiment on radio and television: a "University of the Air" for serious, planned, adult education' (2011: 100).

[11] Mechanics' Institutes formed from 1821 set up their own libraries and from 1850 public libraries began to be provided by local councils (McMenemy 2009: 23–29).

30   J. WHITE

to be seen alongside the continuing vibrancy and inventiveness of popular culture?

Later, continuing the theme of books, learning and culture, and in a significant symbolic gesture for the film, we are shown Dan, a joiner by trade, making a bookcase for Katie. And, Dan's interest in working with wood is of further significance. Within the terms with which the idea of 'culture' is employed in *Le Week-end*, an interest in working in wood is not something that would be deemed a cultural reference. However, what we see at several points in *I, Daniel Blake* is our central character's deep sensitivity towards the look and feel of a piece of wood. When he returns to his place of work where he had his heart attack some of his old workmates have left him a small plank of wood. One of his former colleagues now shows him this length of wood and together they stand the plank on end to touch it, look at it and admire it. What we are being shown is the ability of Dan and his workmates (and by extension, working class people in general) to take part in aesthetic contemplation and to know for themselves, and in their lives, aesthetic value. This appreciation of shape, form, colour and pattern is also, significantly, shown as being shared by children from this intensely poor background. When Dan presents Daisy, Katie's daughter, with a mobile he has made to hang in her bedroom her pleasure is clear, not only in the way she describes it as 'gorgeous' but in her demeanour before it. Where *Le Week-end* has places like the Musée Rodin and the high-quality bookshop, Tschann Libraire,[12] *I, Daniel Blake* has Newcastle public library and a working man crafting a bookcase. The films are distinctively different in their approaches to these things, but both might be said to be intensely interested in culture. It is just that what is seen as culture, understood as culture and taken to be culture in the two films would seem to be two different things. *Le Week-end* is much more obviously about culture and learning and *I, Daniel Blake* would seem at first to deal with these things barely at all. On closer examination, we find that while *Le Week*-end looks at middle-class ideas of culture and learning, *I, Daniel Blake* shows its own interest in these areas but very much in relation to the working class. Our immediate awareness of these things in one film and our initial failure to appreciate the presence of these things in the other is an expression of the dominance of particular forms and understandings of culture.

[12] Take what you want… I'll pay,' says Meg to Nick.

CLASS AND LANDSCAPES

When considering the events that take place in these films, the linkage of *Le Week-end* to places beyond the UK is, again, more immediately apparent. The film is a challenge to any viewers who reject the importance of a European outlook, or who disdain European culture. The opening at once takes us beyond Britain's borders as we emerge from the Channel Tunnel in France. Political impulses embodied in the 2017 UK referendum vote to leave the European Union, and in the success of the UK Independence Party (UKIP) during the years preceding Brexit, are implicitly questioned by the outlook of a film revelling in a keynote sense of cosmopolitanism.[13] An awareness of some of the main Parisian landmarks is assumed from the outset, an at least rudimentary knowledge of French is presumed, and a basic knowledge of European cultural references is taken for granted. By contrast, *I, Daniel Blake* appears to be parochial and inward-looking, concerned with socio-political events in the UK and confined to run-of-the-mill locations in Newcastle. In *Le Week-end*, within the first ten minutes, we are on the Eurostar, arrive in the Gare du Nord, take a taxi with our central couple and listen to them speaking French to the driver, drive past landmarks like the Arc de Triomphe de l'Étoile, and end up in a swanky room in a prestigious Parisian hotel with a view of the Eiffel Tower. Nothing like this happens in the dull, drab environs of Newcastle encountered in the opening to *I, Daniel Blake*. However, as with cultural references, there is more to this than is immediately obvious. The young single mother, Katie, and her two children, who Dan meets within 15 minutes of the start of *I, Daniel Blake*, take us beyond Newcastle in providing a link to London and pointing towards a changed relationship between the UK's capital city and the rest of the country. Current council housing policies have meant Katie has been moved out of London and (effectively) sent to Newcastle. 'We was in a homeless hostel for about two years…,' says Katie. 'The three of us were in one room. They eventually offered me a flat. So,

---

[13] There is not the space here to further investigate the relationship of this film's 'cosmopolitanism' to definitions of 'new cosmopolitanism' in the social sciences post-1989 but, for the purposes of this chapter, the linkage of 'new cosmopolitanism' to liberalism is particularly important. According to Fine: 'While advocates of the new cosmopolitanism are prepared to acknowledge that nationalism may have had value in the past, not least in the pursuit of anti-colonial struggles or in the building of modern welfare states, they renounce the idea that solidarity ties must be conceptually linked to the nation-state and pronounce the death of nationalism as a normative principle in social integration' (Fine 2007: 4).

32   J. WHITE

the good news was it was a flat: bad news was it was up here...They're moving out the likes of me.' Changes in the way in which the housing crisis is being handled in London are linked to the growing importance of that city in recent years as crucial hub of globalisation. The Grenfell Tower fire in the summer of 2017 highlighted the existence of pockets of extreme poverty in London but also, in line with Katie's fictional experience, the way in which deprived social groups have been marginalised in the capital. As London has become increasingly important as a centre of global investment the debate over how open the city should be as a financial marketplace has intensified.[14] In *I, Daniel Blake*, this theme is built on when Dan's young neighbours, 'China' and Piper (Steven Richens), enter the film. These two characters are involved in an entrepreneurial enterprise that positions them within the global marketplace. They are receiving trainers direct from their source, a worker in China, and selling them for half the price they would normally cost on the High Street. Providing a further global link, 'China' describes his usual employment at a warehouse where he can be called in at a moment's notice and then sent home as 'worse than China'.

Loach and Laverty, could potentially have created a film that identified Katie's plight as being in various ways the fault of foreigners. But, instead they highlight the fact that, for them as socialists, divisions within the world should not be seen as being between nationalities but between classes. For them, it has historically ever been thus and the evidence is in the film. The Central Arcade in Newcastle that Dan is seen walking through was built in 1837 by a property developer who managed to persuade the council to agree to his redevelopment plans for a 12-acre site in this part of Newcastle. As has been suggested, the places Dan is seen standing next to or walking past are not down to chance; these locations have been deliberately chosen. The Central Arcade is part of what has

---

[14] *London: Winning in a Changing World, Review of the Competitiveness of London's Financial Centre*, described London as 'a hub for international wholesale finance,' and 'a magnet for capital and talented people,' giving the UK 'the largest international capital flows of any country in the world' (Merrill Lynch Europe 2008: 6). In 2014, in the *Financial Times*, Janan Ganesh identified an 'insistent feeling' that 'London has become too hospitable to foreign (especially Russian) money, too tolerant of various strains of extremism, too indifferent to British citizens priced out of their own capital city.' The article went on to suggest the rise of the UK Independence Party was 'ultimately a reaction against everything the city embodies', but said the city was also 'the last trump card that Britain has to play within the world' and that the one 'globally coveted asset Britain has left is this city' (Ganesh 2014).

THE 'LIBERAL LEFT' RESPONSE TO TWENTY-FIRST CENTURY... 33

become known as the Grainger Town area of Newcastle. This part of the city was redeveloped in the middle of the nineteenth century by Richard Grainger, 'a builder and speculator unparalleled in the region,' (Cullen and Lovie 2003: 3) and, more recently, in a project started in the 1990s, has been regenerated to provide 'a centre second to none among great European cities' (Cossons 2003: 1). Grainger was an entrepreneur with the vision of 'China', the character in *I, Daniel Blake*, to escape his roots. 'See these trainers,' says 'China' to Dan, 'these are the future. No more crap jobs.' Grainger's father was a labourer in Newcastle who with his family 'occupied rooms in a poor tenement' (Cullen and Lovie 2003: 12). But the son became a builder, married into a family with money, and between 1834 and 1842 created a new city centre for Newcastle. In their book on the recent redevelopment of this area, *Newcastle's Grainger Town: An Urban Renaissance*, Fiona Cullen and David Lovie assess him in this way: 'Like many entrepreneurs of the period Grainger was essentially a man of business, ruthless when necessary in pushing through his vision. He was not particularly philanthropic – he never built for the lower classes – but he improved everyone's life, risking bankruptcy in the process' (ibid: 17). For Loach and Laverty little has changed: an entrepreneur may come from humble roots but the outcome of his or her commercial efforts will, in fact, not improve everyone's lives but only the lives of some.[15] In the late 1990s a plan was put together to rebuild this area of Newcastle alongside 'an effective strategy of long-term economic development' (ibid: 37). Top of a list of objectives was 'to develop existing businesses and promote the formation of new businesses' (ibid: 38). The project 'is now widely recognised as an exemplary regeneration scheme and its approach is being applied both in the UK and abroad' (ibid: 43).[16] Fundamental differences between liberalism and socialism highlighted earlier in this chapter, cen-

[15] Cullen and Lovie record Harriet Martineau in 1840 reporting that, 'nearly a million pounds had been added to the value of the town by Grainger's work in just five years' (2003: 23). J.R. Leifchild, in a book first printed in 1853 by Frank Cass and reprinted again in 1968, highlights Grainger's approach to opposition to his business plans: 'Some folk wanted to put a stop to his pulling down the old theatre, and intended to apply for a legal injunction; but within three hours from the sealing of the contract, the chimneys of the theatre were down, and, before any message could have reached London, the whole building had disappeared!' (Leifchild 1853/2012: 63).

[16] In July of the year *I, Daniel Blake* was filmed *ChronicleLive*, the online version of the Newcastle Chronicle, reported the unemployment rate in the North East had fallen to 7.4% but this meant it was 'still by some distance the highest in the country' (Kelly 2016). Newcastle City Council's website with its focus on the city itself says: 'Newcastle has a large

tring on liberalism's linkage with capitalism and socialism's concern to either reform or overthrow capitalism, clearly come to a head when considering these sorts of issues.

Whether it is in the field of culture, as we saw earlier, or that of business, *I, Daniel Blake* announces powerfully that given opportunities the working class are just as capable (of creating things of beauty, or achieving entrepreneurial success) as those from the more privileged middle classes. The cultural and social references in *I, Daniel Blake* are just as strong as those in *Le Week-end* but in *I, Daniel Blake* they are to a history and continuity of working-class solidarity and self-help, to a working-class willingness to work and take pride in their work, and to the post-war development of a welfare state built around social housing, a caring benefits system, health care, valued libraries and education. For the makers of this film this represents a rich culture at least as valuable and worth celebrating as the elite art seemingly valued by *Le Week-end*. *I, Daniel Blake* works to remind the audience of social values and possibilities, and to challenge audiences to face the realities of contemporary UK society. There is a starkness about the way in which the attack by the state on the poorest and most vulnerable is portrayed in Loach's film that takes us back (and Loach full circle) to *Cathy Come Home* (1966).

I, Daniel Blake puts forward a clear political position, contests nationalist attitudes and, therefore, indicates a way forward towards redefining some form of union with Europe. *Le Week-end* presents us with the tired state of a generation of activists who have lost faith in their earlier ideals. *I, Daniel Blake* displays the contemporary resurgence of socialist ideas. Why would Nick, given his youthful enthusiasm for changing society, describe himself as working in a second-rate former polytechnic? In his speech to the assembled dinner guests in Morgan's apartment, he says: 'the university where I teach is not a proper university. It is an ex-polytechnic which is a factory on the outskirts of Birmingham set up only to produce idiocy.' Should he not think that he is in exactly the right place to speak to young people coming to higher education for the first time in their family history? The working class are a frustration to Nick. He has told one of his students, 'If you spent as long on your studies as you do on your hair you might have a chance of escaping your background.'

number of people who are without work and claiming benefits. This represents 27,870 people or 15.6% of the working age population' (Newcastle City Council 2017).

REALISM AND DISTANCIATION

At the end of *Le Week-end* we are given a chirpy reprise of the dance sequence from *Bande à part* that is almost like the cast celebrating the end of a successful shoot and which operates like a Brechtian distanciation device to remind us we are watching a film. Moments like this suggest that this is the film in this pairing that opens up space for the audience to reflect on what they are seeing. They also remind us of long-standing difficulties within film theory in relation to realism and Loach's work. Colin MacCabe famously looked at the relationship between realism and cinema in an article in *Screen* in 1974, suggesting that realist texts (he mentioned Loach's *Cathy Come Home*) were deceptive in that they pretended to be reality itself while actually being just as constructed as any other text (1974: 7–27). For MacCabe it was modernist techniques—drawing attention to film as film—that created critical distance for the audience and, thereby, enabled them to reflect on what they were watching.[17] In his study of Loach's work, *The Cinema of Ken Loach: Art in the Service of the People*, Jacob Leigh identifies the way in which, for MacCabe, 'the form of classic realism undermines radical political intentions' (2002: 14). In discussing *Days of Hope* (Loach 1975), a four-part historical drama made for television, John Hill identifies a position Loach has found himself in on more than one occasion. This TV drama was 'criticised by one group of (liberal) critics for its advocacy of political revolution over reformism' while also being 'criticised by another (Marxist) group for itself being insufficiently revolutionary in its approach to form' (2011: 150).

Following Julian Petley (1992: 101), Leigh identifies something closer to 'naturalism' as opposed to 'realism' in Loach's work. This involves 'a searching out and detailed observation of elements of the social environment frequently excluded from systems of representation' (2002: 14). This, it is suggested, takes Loach's use of realism beyond mainstream film's expectation that we should take the events happening before us as 'real'. Going further, Hill contends that in Loach's work, 'the visual style of the films, and its debt to elements of documentary, may...be seen to

---

[17] More recently, while attacking *The Wind That Shakes the Barley* (Loach 2006) for its simplistic view of history, MacCabe identified Loach as 'perhaps the most important heir of that realist tradition which finds its roots in Rossellini and its justification in the representation of hitherto unrecognised elements of social reality' and acknowledged Loach's 'unreconstructed left politics' as 'an enormous asset in refusing the comforting lies of the present' (2006: 105).

36   J. WHITE

involve a degree of "distanciation" by virtue of the way in which the audience is both encouraged into an engagement with characters but also held at a certain distance from them' (2011: 152). Hill points to the way in which Loach holds shots, avoids excessive cutting, and places the emphasis on 'conversation rather than action' (2011: 153). Certainly, *I, Daniel Blake* does depend on the viewer feeling themselves to be positioned as a detached observer, present within the setting but watching voyeuristically, that is to say, simultaneously aware of the powerlessness that accompanies the disembodied presence of cinema viewing. We are left with two questions, firstly, whether in order to present social challenge and to impact this on the audience it is necessary to challenge the realist form, and, secondly, whether Loach's techniques actually do in some way move beyond conventional social realism.

As regards *Le Week-end*, we might question whether any distanciation techniques we might find here are more than post-modernist tics. Certainly, if we consider the dinner party scenes in this film, the attack on the bourgeoisie is intensely barbed. Through Morgan and his guests the middle classes are mercilessly parodied. As Meg and Nick are entering the apartment he mutters to her, 'What gorgeous hell is this?' and, maybe, in Kureishi's frame of references they are at Rodin's *Gates of Hell*, a version of which is at the Musée Rodin. However, even if we consider much of what we have in *Le Week-end* as heavily ironic and as amounting to an attack on the complacent, self-absorbed middle classes[18]—in other words, an attack on the very people most likely to be watching it—as a film it remains unable to escape its boundaries of art and culture. As with the characters it portrays, it has accepted the reduced frontiers of an intellectual chessboard that at one stage had seemed to be a real political battlefield. It moves with great complexity of referencing but ultimately meaninglessly within the same bounded intellectual field it wishes to attack. This is not to doubt the 'liberal left' leanings of the filmmakers, nor even that they may, as Nick puts it, still feel themselves, 'anarchists of the Left.' But it is to take us back to Mouffe's concerns with liberalism, and it is to highlight the inherent problems in yoking together 'liberal' and 'left' as in the title to this chapter. The unspoken presence in Michell and

---

[18] Notice the roles given to servants in these scenes; Stéphane who is condescendingly and dismissively thanked by Morgan while handing out glasses of champagne, the servant who takes Meg and Nick's coats, and then, Julie, the servant with snacks on a silver salver whose name Morgan repeats several times in what seem to be attempted tones of seduction.

Kureishi's film is Paris in May 1968, which had a strong anarchist aspect to it in that much of the student and worker protest of that period erupted spontaneously and without being controlled centrally. This is the pinnacle moment for Nick and Morgan's generation of student activists. Nick, in particular, is taken back to his lost hopes and beliefs, to a period of promise, potential and possibilities. The lines from Bob Dylan's song, 'Like a Rolling Stone' (1965), that Nick sings as he gets drunk in his hotel room are, 'How does it feel?/How does it feel?/To be without a home/Like a complete unknown.' In this comedy, the sense of the tragic loss of potential of Nick, but also of a whole generation, is laid horribly bare.

Beyond this, Michell and Kureishi will know that the Montmarte area where much of the film is shot saw the start of the Paris Commune uprising in 1871, which ended in mass executions. They will also know that the Sacré-Cœur was built to tower as a conservative reminder over this area that had been a seat of revolutionary ideas. Interestingly, when we see Meg at Morgan's dinner party she is flicking through a book about L'École de Barbizon, an art movement in France in the mid-1800s that began to emphasise the importance of realism in painting. Some members of the school, most famously Jean-François Millet, began to shift the subject matter of their work away from mythological figures and portraits of the bourgeoisie towards authentic images of peasant workers.[19] Although the artists at Barbizon might more correctly be seen as members of the liberal bourgeoisie rather than truly revolutionary, they were challenging both social norms and artistic conventions. *Le Week-end* places before us a complex of liberal and socialist ideas. The film is a product of the liberal wing of the arts community, but it is, in keeping with this tradition, open to more socially challenging interpretations.

Democracy and Antagonism

In juxtaposing the intellectually stimulating but, in the final analysis, comfortable embrace of elite liberal discussion with the in-your-face, confrontational, socialist politics of the streets, these two films identify the split

---

[19] For the primary example of this style see Millet's *Les glaneuses/The Gleaners* (1857) held in the Musée d'Orsay (Musée d'Orsay, Jean-François Millet – *Gleaners*, n.p.). 'Millet's representation of class strife on a large-scale farm was…uniquely modern in the 1850s' (Fratello 2003: 686). There was an influx of artists (including Millet) into Barbizon in 1848 during the Year of Revolutions but this was more likely to escape the political turmoil of Paris rather than to come together to emphasise any revolutionary intent in their art.

38   J. WHITE

that inevitably exists within any attempt to conceptualise a 'liberal left'. From a strongly socialist perspective, Mouffe has argued: 'To be able to mobilise passions towards democratic designs, democratic politics must have a partisan character' (Mouffe 2005: 6). In *On the Political*, she sees liberalism by and large as being 'characterised by a rationalist and individualistic approach which forecloses acknowledging the nature of collective identities' (Mouffe 2005: 10). *Le Week-end* focuses on Nick, and Meg, and Morgan as individuals; *I, Daniel Blake* focuses on Dan but on Dan as a member of a strongly delineated working class. *I, Daniel Blake* is capable of subtlety: notice, for example, the way in which his observational camera technique is used when filming the food bank scene, so that we feel we are watching and over-hearing Katie's shame from a distance. Loach does frame shots and choose locations in such a way as to create meanings that depend on careful use of film language: notice, for example, the way in which when Dan spray-paints his demand to be heard he is placed before a huge, bland wall that is metaphorically the monolithic face of the state and is then filmed small within the frame and penned behind railings. But, in the end, *I, Daniel Blake* is time and again direct and forthright in what it has to say: 'It's all a monumental farce, isn't it?' says Dan, summing-up the Kafkaesque state of the benefits system. Dan's words read at his funeral make the case for the honesty of the ordinary person: 'I'm not a shirker, a scrounger, a beggar, nor a thief...I paid my dues, never a penny short...I don't tug the forelock but look my neighbour in the eye and help him if I can. I don't accept or seek charity. My name is Daniel Blake. I am a man, not a dog.' If we are not currently seeing the end of nation states as new cosmopolitanism predicted,[20] the question then becomes, who is going to define 'the nation' and in the process express a collective sense of 'national identity'?

I, Daniel Blake makes a strong play for defining Britain in terms of a cohesive, inclusive, working-class tradition that it sees as having shaped the post-war state, alongside a dissenting tradition that defends the rights of the individual against the power of the state. Mouffe dismisses 'the post-political perspective' that makes claims for antagonism to have disappeared, and she is correct to do so. The key question, and it is the one *I, Daniel Blake* recognises most strongly, is whether the 'antagonism' will be defined as being between 'Us' and the racial/ethnic/religious 'Other', or between 'Rich' and 'Poor'. Liberalism has no answer to nationalism

---

[20] Mouffe describes the mistaken belief that 'thanks to globalisation and the universalisation of liberal democracy, we can expect a cosmopolitan future bringing peace, prosperity and the implementation of human rights worldwide' (2005: 1).

because it believes in rational reason as a solution to political conflict. The left has the only possible answer to nationalism within the real political world as defined by Mouffe, which is direct antagonistic confrontation.

In conclusion, we might note that this is not to invalidate *Le Week-end*. In a curious way, *I, Daniel Blake* could not exist without *Le Week-end*. The discussion of different approaches, different content and different political positions that has been had here with regard to these two films depends upon viewing films as existing in relation to each other. The term 'liberal left' does yoke together contrary political positions, but the clash of ideas that is therein contained is actually *the* crucial component of any response towards resurgent nationalism. Laclau and Mouffe have highlighted the importance of debate/antagonism between positions. Pointing out how they are in accord with Jürgen Habermas's concept of the public sphere, they have emphasised the way in which 'political identities are not pre-given but constituted and re-constituted through debate in the public sphere' and that they agree 'on the need to take account of the many different voices that a democratic society encompasses and to widen the field of democratic struggles' (Laclau and Mouffe 2001: xvii). But, for them, the debate, even the conflict, between positions is the very nature of democracy:

> The central role that the notion of antagonism plays in our work forecloses any possibility of a final reconciliation, of any kind of rational consensus, of a fully inclusive 'we'. For us, a non-exclusive public sphere of rational argument is a conceptual impossibility. Conflict and division, in our view, are neither disturbances that unfortunately cannot be eliminated nor empirical impediments that render impossible the full realization of a harmony that we cannot attain because we will never be able to leave our particularities completely aside in order to act in accordance with our rational self – a harmony which should nonetheless constitute the ideal towards which we strive. Indeed, we maintain that without conflict and division, a pluralist democratic politics would be impossible. (ibid.: xvii)

BIBLIOGRAPHY

Adler, Katya. 2016. Is Europe lurching to the far right? *BBC*. 28 Apr 2016. http://www.bbc.co.uk/news/world-europe-36150807. Accessed 9 Apr 2017.

Bradshaw, Peter. 2013. Le Week-end – review. *The Guardian*. 10 Oct 2013. https://www.theguardian.com/film/2013/oct/10/le-week-end-review. Accessed 18 July 2017.

40 J. WHITE

Cossons N. 2003. Foreword. In *Newcastle's Grainger Town: an urban renaissance*. Ed. Cullen, Fiona and Lovie, David. London: English Heritage.

Cubitt, Sean. 2016. Ecopolitics of cinema. In *The Routledge companion to cinema and politics*. Ed. Tzioumakis, Yannis and Molloy, Claire. London: Routledge.

Cullen, Fiona and Lovie, David. 2003. *Newcastle's Grainger town: an urban renaissance*. London: English Heritage.

Fine, Robert. 2007. *Cosmopolitanism*. London: Routledge

Fratello, Bradley. 2003. France embraces Millet: the intertwined fates of "The Gleaners" and "The Angelus". *The Art Bulletin* 85(4): 686.

Freeden Michael. 2015. *Liberalism: a very short introduction*. Oxford: Oxford University Press.

Ganesh, Janan. 2014. London: the capital of globalisation. *Financial Times*. 29 Sept 2014. https://www.ft.com/content/40e307c2-3aa1-11e4-bd08-00144feabdc0?mhq5j=e1. Accessed 18 July 2017.

Gant, Charles. 2013. Third time lucky for *Prisoners*, and UK box office has its worst weekend of 2013. *The Guardian*. 16 Oct 2013. https://www.theguardian.com/film/filmblog/2013/oct/16/prisoners-sunshine-leith-uk-box-office. Accessed 18 July 2017

Gant, Charles. 2016. *I, Daniel Blake* scores impressive result at UK box office as Trolls takes top spot. *The Guardian*. 25 Oct 2016. https://www.theguardian.com/film/2016/oct/25/i-daniel-blake-ken-loach-uk-box-office-trolls-top-spot. Accessed 18 July 2017 .

Heywood, Andrew. 2007. *Political ideologies: an introduction*. London: Palgrave Macmillan.

Hill, John. 2011. *Ken Loach: the politics of film and television* London: BFI/Palgrave Macmillan.

Hobsbawm, Eric. J. 1990. *Nations and nationalism since 1780: programme, myth, reality*. Cambridge: Cambridge University Press.

Hutchinson, Lisa. 2015. Over one million people in the UK are using food banks, new figures show. And the busiest food bank in the UK is in the West End of Newcastle where thousands attend each month. *ChronicleLive*. 22 Apr 2015. http://www.chroniclelive.co.uk/news/north-east-news/over-one-million-people-uk-9094302. Accessed 4 July 2017.

I, Daniel Blake. Box Office Mojo. http://www.boxofficemojo.com/movies/?pag e=intl&country=UK&id=i,danielblake.htm Accessed 18 July 2017.

International Monetary Fund. 2009. *World Economic Outlook: Crisis and Recovery*. 24 Apr 2009. IMF, Washington, p.xii. 15 July 2017.

Kelly, Mike. 2016. North East unemployment still the worst in the UK – figures reveal. *ChronicleLive*. 20 July 2016. http://www.chroniclelive.co.uk/news/north-east-news/north-east-unemployment-still-worst-11640943. Accessed 11 July 2017.

Laclau, Ernesto and Mouffe, Chantal. 2001. *Hegemony and socialist strategy: towards a radical democratic politics*. London. Verso.

Laclau, Ernesto. 2005. *On populist reason*. London. Verso.

Leifchild, John, R. (2012) *Our coal and our coal-pits*. London: Routledge.

Leigh, Jacob. 2002. *The cinema of Ken Loach: art in the service of the people*. London: Wallflower Press.

Loach, Ken. 2017. *I, Daniel Blake* – winner's acceptance speech, Outstanding British Film, British Academy Film Awards in 2017. *BAFTA*. 12 Feb 2017. http://www.bafta.org/media-centre/transcripts/i-daniel-blake-winner-acceptance-speech-outstanding-british-film-2017. Accessed 9 Apr 2017.

MacCabe, Colin. 1974. Realism and the cinema: notes on some Brechtian theses. *Screen* 15 (2) Summer: 7–27.

MacCabe, Colin. 2006. Film: Cannes 2006. *Critical Quarterly* 48 (3) Autumn: 105–109.

McMenemy David. 2009. *The public library*. London: Facet.

Merrill Lynch Europe. 2008. London: winning in a changing world. Review of the competiveness of London's financial centre. https://www.theinvestmentassociation.org/assets/components/ima_filesecurity/secure.php?f=press/2008/20081212-01.pdf. Accessed 17 July 2017.

Mouffe, Chantal. 2005. *On the political*. London: Routledge.

Musée d'Orsay. Jean-François Millet – *Gleaners*. http://www.musee-orsay.fr/index.php?id=851&L=1&tx_commentaire_pi1%5BshowUid%5D=341. Accessed 20 July 2017.

Newcastle City Council. 2017. Equality statistics, research and information. 30 May 2017. https://www.newcastle.gov.uk/your-council-and-democracy/statistics-and-census-information/equality-statistics-research-and-information #employment. Accessed 11 July 2017.

Newman, Michael. 2005. *Socialism: a very short introduction*. Oxford: Oxford University Press.

O'Neill, Deirdre. 2016. *Film and the politics of working class representation: the Inside Film project*. In *The Routledge companion to cinema and politics*. Ed. Tzioumakis, Yannis and Molloy, Claire. London: Routledge.

Pantucci, Rafaello. 2016. Ignored by the authorities, emboldened by Brexit, Europe's far right is surging. *The Guardian*. 28 June 2016. https://www.theguardian.com/commentisfree/2016/jun/28/brexit-europe-far-right-rightwing-extremists-politics-terrorism. Accessed 9 Apr 2017.

Pearce, Nick. 2016. How the left should respond to the steady march of nationalism. *New Statesman*. 15 Dec 2016. http://www.newstatesman.com/politics/2016/12/how-left-should-respond-steady-march-nationalism. Accessed 9 Apr 2017.

Petley, Julian. 1992. *The lost continent*. In *All our yesterdays: 90 years of British cinema*. Ed. Barr, Charles. London: BFI, 98–119.

Raffaello, P. 2016. Ignored by the authorities, emboldened by Brexit, Europe's far right is surging. *The Guardian.* 28 June 2016. https://www.theguardian.com/commentisfree/2016/jun/28/brexit-europe-far-right-rightwingextremists-politics-terrorism. Accessed 9 Apr 2017.

Sterritt, David. 1999. *The films of Jean-Luc Godard: seeing the invisible.* Cambridge: Cambridge University Press.

Taylor, Richard and Steele, Tom. 2011. *British Labour and higher education, 1945–2000: ideologies, policies and practice.* London: Continuum.

The Pearl, Newcastle. http://www.thepearlnewcastle.co.uk/. Accessed 18 July 2017.

Vincent, Andrew. 1995. *Modern political ideologies.* Oxford. Blackwell.

Wootton, David. 1993. *John Locke: political writings* Indianapolis Hackett.

CHAPTER 3

From *Down Terrace* to *High-Rise*: The 'Unreal Estate' Cinema of Ben Wheatley

William Brown

On 14 June 2017, the 24-storey Grenfell Tower block in London's North Kensington caught fire, leading to at least 80 deaths and 70 injuries. As has been widely reported, the local council responsible for the tower's upkeep had recently invested in cheap, flammable cladding, which likely caused the fire to spread more rapidly than it could or would have done otherwise, thereby worsening the death toll (Reed and Clare 2017). This sparked debate concerning the way in which working-class residential areas suffer relative neglect compared to more affluent areas, including those that surround the Grenfell Tower in Kensington, suggesting that lives in the UK are valued and protected according to class. Indeed, undocumented migrant workers believed to be living in Grenfell Tower have thus far been excluded from the reported death toll, which in turn suggests that some of the very poorest residents in the UK literally do not count as human beings (Bulman 2017).

The Grenfell Tower fire is simply the most visible recent example of how class correlates with living conditions and the value of life in the UK, as nearly two months after the incident only 12 Grenfell families had been

W. Brown (✉)
University of Roehampton, London, UK
e-mail: William.brown@roehampton.ac.uk

© The Author(s) 2018
J. Harvey (ed.), *Nationalism in Contemporary Western European Cinema*, Palgrave European Film and Media Studies,
https://doi.org/10.1007/978-3-319-73667-9_3

44 W. BROWN

rehoused, while 1652 properties were listed as unoccupied in the local borough of Kensington and Chelsea alone—with 603 of these vacant for more than two years (see Batty et al. 2017). Together with issues of gentrification, the buying of properties by foreign investors and the perception that 'affordable housing' schemes regularly are anything but, it would seem that real estate remains among the most pressing issues in contemporary British life, especially as it relates to class. It is no surprise, then, that British cinema involves a history of films that feature, and which sometimes are about property and real estate, from Edgar Anstey and Arthur Elton's *Housing Problems* (1935) through to *Breaking and Entering* (Anthony Minghella 2006) and *Red Road* (Andrea Arnold 2006). The most recent British cinema has been no different, with the 2010s seeing a 'cluster of tower horror films – *Attack the Block* (Joe Cornish 2011, shot in part on the condemned Heygate Estate in Elephant and Castle), *The Raid* (Gareth Evans 2011), *Dredd* (Pete Travis 2012) and *Containment* (Neil McEnery-West 2015) – all of which literalised social stratification in ascents or escapes from tower blocks' (Luckhurst 2016: 68). This is not to mention documentaries and short films on the topic, including *Home Sweet Home* (Enrica Colusso 2012— about the last residents of the Heygate Estate), *Estate, A Reverie* (Andrea Luka Zimmerman 2015—an experimental documentary about the last days of the Haggerston Estate in Hackney) and *Aylesbury Estate* (Maja Yagoda 2013—a short film about the history and future of the eponymous estate in Walworth).

Ben Wheatley's *High-Rise* (2015) is another film that could be added to the list, since it tells the story of life in a high-rise for various characters from a range of socioeconomic backgrounds (with Luckhurst seeing the Aylesbury Estate as a direct influence on J.G. Ballard's novel, which provides the source material for Wheatley's film; see Luckhurst 2016: 64). What is more, while *High-Rise* is set specifically in a tower block, all of Wheatley's films demonstrate a critical interest in property and real estate. Indeed, various of the essays gathered together in a special issue on Wheatley's films in a 2016 issue of *Critical Quarterly* attest to his interest in these issues. Rosalind Galt, for example, talks about the importance of 'domestic architecture' in *Down Terrace* (2009), noting how the 'shabby terraced house' in which this tale of criminal hoods predominantly unfolds, seems to 'resist the extreme acts that take place in it' (Galt 2016: 23 and 27). Meanwhile, Adam Lowenstein identifies a 'pattern of disorientation' in Wheatley's films as he attempts to 'space out' his viewers (Lowenstein

2016: 5). In this chapter, I should like to pick up and to expand upon Lowenstein's analysis by suggesting that Wheatley's films constitute a subversive 'unreal estate' cinema. That is, through the hallucinatory qualities of his work, Wheatley challenges the 'reality' of 'real estate', thereby undermining the way in which the term is used to legitimise certain ways of organising and owning space in the contemporary world. Furthermore, I shall argue that the violence that commonly erupts in Wheatley's films functions as an expression of the violence inherent in the organisation of space that he identifies—including the organisation of space that is the nation. While Wheatley might be accused of glorifying violence, and thus implicitly of endorsing an organisation of space and real estate that is divisive and thus also violent, the disturbing nature of his films instead highlights and thus opens space for critique of the violent organisation of (space in) the UK.

However, before explaining more fully how Wheatley's 'unreal estate' cinema helps us to think about space and property in the era of Grenfell Tower and of course Brexit, let us first introduce his films and the role that houses and housing play in his cinematic universe.

A Cinema of Real Estate

By 2017, Ben Wheatley had made six feature films as well as various television shows, adverts and online videos. The first of the feature films is the aforementioned *Down Terrace*, which tells the story of a Brighton-based family of gangsters, including Karl (Robin Hill), who has just come back from prison. Set largely in the family home on the street from which the film takes its name, Karl and his father Bill (Robert Hill) must uncover which of their associates is a police informant. Initially suspecting local club owner Garvey (Tony Way), Bill, Karl and Bill's wife Maggie (Julia Deakin) employ local hitman Pringle (Michael Smiley) to kill him, before the latter botches the job. Karl himself kills Garvey, a childhood friend, for implying that Karl's girlfriend Valda (Kerry Peacock) may not have been faithful to him while in prison—and that the child that she is expecting is not therefore his. Karl hides the body with his uncle, Eric (David Schaal), who then kills Pringle and his family since they cannot be trusted to keep Garvey's disappearance a secret. Under pressure from their superiors in London, the family then tries to clear up the mess as Maggie poisons Eric and a hitman attempts to kill Karl in an underpass. In revenge, Valda and Karl murder Maggie and Bill, not least because dying family lawyer Berman (Mark Kempner) says that it is Bill who 'talks to plod'.

46   W. BROWN

Shot primarily using a handheld camera, *Down Terrace* offers to us a claustrophobic world of interior space, where secrets are nigh impossible to keep as characters can hear each other through the walls—with Bill complaining about Karl's music just as we hear various characters listen to arguments and Pringle talking to Garvey through the door to the upstairs bathroom, where the latter hides from the former during his unsuccessful hit. 'You don't want to leave this house. It's not safe for you out there on your own', says Maggie to Karl towards the end of the film, in the process revealing the ongoing psychological trauma that his parents inflict on their son, who features in no photographs from the family's past. Cloistered in the house on Down Terrace, it is no wonder that Karl is prone to substance abuse and violent outbursts. 'You've grown up privileged and spoiled and soft', Bill affirms as he asks Karl to kill Valda. 'I don't want your fucking house', Karl later declares, before shooting his father in the unfinished 'breakfast room' that is at the centre of the family's space. Whether he wants it or not, the house now belongs to him and Valda.

If *Down Terrace* has at its centre an unfinished breakfast room, it is an unrepaired Jacuzzi that sets in motion the plot of *Kill List* (2011). For, hard-up former soldier and hitman Jay (Neil Maskell) comes out of retirement to assassinate various people with his partner Gal (Michael Smiley) in order to maintain his wife Shel (MyAnna Buring) and his son Sam (Harry Simpson) in the manner—and the house—to which they have become accustomed. Killing first a Priest (Gareth Tunley) and then an archivist referred to in the film's intertitles as the Librarian (Mark Kempner), Jay and Gal seem to be doing the dirty work of some occult organisation, not least because both targets thank Jay before he kills them. Indeed, the Librarian has in his possession videos so horrific in content that Jay finds his associates and murders them, too, before reluctantly continuing down the 'kill list' by going to a country estate to murder someone referred to as the Politician. Interrupting a Satanic ritual, Jay and Gal open fire indiscriminately on those in attendance, before being chased and the latter killed. Jay then is forced to fight a figure called the Hunchback in a knife duel, only to discover that the Hunchback is Shel with Sam strapped to her back.

'We should do this more often', says Gal, as he and Jay stomp through the sizeable estate of the politician. 'What? Kill rich people', the latter responds, before Gal rebuffs him: 'No. Get some fresh air.' While wryly amusing, the moment also bespeaks the claustrophobic life that Jay and Gal lead. 'It's not right – one man living in all of that', Gal continues to

FROM *DOWN TERRACE* TO *HIGH-RISE*: THE 'UNREAL... 47

Jay as they observe the mansion on the Politician's estate, a single light illuminated in an otherwise dark building. Earlier, Gal had recalled how the recession of the 1980s was 'a lot more glamorous' than the one that he and Jay are living through now, thereby placing *Kill List* against an economic backdrop that links to the difficulty that Jay has in maintaining his domestic space—all the while corrupt politicians use him for their own gains, as suggested by the role that Jay plays in the occultists' entertainment at the film's climax, where many of the previously masked observers reveal themselves to be figures whom Jay and Gal have encountered over the course of the film, including their employers and Gal's seeming girlfriend Fiona (Emma Fryer).

While *Sightseers* (2012) ostensibly is a road movie and thus not a film confined to domestic spaces, it nonetheless is also heavily concerned with architecture as it follows lovers Chris (Steve Oram) and Tina (Alice Lowe) as they go on a murder-spree caravan holiday across the north of England. Taking in such tourist delights as the Crich Tramway Museum in Derbyshire and the Derwent Pencil Museum in Cumbria, Chris also kills anyone who contradicts him, especially if they are ostensibly posher than him. Meanwhile, Tina begins to kill people much more indiscriminately. This leads to tension between the couple, before they destroy their caravan and head to the Ribblehead Viaduct in Yorkshire. Although they are supposed to jump to their deaths together, Tina lets go of Chris's hand at the last minute and lets him jump to his death alone.

While *Sightseers* is like a cross between *Nuts in May* (Mike Leigh 1975), *Butterfly Kiss* (Michael Winterbottom 1995) and *The Trip* (Michael Winterbottom 2010) in its comically murderous journey across England's quirkier northern tourist destinations, it nonetheless starts out in and regularly takes us back to the chintz-filled domestic space of Tina's mother, Carol (Eileen Davies), in Redditch in Worcestershire. As they leave Carol, who declares that she does not like Chris and that Tina is a murderer, Soft Cell's cover of 'Tainted Love' plays on the car radio and the film's soundtrack. The lyrics 'I've got to run away' and 'I've got to get away' seem particularly resonant in relation to Tina's need to escape her abusive mother. Furthermore, when eating at a restaurant with a group of women on a hen-do, Tina explains that she 'gets' Chris's predilection for killing people: 'Because it's just about personal empowerment, isn't it? It's just expressing yourself and thinking outside the box. And I've been in the box and I don't want to go back to the box, Chris. I'd rather die. Do you know that?' The box, then, is at first Tina's Redditch home and her life

48   W. BROWN

with her mother, with whom she still lives at 35 years of age—before then becoming the caravan that she inhabits with Chris. As per James B Twitchell's analysis of the Winnebago in American culture, the caravan promises freedom and mobility, but in fact brings domesticity on to the road, thereby creating a contradiction that *Sightseers* finds unsustainable as Tina must not only escape Redditch, but also destroy the caravan and kill Chris in order to be free (see Twitchell 2014).

A Field in England (2013) might also seem not to be about real estate, since the film is set entirely outside in a seemingly never-ending field that nonetheless is bounded by hedgerows and woodland. The film tells the story of Whitehead (Reece Shearsmith), a cowardly scholar and a seer who escapes from combat during the English Civil War (1642–1651) only to be taken in by a soldier, Cutler (Ryan Pope), who leads him and two other men, Jacob (Peter Ferdinando) and Friend (Richard Glover), to O'Neil (Michael Smiley), an Irish loyalist who has stolen books on alchemy from Whitehead's former master, but who needs Whitehead in order to divine the location of treasure supposedly buried in the titular field. Refusing magic mushrooms, Whitehead is tortured by O'Neil into a visionary trance. He leads the group to a spot in the field where Jacob and Friend are forced to dig, before eventually rebelling and the group disintegrating into violence.

If not overtly about housing, the film is nonetheless about land and property, including the concept of humans as property, since at various points in the film characters assert how they are not slaves and/or that they are their own masters. In this way, the film's Civil War setting reflects a wider sense of rebellion against a system of property and ownership and which is linked to Royalty: 'real estate' here is Royal, since real may not just be derived etymologically from the Latin term *res*, meaning a material thing, but also from *rex*, meaning king. That is, the estate or the field is the field of the king, and which the characters seek to undermine (or literally to mine under) in order to find their own treasure. It is perhaps apt that O'Neil and company find nothing but a skeleton at the bottom of the hole that they dig: there is no treasure or power to help the Loyalists; Royals are simply human beings like any other, whose flesh will rot like any other.

In *High-Rise* (2015), Anthony Royal (Jeremy Irons) is in Wheatley's Ballard adaptation the architect who has designed and who lives in the penthouse of the high-rise apartment block that is the new home of neurosurgeon Robert Laing (Tom Hiddleston). Living on the 25th floor, Laing nonetheless aspires to make it higher in the building, the storeys of which correspond to social standing. His ambitions are thwarted both by one of his medical students, Munrow (Augustus Prew), who lives on the 39th floor, and by Royal's thuggish servant, Simmons (Dan Skinner), who forcibly ejects Laing from Royal's penthouse suite when he arrives at a party in a suit rather than in the aristocratic Restoration attire worn by the other guests (with the Restoration being the restoration of the monarchy after the failure of Oliver Cromwell's son, Richard, to carry on his father's policies). Laing is trapped in a lift—an early sign of the power and other failures that will soon blight the high-rise. Indeed, power shortages lead to an uprising by tenants from the lower levels, who are led by debt-ridden television producer Richard Wilder (Luke Evans) to the upper floors to use the swimming pool, supermarket and other amenities. Social decorum descends into savagery, in particular after the suicide of Munrow, whom Laing deceives into believing that he has a brain tumour. In effect, the upper and lower levels come to blows, with Pangbourne (James Purefoy) and Wilder as their respective ringleaders. The film ends with Wilder killing Royal, before himself being killed by the various women living in the penthouse. As the credits roll, we pan up from the high-rise to blue skies as The Fall's song, 'Industrial Estate', appears on the soundtrack, together with Margaret Thatcher's voice explaining that 'where there is restrained capital, there will never be political freedom'.

From the above synopses it should be clear that real estate and property are a core concern for Wheatley. Before I begin to integrate my analyses of the films (as opposed to considering them separately), I might briefly mention that Wheatley has since directed *Free Fire* (2016), a film set in a warehouse in Boston, Massachusetts, in 1978, which sees an arms deal between a South African seller and IRA buyers go wrong after Harry (Jack Reynor) and Stevo (Sam Riley), who are working on different sides of the deal, recognise each other from a brawl the night before and begin to fight again. The film then basically consists of a continuous gunfight within the single warehouse setting. Given its American setting, together with the presence of international stars like Sharlto Copley, Armie Hammer, Brie Larsen and Cillian Murphy, the film marks something of a departure from Wheatley's earlier work. Even though the film is clearly invested in the meaning of industrial space in 1970s Boston, it does not involve the emphasis on domestic and/or the specifically English space(s) of his earlier work, and so I shall only refer to it on occasion in what follows. But having established how Wheatley's is a cinema of real estate, let us now look at how his work involves various consistent themes, and particularly an interest in esoterica and the occult.

DARK, SATANIC THEMES

There are various tropes that appear consistently in Wheatley's films, including performers, spaces and stylistic elements. Michael Smiley, for example, remains a consistent presence in nearly all of Wheatley's feature films—as well as taking a role in his short 'U for Unearthed', which Wheatley made for the compilation horror film, *The ABCs of Death* (Various 2012). Furthermore, he works consistently with writer (and wife) Amy Jump, cinematographer Laurie Rose and—at least in the earlier films, actor and editor Robin Hill.

As mentioned, domestic spaces are common in Wheatley's films, as are woodlands and hedgerows. Even a film as claustrophobic as *Down Terrace* features Karl and Eric trying to bury Garvey in a hedge, while woodland marks a transition from the cramped suburban spaces that dominate the early sections of *Kill List* to the nightmarish occult ending. The rural also pervades *Sightseers*, with Chris killing a writer, Ian (Jonathan Aris) by throwing him from a cliff, a fate that also befalls Martin (Richard Glover), as Tina shoves him from a cliff in his specially adapted bike and plastic trailer ('a whole new way of living for economic migrants') after Chris seems to prefer Martin's company to hers.

What is more, it is at a National Trust monument, which resembles the Birkrigg stone circle near Ulverston in Cumbria, that Chris bashes to death a man (Richard Lumsden) after he tells Tina to pick up the excrement left by her dog Poppy, who is in fact a dog called Benjy that used to belong to Ian and his wife Janice (Monica Dolan), and which they rename Banjo before Tina believes the beast to be the reincarnation of Poppy, a dog that she accidentally killed a year earlier (and which is the reason why Carol brands her a murderer). 'Did you go to private school?' asks Chris of the man, whom he accuses of 'still thinking that it's their country', as Chris, post-murder, imagines a history of serfdom in which the man would just have raped Tina because he felt entitled to do so.

During the murder itself, we hear strains of Edward Elgar's 'Nimrod' (1898–1899) as a voiceover by John Hurt recites 'Jerusalem', a poem written by William Blake as part of the preface to *Milton a Poem* (1808). That poem famously features the words 'And was Jerusalem builded here, / Among those dark Satanic mills?' – a reference typically made to the factories and mills created during the era of industrialisation in the UK (Wheatley cuts Hurt's recital off after the word 'Satanic'). In other words, for Blake heavy industry is 'Satanic', meaning that by extension the class

FROM *DOWN TERRACE* TO *HIGH-RISE*: THE 'UNREAL... 51

system and geopolitical domination of the British Empire are equally anti-Christian (for more on the Blakean resonances of Wheatley's work, see Flanagan 2016).

There is a strong interest in the esoteric and the occult that runs throughout Wheatley's work, which we can identify presently. In *Down Terrace*, Bill professes to have a strong interest in *The Tibetan Book of the Dead*, before proposing that his interest in drugs is not driven by money but by the mental expansion that they can afford. This claim to a Zen-like enlightenment is undercut by Bill's snobbery, describing Garvey as of 'working class stock' and Valda as unsuitable for his family, but it nonetheless is reflected by hallucinatory sequences that blur sound and image as he, Karl and Eric take a 'double dip' (a drug cocktail, the contents of which are unclear, but which may include crack and/or PCP, which sometimes are respectively referred to in street slang as 'dip' and 'dipper')—even though in the film the pills that they mix with water look suspiciously like Alka Seltzer. Finally, Bill also has a strong interest in folk music, including 'Scarborough Fair', a song famously covered by Simon and Garfunkel, but which has its origins in the Middle Ages, and in which a woman at one point explains that she has an 'an aiker of good ley-land'.

In *Sightseers*, Janice explains that Ian is himself writing a book entitled *Walks along the Ley-lines of Britain*, which equally represents a history of British spiritual beliefs that give meaning to the space of the country. Often associated with water, and thus by extension with fertility (plants and animals need water to live), ley lines suggest a kind of 'deep history' of the UK: the paths that the earliest inhabitants followed in order not to find themselves stranded without water, or in effect a mapping of the nation defined by humans responding to geography rather than by humans shaping geography. A similar elemental geography is explained at the Derwent Pencil Museum, where Tina learns how in the early 1500s a storm exposed a strange black material that would come to be known as graphite. This material geography, then, suggests a chthonic as opposed to intellectual or religious history of the UK; tourists should not intellectualise and respect the monuments of history from a distance, but rather should live in and interact with them, as happens when Chris kills the man in the stone circle.

Finally, as the stone circle equally evokes a non-/pre-Christian British history of Druidic beliefs, *Sightseers* also features a group of shamen at one of the campsites where Chris and Tina stay, and who are arrested for sacrificing the chickens of the campsite owner to the goddess Kali, the Hindu

52   W. BROWN

destroyer of evil forces. Although potentially an object of ridicule for their new age hip(pi)ness, we nonetheless see Tina in a typically hallucinatory sequence dancing with the shamen, before then seeing her in what appears to be a dream sequence walking through woodland in a wedding dress, as Chris follows her dressed as a serf from the Middle Ages. Not only might this connect Tina visually with a history of unofficial belief systems like witchcraft (an association reinforced by the appearance on the soundtrack of 'Season of the Witch' by Vanilla Fudge), but it also helps to convey her 'chaotic' approach to killing (while Chris professes to be more reasoned and methodical in his murder, a claim that is not strictly true as he basically kills people whom he does not like and/or who slight him somehow).

Witchcraft looms large in *Kill List*, where Fiona arrives with Gal for a dinner party at Jay and Shel's house, only at one point to carve an occult shape into the back of a mirror. Although Fiona and Gal supposedly split, Fiona befriends Shel, before also appearing in a field outside Jay's house at night, staring at him as he stands in his window. Her presence at the Satanic ritual at the film's climax would suggest that she is indeed a witch, as we see the carved shape appear once again. At one point in the ritual, a woman hangs herself, only for the assembled crowd of naked people wearing straw masks to start clapping. Shocked, Jay and Gal begin to fire upon the occultists, who squeal like pigs as they run not away from the gunfire but towards it. Although never explained, *Kill List* suggests a UK in which those in power (the Politician and his ilk) have obtained it *à la* Blake through anti-Christian values, feeding off the complicity and blood of working men like Jay, who strives to maintain a house with a Jacuzzi.

The esoteric and the occult also define *A Field in England*. Not only do we have discussions of alchemy, but we also have hallucinogenic sequences after Cutler drugs Jacob and Friend with a mushroom-based concoction that Whitehead initially refuses, although he, too, grabs and eats mushrooms before his final showdown with O'Neil. This prompts upside-down images that reflect the idea of revolution—with O'Neil declaring at one point that 'the world is turned upside-down, Whitehead, and so is its puppets', referring thus to the possibility for social change as the ruling monarchy are revealed to be puppets, figures whose power is in fact unjustified and empty. *A Field in England* also features regular *tableau vivant*-style images, in which the characters assume static postures even though the camera is recording moving images. Furthermore, we memorably see one of Whitehead's visions, featuring a black sun approaching the Earth. In other words, Wheatley adopts a regularly experimental style that mirrors the links that the film makes to unconventional perspectives and beliefs, with the film also featuring a folk music score on which 'Lady Anne Bothwell's Lament' plays a prominent part. Also known as 'Baloo, My Boy', the song is about the ghost of a husband visiting his wife and child at night having died in war. The use of folk music would seem also to situate Wheatley's film within a folk history of England, one defined not by major historical figures, but by everyday folk with their esoteric beliefs and bodily malfunctions.

Although references to esoterica are less pronounced in *High-Rise*, the film nonetheless also features much surreal imagery, such as Laing covered in paint and Royal's architectural plans of the building itself. Laing likens the plans to 'the unconscious diagram of some kind of psychic event', while they also loosely recall the occult pattern drawn by Fiona on the back of Jay's mirror in *Kill List*. *High-Rise* also provides us with the perspective of a kaleidoscope that belongs to Toby (Louis Suc), the son of Charlotte Melville (Sienna Miller), a woman with whom Laing has a brief initial affair and who is the object of Wilder's attention (with Wilder eventually raping her). We discover that Charlotte has also had an affair with Royal, who turns out to be Toby's father (Royal: 'she has quite a tight cunt, as far as I recall'). 'What can you see in there?' Laing asks Toby as he looks through the kaleidoscope. 'The future', the boy announces, soon after they first meet—before, at the end of the film, we return to kaleidoscopic imagery as Wilder is killed by the coven of women who now take over Royal's penthouse. If these are images of the future, then Wheatley's film might loosely imply a future of a world become woman, perhaps even become witch—even if one of the residents, Steele (Reece Shearsmith), believes that the world would be a better place if women 'kept their legs crossed'.

If there are consistently dark, Satanic themes in Wheatley's films, what are we to make of these? That is, what does the presence of such themes mean? It is not so much that Wheatley believes the world to be governed by Satan-worshipping occultists, but rather that his anti-Christian vision of the world suggests a godless, chaotic universe in which no hierarchies need to be respected—as we shall see in the next section. Establishing Wheatley's 'godless' vision will help us to understand how his cinema is a cinema of 'unreal estate' that undercuts the claims to reality—and thus to legitimacy and power—involved in the term real estate.

Sudden Death

Violence erupts out of nowhere in Wheatley's films. The house on Down Terrace does not strike one immediately as a home for a gangster family, while the murder spree of *Sightseers* starts when Chris runs over a man (Tony Way) for nothing more offensive than littering (and for ignoring Chris's admonitions that he stop doing so). In other words, Wheatley's universe is one in which chaos and death are never but an instant away (or what Adam Nayman would call a universe of confusion and carnage; see Nayman 2017). Indeed, this is remarkable in even Wheatley's earliest work. In 2005, Wheatley made a video called *cunning stunt*, in which a man (Robin Hill) jumps over an oncoming car before then turning to camera in search of acknowledgement for his virtuosity. Before he can celebrate, however, blam! He is run over by a car travelling in the opposite direction. Not only is death by getting run over common in Wheatley's films (*Down Terrace* sees Eric push Pringle's mother in front of a car, while *Sightseers* also sees Tina run-down a random jogger when Chris tells her to stop the car; *Free Fire* involves Harry running-over Stevo towards the film's end). But also, death is, or at least can be, sudden and without warning.

If chaos is never far from Wheatley's world, then this is because this is not a world governed by a god. Indeed, if anything, Wheatley's is a cinema that is deliberately irreverent towards authority, and as such is godless. We can see this in various different forms, including the trajectory of Wheatley's career itself. Having started outside cinema with viral videos and then television, it would seem that Wheatley is atheistic towards cinema as a form. Furthermore, he shot *Down Terrace* over the course of eight days and with a minimal budget. Wheatley thus refuses to conform piously to the rules of the film industry, instead forcing his own way into it like a revolutionary, and bringing to this medium a sensibility honed in other, supposedly inferior, media.

Wheatley's 'atheism' is seen also in the films' plots. In *Down Terrace*, a son kills his own parents in order to take over the family business—but without any recourse to the patriarchal law of the Oedipus myth, as Karl seems to hate Maggie as much as he hates Bill. Meanwhile, *Sightseers* sees Chris subvert social hierarchy by murdering all those who are posher than him, specifically Ian and the man at the stone circle. But where Chris subverts the social order in a bid to reverse it, Tina utterly destroys it. As she explains that she does not want to return to the 'box' that is life with Carol

FROM *DOWN TERRACE* TO *HIGH-RISE*: THE 'UNREAL... 55

in Redditch (or Chris in the caravan), Tina mentions how it might be romantic for the two of them to jump to their own deaths. Chris responds negatively to this: '[w]ell, I mean, going to salsa's romantic. We could maybe try that first.' And yet, come the film's climax on Ribblehead Viaduct, Chris is indeed prepared to die with Tina and jumps to his own death. That is, Chris ultimately buys into the guiding narrative of the tragic lovers, in this sense believing in the 'god' of narrative such that it structures his behaviour. It is Tina who is godless towards narrative, denying the classical 'tragic' ending of the double suicide, and instead letting Chris drop to his death—precisely for getting suckered into the belief that such a death would bring 'meaning' to his existence. Tina sees that the universe is meaningless, and acts accordingly.

Laing suffers from a similar sense of godlessness. He has moved to the high-rise following the death of his sister, and he clearly aims to subvert the established social order by 'climbing' his way to the top of the tower, much to the irritation of Simmons, for example, who has undertaken a similar trajectory of his own (and who thus sees Laing as a threat). If Laing initially wants to subvert the social order by climbing it (a subversion that in fact reinforces the social order—as per Simmons's attempts to conform to those in power), by the end his atheism towards the social order is more complete: Laing does not believe in private property or possessions, beating up a resident to steal some paint from the supermarket and sleeping with Helen while Wilder finds a way to reach the penthouse. As those at the top of the tower eat a horse as order breaks down, Laing also kills and eats a dog. But more pointedly, Laing begins referring to himself in voiceover via the third person ('[f]or all its inconveniences, Laing was satisfied with life in the high-rise'). In other words, where many characters seek consolation for the meaninglessness/godless nature of the universe through social order, consumerism and/or new age self-help—the latter of which demonstrates how the self is a construct designed precisely to give order to the chaos of the world—Laing does not even believe in (the concept of) his self.

Beyond the plots of his films, Wheatley would also seem to suggest an atheism towards established order through the forms that his films take. Rather than a cinema of clarity, and in which loose ends are tied up, thereby giving order to the narrative universe, Wheatley's films regularly descend into chaos, not even making sense at times. How is it that Friend comes back to life—twice—after being killed in *A Field in England*? What exactly is the state of affairs at the end of *High-Rise*? And what is the conspiracy in *Kill List*? If Wheatley's films are occasionally accused of being or becoming jumbled and hard to follow (see, for example, Barnes 2015), then this is because he himself is atheistic towards the 'rules' of cinema and the necessity for the narrative always to make sense—hence the regular insertion of hallucinogenic sequences into his films, featuring experimental moments that interrupt the narrative.

One might argue that the end of *Kill List* reasserts a sinister god, in that the world is indeed governed by forces beyond our ken as Jay murders his own wife and child. And yet, as Jay murders his family, do we not also see precisely an anti-Christian vision of the world, in which father now kills son and wife—where son in *Down Terrace* had killed father and mother? In Wheatley's universe, there is no authority before which to bow down and there are no rules structuring behaviour. Indeed, in *A Field in England* history is not the work of 'Great Men', but instead is reduced to the plight of a handful of opportunists in a field, tripping on mushrooms and giving scant regard to the monarchy and its supposedly ordered world of real estate (see also Miller 2016).

Unreal Estate

Having established Wheatley's 'atheism' of form and content (he is atheistic towards the dominant form of cinema as narrative breaks down, while his stories feature people who are atheistic towards the dominant structure of the world as a result of their understanding of the chaotic nature of the universe), we can now establish how this ties in with his treatment of real estate in his British films. For, while Wheatley is 'atheistic', it is worth reminding readers that we nonetheless live in a world in which people seek power and domination, and who seek to maintain that power and domination through the imposition of order. This imposition of order, or the attempt to present one's authority as unquestionable (i.e. the attempt to make oneself a god—a theism that Wheatley does not respect and towards which he is atheistic), is inscribed into the organisation of space—from the division of space into the British nation to the division of British space into houses and apartments. This process of division, which is linked to processes of real estate and property, is inherently violent.

Without necessarily evoking the cliché that 'every Englishman's home is his castle', we nonetheless get a sense that the division of space that is the home in *Down Terrace*, *Kill List* and *Sightseers* is a tool for exclusion. Garvey, Pringle and Valda are in effect not welcome in Bill's home—as is increasingly the case for Karl, it would seem, as he sides with Valda over his parents. This sense of exclusion is most literal when Garvey's wife Helen (Kali Peacock) demands to know where her husband is after he has disappeared; she is neither invited nor seeks to enter into the house, where invitations into different rooms might well involve death. Similarly, Carol in *Sightseers* cannot stand Chris's intrusion into the room where she does her painting (her 'sanctum'), responding by saying—as mentioned—that she does not like him. Furthermore, it is when a charity collector interrupts their home life that Poppy dies because Tina is no longer looking after him. Finally, Fiona's presence in Jay's home in *Kill List* is clearly an intrusion as she marks the back of his mirror—with Jay even saying that he is glad for his old friend Gal to have gone when the dinner party has finished. The home, then, divides space and people from each other—with Wheatley not so much investigating the distinction between private lives and the public sphere as demonstrating how the concept of privacy, and by extension private property and privatisation more generally, are the dominant, divisive and thus controlling policies of British life.

This organisation of space is most clear in *High-Rise*, where the upper level apartments are kept separate from the lower levels. The architect Royal professes that he has built this and the other surrounding high-rises for 'the vanguard of the well-to-do to live', and that he 'conceived of this building as a crucible for change. I mustn't disappoint her'. And yet, Charlotte explains that 'there's a rigid social hierarchy whether Royal likes it or not.' Wilder at a later point adds: 'living in a high-rise requires a special type of behaviour. Acquiescent, restrained, perhaps even slightly mad', while Pangbourne argues that the high-rise requires a 'firmer hand' if order is to be maintained. When the latter demands that Laing lobotomises Wilder in order to restrain him, Laing refuses, claiming that Wilder is the 'possibly the sanest man in the building', since he, like Laing, refuses to accept the social order, having lived a life of debt 'among the shadows'. As the late Mark Fisher summarises, the film critiques 'a glorious shedding of all obligations to the poor and the vulnerable' on the part of Royal, Pangbourne and their acolytes, as the ethos becomes: '*[t]he masses have got above themselves – time to put them back in their place*' (Fisher 2016: 87, original italics). In other words, Royal wanted to see change imposed from the top down, which led rapidly to class war waged from the bottom up, which in turn leads to violent attempts once again to contain the masses from the top down. As Fisher notes, we therefore witness the 'revolt of the elites', with Royal himself increasingly ignored, perhaps especially by

Simmons, who claims to serve the building and not the architect (Fisher 2016: 84). However, this revolt of the elites is not entirely successful, and by the end a confusing chaos reigns—and what Wheatley achieves in this chaos is not just a revolution as some humans climb the tower to replace those already in power, but rather the revolutionary establishment of chaos itself.

Towards the end of *High-Rise*, Laing describes the building to Royal as follows: '[w]ell, the lights fire like neurons in a great brain. The lifts seem like the chambers of a heart. And when I move, I move along its corridors like a cell in a network of arteries.' In other words, the high-rise is an organism with its own life and its own brain. Is the building therefore thinking or dreaming these events? Or are the scenes of orgies and looting real? As per *Kill List, A Field in England* and perhaps even *Down Terrace* and *Sightseers*, it becomes hard to tell what is real and what is hallucinated, dreamed or imagined. But the effect of this ambiguity is not simply to allow viewers to dismiss all that they see as unreal, untrustworthy and thus deniable or something to be ignored. On the contrary, in the tradition of good surrealist art—as well as perhaps Gilles Deleuze's concept of time-image cinema (see Deleuze 2005)—what Wheatley achieves through this untrustworthiness is to expose the untrustworthiness of any and all claims to reality, including the claim that the estate is real. Real estate is an illusion—hence Wheatley's creation of a cinema of unreal estate.

To clarify this further, let us recall how earlier I linked the term 'real estate' to the Latin words *res*, meaning material thing, and *rex*, meaning king. I should like now to argue for a further, political dimension for the term. Robert Campbell has argued that the term 'real time' is used in the contemporary era not simply to signal that we can see what is happening on the far side of the planet right now, or in 'real time'. Rather, for Campbell the term 'real time' also suggests the way in which any time—in the sense of temporality, or pace of life—that runs counter to the time of mass media, telecommunications and capital is rendered 'unreal', in the sense of being discounted, discarded and/or deprived of its reality status. The result is that only the time of capital is considered to be a real time, a political manoeuvre that ensures its hegemony, since to believe in any other time is not to think in a 'realistic' fashion (see Campbell forthcoming).

Here, therefore, I shall argue that the 'real' in 'real estate' serves a similar function: it serves to legitimise as the only reality that organisation of space and property in its current iteration. That is, it serves to cement those who own space—be that the space of a nation or the space of a house, as well as to cement the concept of ownership, property, the private and the self. In creating a cinema of 'unreal estate', however, Wheatley exposes the contingent and political nature of 'real estate', cocking a snook at those who use the term in order to maintain power, and demonstrating atheism towards the would-be 'gods' who would have us believe that space and property are organised in the only way possible and which therefore is not to be questioned. In demonstrating a cinema of 'unreal estate', Wheatley puts in place an atheistic, chaotic cinema that can help us to think of a different space, one organised not through private property or real estate, but which perhaps involves a reconnection with the earth and the creation not of an eternal present that never changes (this time is the only real time), but which, as Toby in *High-Rise* might put, presents us a kaleidoscopic, hallucinogenic vision of the future.

CONCLUSION: FROM BREXIT TO GRENFELL

On 23 June 2016, the UK voted with a narrow majority to leave the European Union, an event that commentators have since struggled to understand and/or explain in a coherent fashion. What is certain is that the rhetoric deployed by various of those leading the leave campaign was that success would involve 'taking back control' of the nation.

In some senses, then, Brexit can itself be considered a 'revolt of the elites', in that those who voted to leave wished to separate themselves from what at the time were their fellow Europeans—out of a sense of superiority to them ('they are worsening our lives'). In reaffirming the sovereignty or the privacy of the nation, the vote can be seen not as an act of atheism (even if it refuses to accept the authority of the EU), but as an act of theism (as it reaffirms the authority of the UK—with the UK being the binding 'divinity' of many of the people that voted to leave). While at time of writing the exit negotiations have barely begun, it would seem, though, that the desire to 'take back control' in some senses expresses a desire to be controlled; to lead an ordered life in the kind of terraced housing that was the bedrock of the British working class when developed in the early twentieth century. These were sovereign, privatised spaces, or real estates, that legitimised those in power.

Moving forward a year, we see in the destruction of Grenfell Tower, including the loss of the lives of the 'non-human' migrants living within it, an aspect of Brexit that was perhaps previously concealed. For, the Grenfell disaster reaffirms class distinctions as families are not rehoused in spite of vast swathes of real estate remaining unoccupied in the tower's very own borough: the privacy of those estates takes precedence over/is respected more than the plight of the humans displaced by the fire, itself so calamitous because of the greed of the tower's owners. Wheatley's films help to expose as illusory the authority (or theism) both of those who own space, as well as the concept of ownership itself, such that he exposes the estate to be not real, but utterly unreal. By mining the past in his films—from the druidic stone circles in *Sightseers*, to the Civil War in *A Field in England* and the 1970s literature of J.G. Ballard—Wheatley might well give us a folk cinematic glimpse of a chaotic but revolutionary future in which private/real estate crumbles, and in which all humans might find each other on common ground.

BIBLIOGRAPHY

Barnes, Henry. 2015. *High-Rise* review – Tom Hiddleston surfs through a confused, and confusing, tower block class-hop. *The Guardian*, 14 September, https://www.theguardian.com/film/2015/sep/14/high-rise-review-tom-hiddleston-ben-wheatley-jg-ballard-film-toronto-tiff. Accessed 15 August 2017.

Batty, David, Niamh McIntyre, David Pegg and Anushka Asthana. 2017. Grenfell: Names of wealthy empty-home owners in borough revealed. *The Guardian*, 2 August, https://www.theguardian.com/society/2017/aug/01/names-of-wealthy-empty-home-owners-in-grenfell-borough-revealed. Accessed 13 August 2017.

Bulman, May. 2017. Grenfell Tower Fire: Undocumented migrants could still be missing. *The Independent*, 19 June. http://www.independent.co.uk/news/uk/home-news/grenfell-tower-fire-disaster-latest-residents-families-victims-homeless-immigration-status-migrants-a7798051.html. Accessed 13 August 2017.

Campbell, Robert. Forthcoming. Drone Film Theory: The Immanentisation of Kinocentrism. currently seeking publication.

Deleuze, Gilles. 2005. *Cinema 2: The Time-Image*. trans. Tomlinson, Hugh and Robert Galeta. London: Continuum.

Fisher, Mark. 2016. The revolt of the elites. *Critical Quarterly*, 58:1. April: 84–89.

Flanagan, Kevin M. 2016. "Green and pleasant land"?: Ben Wheatley's British cinema between romanticism and modernism. *Critical Quarterly*, 58:1. April: 16–22.

Galt, Rosalind. 2016. *Down Terrace*'s duplicitous geographies. *Critical Quarterly*, 58:1. April: 23–28.

Lowenstein, Adam. 2016. A cinema of disorientation: Space, genre, Wheatley. *Critical Quarterly*. 58:1. April: 5–15.

Luckhurst, Roger. 2016. *High-Rise* 1975/2015. *Critical Quarterly*, 58:1. April: 63–69.

Miller, Henry K. 2016. On the edge of history: *A Field in England*. *Critical Quarterly*, 58:1. April: 41–45.

Nayman, Adam. 2017. *Ben Wheatley: Confusion and Carnage*. Philadelphia: The Critical Press.

Reed, Jim, and Sean Clare. 2017. Grenfell cladding "14 times combustibility limit". *BBC News*. 19 July. http://www.bbc.co.uk/news/uk-40645205. Accessed 13 August 2017.

Twitchell, James B. 2014. *Winnebago Nation: The RV in American Culture*. New York: Columbia University Press.

CHAPTER 4

Approaches to Othered Identities and Spaces in French Cinema

Şirin Fulya Erensoy

In January 2015, 17 people were killed during the attack carried out on the satirical newspaper *Charlie Hebdo* and a Jewish supermarket nearby. Members of the editorial board, a police officer and customers of the shop were killed by perpetrators Chérif Kouachi, Said Kouachi and Amedy Coulibaly. The perpetrators were all French citizens who grew up on the outskirts of Paris. The attack triggered collective action in France: the people united, determined to reaffirm the values of the French Republic. Marches across the country denounced terrorism and celebrated press freedom. These marches, specifically the ones called by the government for 11 January 2015, were declared to be the largest gatherings on the streets of France since the Liberation from Nazi occupation in 1944 (Le Monde 2015).[1] In Paris, it was La Place de la République that was designated as the central gathering point, "in the spirit of those previous occupations of the square at the moments of republican crisis" (Welch and Perivolaris 2016: 282). Indeed, there was a need to reassert the values that

---

[1] All translations are mine, unless stated otherwise.

Ş. F. Erensoy (✉)
Independent Scholar, Istanbul, Turkey

© The Author(s) 2018   63
J. Harvey (ed.), *Nationalism in Contemporary Western European Cinema*, Palgrave European Film and Media Studies,
https://doi.org/10.1007/978-3-319-73667-9_4

64   Ş. F. ERENSOY

the Republic stands for, because this attack exposed and threatened not only the victims but the Republic itself.

In November of the same year, six separate but coordinated terrorist attacks in the tenth and eleventh arrondissements of Paris caused the deaths of 130 people. In the aftermath, President François Hollande declared a state of emergency. Again, some of the terrorists were French citizens. These tragedies have led to public outcry from all factions of society, as well as the political spectrum. Public expression of religious difference had long been an undebatable issue; any overt expression of religious or cultural differences was seen as a betrayal of the Republican ideals. Indeed, Muslims who did not publicly denounce the attacks were targets of Islamophobic attacks and labelled pro-terrorist. But then Emmanuel Todd's book entitled *Who is Charlie?* (2015) came out, labelling the post-attack spectacles of unity themselves as a reaffirmation of Christian middle-class values and Islamophobia. He stated in his book that national attitudes after the attacks were self-glorifying and did not look at the real reasons that might have led to the attacks.

Islamophobic responses to events within the nation occurred on several occasions in the recent past of France. Starting in the 1980s, outcry from the *banlieue*[2] of big cities has occurred periodically, for several different reasons. While the ruling governments of both left and right have made attempts to appease grievances, they have been very limited and superficial, and eventually abandoned.[3] Todd's claim resonates when looking at

---

[2] *Banlieue* literally means suburb. It designates urbanised areas located outside the cities. The *banlieues* in France are large housing estates constructed in the 1950s, due the growing population and as a response to the housing crisis. Today, while there are some wealthy *banlieues,* they have mostly become a source of anxiety for French Republic ideals, where secular values have to be negotiated. The word *banlieue* will be used as opposed to suburb as suburb does not necessarily hold the negative connotations that *banlieue* does.

[3] As a response to the massive revolt that took place in Les Minguettes in 1981, François Mitterrand's socialist government wanted to recognise cultural pluralism. However, instead of doing that, the differentialist policies undertook led to ethnicisation and urban marginalisation of the *beur* community (Echchaibi 2007: 302). Policies such as *politique de la ville* aimed at subsidising housing estates, but the disconnection between the central government and local authorities caused actions to not be regulated and enforced. In 2002, the *Conseil Français du Culte Musulman* was established and aimed to adapt Islam to Europe by managing differences. The government referred all issues relating to the immigrant community to them, wanting them to resolve and deal with problems in times of crisis. Yet, they refused to take the *Conseil*'s on other occasions, such as in 2004 when the ban on religious symbols was enacted. This showed finally, how little influence the *Conseil* has on policy.

this history and the failure of the state officials to deal with problems relating to the immigrant population in a timely manner; "cast[ing] Muslims out of the national community, is both the cause and effect of terrorism" (Todd 2015: 21). It has been claimed that exclusion from citizenship in the Republican sense, and discrimination, has led immigrant communities to turn to and embrace other forms of identities; Islam, for some has been such an identity that has allowed for "constructing a positive identity, of building supportive social networks and more broadly acquiring a code of ethics that enables them to live peacefully alongside mainstream society" (Doyle 2011: 486).

Cinema has also addressed the escalating crisis relating to French citizens of North- and West-African descent. Films such as *La Haine*[4] (Matthieu Kassovitz 1995) were directly influenced by the events happening in the *banlieues* in the late 1980s. *La Haine* refers to the murder of Malik Oussekinem by riot police during a mass demonstration, which he was not even participating in, through the use of documentary footage of police brutality in the *banlieues* in the opening sequence. *La Haine* and other films brought to the screen "sentiments of injustice against social misery, the indifference of those holding political power, police brutality and the contempt the rest of the population feels towards the inhabitants of the *cites*"[5] (Milleliri 2012).

This chapter will investigate two contemporary French productions, *Dheepan* (Jacques Audiard 2015) and *Fatima* (Philippe Faucon 2016) in order to identify which national sensibilities relating to the foundational principles of the Republic are being targeted by the films and whether they offer solutions or retreat to the safety of the status quo. I will argue that while *Dheepan* repeats the clichéd representations of the *banlieues* that cinema has perpetuated, reaffirming and aggravating anxieties regarding

---

[4] The film foregrounds the ethnic differences within the *banlieue* through a *Blanc-Black-Beur* trio. Kassovitz as a director is aware of the ethnicity problem in France and believes it is a question that needs to be addressed and not ignored. While the director's motivation to make the film comes from the social reality in the *banlieue*, it is important to note that one of the narrative privilege is placed on the character of Vinz who is of Eastern European descent and Jewish, as opposed to the *Black* or the *Beur* characters. While Vinz does take on a hybrid identity, Kassovitz has been criticised for eclipsing the issue away from the ethnic difference. Nonetheless, Kassovitz emphasises the commonality of the experiences in the *banlieue* in the face of unemployment, police violence and social discrimination (Tarr 2005: 68).

[5] This term refers to the uniform housing estates built in the *banlieues*.

the peri-urban space, *Fatima* opens a discursive space to discuss the lack of compatibility between Republican ideals and policies of integration with social reality, where a shift in perception is yet to occur. Furthermore, *Girlhood* (Céline Sciamma 2014) will be brought into the reading of *Dheepan* to demonstrate how certain clichéd representations can be reworked to allow for more positive messages.

PRINCIPLES OF THE REPUBLIC

French collective consciousness is built on the promotion of certain ideals that make up the foundation of the Republic. Two of these principles are *laïcité* and *égalité*. *Laïcité* initially entailed the separation of Church and State,[6] and while this was the case when the Republic was established in 1794, today the concept of secularism has evolved. As Charles Taylor notes: "[w]e think that secularism (or laïcité) has to do with the relation of the state and religion; whereas in fact it has to do with the (correct) response of the democratic state to diversity" (2011: 36). Indeed, *laïcité* has given rise to an anti-religious discourse, where the government has again and again refused to engage in discussions relating to religion. Yet, religion can also be approached like any other social reality and discussed rationally. The refusal to do so has led to forms of protests against forced identity moulds. Events such as the one in Creil in 1989, where three Muslim girls refused to take off their headscarves to go to state school, highlighted their intolerance towards the intolerance forced upon them. These second-generation immigrants are the biggest challenge to French values because they challenge the very meaning on which "Frenchness" has been constructed, here namely, the division of religion and state. According to Gaspard and Khosrokhavar, this type of situation and the attitude of such immigrants can be interpreted as a form of negotiation: "[f]inally the headscarves of the young women who claim a 'veiled identity' cannot be interpreted as a rejection of French citizenship, but as a desire for integration *without* assimilation, an aspiration to be French and Muslim" (1995: 204).

The French public sphere has no space for these differential identities as a consequence of this secularism that forms the very basis of all French

---

[6] A law was passed in 1905 that officially separated the affairs of the Church from the state. This law forms the basis of French secularism. The aim was to ensure freedom of conscience, while keeping state affairs "neutral".

values. The principle of *égalité* entails that all citizens are equal in the eyes of the law and the state. As a result of this understanding, it is forbidden by law for the government to collect and keep data based on a citizen's race and religion because this would mean that citizens would be distinguished according to differences, which would undermine the principle of equality. Etienne Balibar (2007) argues that this form of universalizing equality holds an intrinsic violence within it as a condition for its existence. He states that the universal is defined more with regards to what it is not, to what it excludes, than to what it is and what it includes. Seen by the makers of the French Revolution as a foundational value, it can lead to the possibility of radical intolerance or internal violence. Those who do not share the same set of values imposed by the universalizing principle of equality are not seen as worthy, they are excluded, "othered". Indeed, policies of integration have led to discrimination especially for Muslim citizens, because the practices of Islam are perceived to run against *laïcité*. As a result of this perception, in 2004, visible religious symbols were banned in state schools. In 2011, the full-face veil was banned from all public spaces. Albeit, an overwhelming majority of French Muslim women did not wear it; a report according to the Ministry of Interior stated that the number was estimated at 2000 (Doyle 2011: 482). Nonetheless, it was not only claimed to be incompatible with *laïcité*, the ban was further legitimised by stating that the veil was a symbol of the oppression of women and was not welcomed on Republican land. So, if the visible modes of practicing Islam are against France's conception of citizenship, how can one identify as both French and Muslim?

French governments have made attempts to "format Islam" (Roy 2013) and accommodate its reality within society. Regardless of these attempts, it can be said that France has mismanaged its post-colonial policies. France's current relationship with citizens of former colonies reflects the difficulties of integrating them into the Republican version of citizenship. The immigrant experience as outsiders and their uncertain status as citizens within the French nation is best described by Pierre Bourdieu:

> Neither citizen nor foreigner, not truly on the side of the Same, nor really on the side of the Other, he exists within that "bastard" place, [...], on the frontier between being and social non-being. Displaced, in the sense of being incongruous and inopportune, he is a source of embarrassment. [...] Always in the wrong place, and now as out of place in his society of origin as he is in the host society, the immigrant obliges us to rethink completely the

68   Ş. F. ERENSOY

question of the legitimate foundations of citizenship and of relations between citizen and state, nation and nationality. (Bourdieu 2004: xiv)

France has been accused of reproducing within the country the colonial conception of the social relations that it practiced long ago overseas, namely in Africa. The promises of the Republican model are not translated into actions of the state and the ruling elites. As Kristin Ross states:

> France's denial of the ways in which it was and is formed by colonialism, its insistence on separating itself off from what it views as an extraneous period irrelevant to its true national heritage, forms the basis of the neo-racist consensus of today: the logic of segregation and expulsion that governs questions of immigration and attitudes towards immigrants in France. (1996: 196)

Indeed, this attitude of excluding French citizens from accessing French citizenship was perceived by these immigrant communities as 'Republican betrayal' (Echchaibi 2007: 302). In 2005, tensions within the nation rose and exploded in riots that took place during the months of October and November in the *banlieues* of Paris, as well as other French cities, where cars were burned as well as public buildings, symbols of state power. Minorities of North- and West-African descent, mostly in their teens, were the ones out on the streets doing these deeds (Echchaibi 2007: 301). These riots resulted in damage estimated at €200 million (Bronner and Ceaux 2005). Furthermore, 4770 people were arrested, 217 police were injured (including 10 who were on sick leave for 10 days or more as a result) (Fassin 2006: 1–2), while three non-rioters died in the clashes. The riots were sparked by an incident that occurred in Clichy-sous-Bois, involving the death of two teenagers of North-African descent, Bounna and Zyed, while trying to escape the police. The follow-up to the deaths of these two teenagers by the Interior Minister Nicolas Sarkozy was the denial of the involvement of the police, where he wrongfully stated that the three were involved in a burglary.[7] His provocative language only intensified during the riots, where, during the French National Assembly

---

[7] During the previous months, Sarkozy had gone on a tour of the *banlieues* where several incidents had occurred, including the shooting of an 11-year-old boy as a result of a gang confrontation. During this tour he declared that he aimed to rid the *banlieues* of "the *racaille*...with *Kärcher*", *racaille*, literally "scum", being a word to designate an undesirable group of people and *Kärcher*, a German brand of cleaning appliances.

on 15 November, he accused rioters of making "crime their main activity to fight against the Republic's ambition of reinstating law and order in its territories" (Canet et al. 2015: 277). The families of the two dead boys refused to meet him, instead meeting with Prime Minister Dominique de Villepin. Outcry rapidly ensued amongst French citizens from former colonies, living in the *banlieues*, who had already been feeling culturally 'different' from the force-fed discourses of their country of residence. The riots quickly spread from the suburbs of Paris to the whole of the country, affecting nearly 300 cities' *banlieues* (Canet et al. 2015: 271). While the trigger for the outburst of riots was the deaths of Bounna and Zyed, there were many underlying reasons for the citizens living in the suburbs to be angry.

According to Gérard Mauger, the riots of 2005 were "a collective revolt against state violence that lacked any form of collective organization and whose members were not politicised" (2006: 82–83). The rioters came from working-class families, impoverished by mass unemployment and insecurity. Protesters stated that they had had enough of living in poor conditions and in fear, citing unemployment and the lack of opportunities in France for them, due to the prejudice and discrimination they face because of their origins. Indeed, unlike how the media labelled the riots, it was not due to a rejection of France and French values, but on the contrary, the will to be integrated that led to revolts. They were worried about the isolation due to geographic segregation, which left them outside society. Rioters are "contesting the behaviour of political leaders who were acting in an unrepublican manner themselves" (Koff and Duprez 2009: 728).

Instead of responding to the problem of *fracture sociale*[8] by looking at their root causes, far-right politicians saw Sarkozy's approach as an opportunity to further discriminatory agendas, going as far as to suggest in parliament that the citizenship of rioters should be revoked. Furthermore, Prime Minister Dominique de Villepin declared a tightening of controls on immigration. Furthermore, certain journalist stated that the riots were proof of Islamicisation and an anti-French generation (Echchaibi 2007: 305), where they only concentrated on the criminal aspect of the riots and not the source of the problem.

---

[8] This is a term, used in France to designate the division amongst members of society based on social class. The term implies a division where certain members—in essence those living in the *banlieue*—are excluded from society due to their low level of income and education.

70 Ş. F. ERENSOY

As can be seen, this perverted form of universalism no longer functions as utopically as hoped for initially. Indeed, according to Max Silverman "the greater the quest for assimilation of differences and the unification of diversity, the more visible difference and diversity became" (1999: 3). The truth of this statement is more than evident in 2017.

CINEMA AND THE REPUBLIC

Like its conception of identity, the French state has perceived the role of culture as a unifying one (Hayward 2005: 16). For the state, it has always been important to "take care" of culture. They introduced the term "cultural exception" in 1993, wherein they advocated that culture was different than other commercial products and thus should be treated differently. This meant that protectionist measures should be implemented in order to keep cultural specificities alive, because these specificities pertain to national identity and values beyond commercial ones. France has established many government bodies and has passed several laws to protect its cultural products and ensure their proliferation and wide-reaching reception. Thus, it can be said that the interventions the state has made with regards to all cultural fields and specifically to the film industry have been for the benefit of the industry's wellbeing, in the sense that the government has a vision of the artist as a cultural missionary that it can economically invest in.

Since the 1980s, the main goals of the Ministry of Culture relating to cinema were to "promote new talent [...] encourage established auteurs [...] and to launch a new quality cinema" (Palmer 2011: 147). This approach led to the emergence of the heritage film, which were productions that were classical in form and inspired by historical events or literary adaptations. These films were the recipients of aid from the Centre National du Cinéma [National Centre for Cinema] and the socialist government of the 1990s, and were seen as a continuation of the *Tradition de Qualité* [Tradition of Quality]), so fiercely attacked by the filmmakers of the *Nouvelle Vague*.[9] In the 1980s and early 1990s, for the Minister of Culture Jack Lang, the heritage film was highly important in differentiating

---

[9] The films designated as films of the *Tradition de Qualité* are the mainstream, studio productions of the 1940s. The directors of the 1960s, namely François Truffaut, detested this type of filmmaking, which he described as sterile literary adaptations that did not capture the true magic of the cinema.

APPROACHES TO OTHERED IDENTITIES AND SPACES IN FRENCH CINEMA   71

French film from that of Hollywood and also in beating Hollywood at its own game, because of its high production values and use of star power (Higbee 2005a: 301). Claude Berri is considered the leading director of the heritage film of this period, due to his literary adaptations; the film *Jean de Florette* (1986) followed by *Manon of the Spring* (1986), both adaptations of Marcel Pagnol novels, are exemplary works both of Berri and the heritage film. Other films such as *Indochine* (Régis Warnier 1992), *Fort Saganne* (Alain Corneau 1984) and *The Lover* (Jean-Jacques Annaud 1992) were all made with huge budgets, winning awards internationally. What all these films did however was "silenc[e] the voice of the colonised and lend themselves to the neo-colonialist project of repossessing the colony fantasy through the visual recapture of its reified landscape" (Carr 1997: 63). Indeed, these films distance the consequences of colonialism from mainland France, depoliticising French history in order to consume it as a spectacle. This Eurocentric approach to France's history was problematic in terms of the way it represented the others of the nation, where "Europe is seen as the unique source of meaning, as the world's centre of gravity, as ontological 'reality' to the rest of the world's shadow" (Shohat and Stam 1994: 3).

Another type of film that emerged in the late 1980s was the cinema *beur*.[10] The films, that were responses to the neo-colonialist master narratives, broke with the illusion of national myths and problematised its symbols. These films represented a form of resistance and returned the overtly political to French filmmaking. The rise of othered voices of the nation in cinema served as a challenge to the essentialising narratives that excluded them from mainstream representation. Their works featured restive youths who struggle with themselves, their families or repressive police officers in an often violent, dystopic, ex-centric suburban space dominated by concrete, their existence punctuated at best by brief moments of community, hope or aesthetic promise (Austin 2009: 81). In this sense, these films can be classified as part of a committed cinema that was different from its predecessors because of both the forms it took and the context to which it was responding (O'Shaughnessy 2010: 39).

---

[10] *Beur* is the term used for French citizens of North-African descent. It entails a bi-cultural belonging and is used for second- and third-generation immigrants. It derives from the rearrangement of the word *arabe*.

72   Ş. F. ERENSOY

The filmmakers of the *cinéma beur* were second-generation immigrants.[11] Their films were critical of the mythology of French *grandeur*[12] and brought out the cracks that lay within it. They began telling stories of their experiences within the French Republic, contradicting the values on which the Republic was founded through the experiences of their protagonists. The triptych "Liberty, Equality, Fraternity" was questioned through the confrontation with daily reality.

They responded to real socio-political developments within the nation, initiated by successive right-wing governments during the 1990s.[13] Unlike the *cinéma du look*,[14] these films stayed away from aestheticisation and preferred a much more 'realist' look, as a kind of "autobiographical" homage, considering that most of the filmmakers were bringing to the screen their own personal observations and experiences.

While the aesthetic innovativeness of *La Haine*[15] means it can be considered an exception to the general tendency of staying away from aestheticisation, it was nonetheless one of the most powerful films made during this time with regards to the representation of the anger and frustration felt by the youth of the *banlieues* and how violence and the expression of anger unleashed became an attempt to find some sort of power and autonomy over their lives. Indeed, the characters of these films represent a multicultural and a multiethnic society, often side-lined in mainstream French cinema or relegated to minor roles; roles that serve the journeys of the essentially "white" protagonists.

---

[11] While at first the term *beur cinéma* demonstrated the agency in the production of representations that challenged the way Frenchness and otherness was represented in mainstream cinema, eventually it led to a form of separation on essentialist lines that could no longer encapsulate the difficulties in identity politics.

[12] Literally translating as French greatness, this term refers to France's mythologised identity as a world superpower.

[13] Several laws were pushed in order to bring restriction on immigrants, such as restricting the citizenship of people born in France but coming from immigrant backgrounds.

[14] This is the name given to films that came out in the 1980s that prioritised style and spectacle, as the name indicates. Leos Carax, Jean-Jacques Beineix and Luc Besson are considered the pioneers of the movement.

[15] An important differentiation needs to be made here. *La Haine* was not part of the *beur cinéma*, but was an example of *banlieue* film. The *banlieue* film foregrounded the *banlieue* as a setting and how this segregated space shaped the often isolated experience of the people living within it. These films depart from the *cinéma beur* in that its directors are not necessarily from North-African descent. Furthermore, *cinéma beur* does not only talk about the *banlieue* experience but also engage in issues of identity in post-colonial France.

Films such as *Hexagone* (Malik Chibane 1994) and *Bye, Bye* (Karim Dridi 1995) enlarged the scope of representations of life in the *banlieues*, reflecting the fact that the people were not the perpetrators of violence, but were the victims of it. They brought to the fore the human dimension of the people living on the periphery, with stories of solidarity and fraternity in the *cité*. This was a change from the media representation of the *banlieue* that depicted these areas as dangerous, and full of shady deals and affairs. The films are characterised by "naturalistic *mise-en-scène*, combining a documentary-like approach with intimate (often hand-held) camerawork that suggests empathy for the characters" (Higbee 2005b: 133). They are political not because of a particular ideology that they support but by virtue of the social realities they choose to represent.

But both *beur* and *banlieue* films had problems accessing funds, even though, in the 1980s, when the *cinema de beur* first started to appear, President François Mitterrand and the Secretary of State in charge of Immigration and the Minister of Culture sent out messages that they wanted to encourage "the creative wealth represented by the culture of the immigrant population" (Lehin 2005: 216). However, the *avances sur recettes*[16] prioritised auteur works or box office success over films that explored social issues. Mehdi Charef was fortunate enough to be funded by Costa-Gavras and his producer wife for his film *Tea in the Harem* (1985), as well as his more recent films *Summer of '62* (2007) and *Graziella* (2015), all films that tell the stories of the oppressed, the othered of society, while Kassovitz was refused the *avances* for *La Haine* due to restrictions that were going to be put on his creative control (Tarr 1997: 60). Malik Chibane struggled for six years in order to find funds for his first feature *Hexagone*, a film about the gap between the aspirations of five young North-African immigrants living in the *banlieue* and their social reality. So, although a public image that embraced directors from all background was perpetuated, the reality of the matter was that the government was still burying its head in the sand regarding the social realities of the *banlieue*. Twenty-two years after *La Haine*, the problems brought to the screen by Kassovitz are still valid, where the grievances of the immigrant

---

[16] A government financial aid instituted in the 1960s that aimed to "promote the creative renewal and to encourage the direction of first films, and to support an independent cinema, audacious in relation to marketplace norms, which could not maintain its financial equilibrium without public aid" (Palmer 2011: 16–17).

communities have not been addressed, thus continuing to accumulate in an unhealthy manner.

DHEEPAN

Dheepan is the story three Sri Lankan refugees fleeing the civil war in their country to find themselves in the Parisian *banlieue*, which turns out not to be that different from their country. Dheepan takes a dead man's identity, creates a fake family with Yalini and Illayaal in order to seek asylum in France. There, Dheepan is given the duty of guardian of a *cité* in the French *banlieue* Pré-Saint-Gervais. The characters want to go to the UK but cannot due to restrictive immigration laws. They are forced to go to France instead, which renders life difficult for them as they do not speak the language. Indeed, most of the film is in the Tamil language; French is only heard when the characters interact with representatives of French institutions, or habitants of the *cité*.

The *banlieue* is ruled by drug deals and gang violence, and there does not appear to be any police presence, suggesting the social isolation of the *banlieue* space. The film was awarded the Palme d'Or at Cannes in May 2015. Critics such as Caspar Salmon stated the irresponsibility of awarding a film that portrays the *banlieue* and those inhabiting in it in such a negative light, five months after terrorist attacks. But Dheepan is a Tamil Tiger fighter and Audiard's decision make the refugees Sri Lankan was a conscious one: "I had this idea of people coming to France who had no connection with the old colonial empire, so had no reference points in terms of language and culture" (Romney 2016). This, accordingly, would prevent any post-colonial readings that would lead to discussions of the oppressed and the oppressor within the French context. Even if this superficial pretext of disassociation is taken to be valid, an analysis of the depiction of the *banlieue* space and the characters that inhabit it can be done to decipher the ideology behind the way of seeing the *banlieue* and its perpetuation of clichéd and dangerous representations.

It needs to be handed to Audiard that he is successful in depicting the realities that refugees experience. *Dheepan* illustrates the foundational steps for all migrants from their forced displacement from their homelands due to war to their placement in an unknown territory. All three characters' alienation in this unfamiliar society, their difficulties in feeling secure, their troubles in learning a new language and their shock at the lack of the presence of authorities within the gang-ridden *banlieue* are all woven together in a touching manner, which makes the audience feel for the plight of the characters. Their displacement, hard as it is, is rendered even more complicated as they end up in one of the worst places they could be in France.

The *banlieue* is marginalised, very much as imagined by the Franco-French,[17] justifying their anxieties with regards to these regions and the people inhabiting them. In *Dheepan*, the *banlieue* is a space in which the laws of the Republic are put on hold and ruled by the self-determined laws of the armed gangs. Indeed, clichés run throughout; when Yalini goes to her new job as a caretaker for an old, disabled man, she is taken into a pitch-black apartment, where, in the darkness, glimpses of threatening-looking men and aggressive pit bulls appear, filmed through point-of-view shots of Yalini as she walks up the staircase. This scene is represented 'like a descent into Dante's Inferno' (Ebert 2016). Illayaal too is confronted with xenophobic violence in her own world. When she goes to school, the other children exclude her from their games. This frustrating situation is a slap in the face as it reminds her of her already othered position, leading her to lash out at the children.

Very much like Dheepan, Yalini and Illayaal, the other people living in this *cité* are alienated from wider society and have thus created their own form of society within the walls of the *cite*. Their social alienation has taken on a physical form as the *banlieue* is also physically excluded from the centre. Shootings happen in broad daylight, and there is no sign of police anywhere. Checkpoints are created at the entrance of the *cité* by gang members. But for Dheepan, Yalini and Illayaal, who have just left a country due to war, they are back at the heart of another form of violent conflict. Audiard attempts to draw parallels between the war-torn Sri Lanka and the Parisian *banlieue*. As a matter of fact, Yalini says so herself; after the first shooting where she and Illayaal are caught in the middle, she decides to leave Paris for the UK. She tells Dheepan that there was a reason they left Sri Lanka but have found themselves once again in the heart of violence. A further analogy between French suburbs and Sri Lanka occurs when Dheepan watches a BBC news report on the continuing war in his homeland, which underlines the impossibility of entering the territory to report on events. Officials are also nowhere to be seen in Pré-Saint-Gervais. The impression given is of a lawless universe left entirely to its own murderous devices. As a result, this representation legitimises the

---

[17] This form of identification entails a narrow and exclusive way of French life.

recourse to violence: since there is no authority to turn to, matters have to be taken into your own hands for your safety and for the safety of your loved ones.

When talking about the making of *Dheepan*, Audiard has stated that his aim was to do a remake of Sam Peckinpah's *Straw Dogs* (1971). The ending of the film where Dheepan goes on a killing spree in order to save Yalini is reminiscent of the ending of Martin Scorsese's *Taxi Driver* (1976), where Audiard dispenses with his film's stylised yet realist atmosphere and very real conditions of living and turning the film into a revenge-thriller; almost in slow-motion, the camera is fixed Dheepan's lower body, as he cuts, shoots and stabs the thugs that attack him, through a smoke that fills the screen. Furthermore, the epilogue of the film is quite reductive in its representation of a multicultural English suburban heaven. The attempt to contrast the French *banlieue* with the bizarrely overly idyllic English suburbs is clumsy in its political implications. Thus, *Dheepan* uses the *banlieue* as a setting for the story and yet fails to address the questions regarding ethnic discrimination previously raised by the *banlieue* film.

GIRLHOOD

The representation of the *banlieue* in *Dheepan* can be contrasted to another recent film that also uses the *banlieue* as setting: *Girlhood*. The film tells the story of Marieme's transformation from a shy and silent girl to a fierce and confident one. This transformation is possible through her refusal to accept what is dictated to her by her mother and her brother, by her school and by the social conceptions of the 'good girl' expected of her. Her confidence grows as she is introduced to Lady, Adiatou and Fily. She learns to act on her desires and to do what she wants. The girls are loud and determined, and their noise is political, fighting against prohibitions. Marieme chooses her own path, even though it is not too certain where it will take her. The police, class differences, ethnic groups, religion and clichés (rap, graffiti) are left outside the narrative in order to concentrate on the positive, controlled and interiorised violence of survival within the *banlieue* (Chevalier 2016: 419). The opening sequence sets the tone for the rest of the film where there will be a reversal of expectations. In this sequence, the audience is presented with an American football game, where the expectation is that men are playing. But when the helmets are removed, it turns out to be women playing. From this group emerges Marieme.

The girls are nonetheless silenced in the *banlieue*. In the scene following the opening sequence, as the girls get closer to the housing blocks where they live, their lively chatter cuts off. All of a sudden, their dialogues and laughter are replaced by comments coming from the darkness surrounding them; male voices that make the girls shut down and head home. Yet in the film, these restrictive public spaces of the *banlieue* are countered with locations that the girls make their own. There is room for negotiation in the film: the opening American football scene and the hotel room sequence demonstrate their dominance in certain spaces in opposition to the oppression within the *cité*, the household and the school.

Nonetheless, Marieme's method of gaining respect is through violence. Violent behaviour is a strength that dominates relations, leading to respect. When she sells drugs, she is able to access the same privileges as her brother for example: a room for herself and a PlayStation. Furthermore, the film still includes scenes that contribute to the negative images present in French cinema of minorities: Marieme's brother hitting her, the girls stealing dresses, playing truant as well as the cliché of a shop assistant suspecting Marieme is stealing something from the shop because she is black. Regardless, Sciamma presents a film where bonding with sisterhood can lead to options and hope for the future; very much like the first *beur* films of the 1980s.[18]

FATIMA

In contrast to *Dheepan*'s perpetuation of clichés regarding the location in which the immigrant population of France lives, as well as the one-dimensional and stereotypical representation of immigrants living within it, Philippe Faucon's 2016 film *Fatima* is a refreshing example to look at.

It is the story of a Moroccan immigrant single mother raising her daughters in Lyon. The film won the César Award for Best Picture in 2016. Nonetheless, for this reason, Guillaume Gallienne accused the César's committee for always wanting to extoll cultural diversity at the

---

[18] The first films of directors Mehdi Charef and Rachid Bouchareb desired to believe in the possibility of integration through assimilation of their characters and thus were hopeful films in that sense. They engaged in several strategies to reveal this hope in their films: "they stress the way *beur* lifestyles are similar to other young French people's lifestyles; they construct a sympathetic understanding of the role played by drugs and delinquency in the lives of the unprivileged; and they confine the representation of Islamic believe to the older generation" (Tarr 2005: 57).

78 Ş. F. ERENSOY

expense of good art, making political decisions as opposed to artistic ones (Pagesy 2016). However, Gallienne made this accusation without himself even having seen the film! On the other hand, other critics have praised the film because it is a film about immigrants but the story does not take place in the *banlieue,* which adds a refreshing dimension to the filmic representation of immigrants. In his review on the film, Grégoir Leménager states that it is an important film because "the film creates a new kind of character, never before seen in French cinema" (Le Figaro 2016). Indeed, the film is refreshing in that instead of looking for the answer as to whether traditions and integration are incompatible or not, it simply explores the seemingly paradoxical relationships that may come out of this situation. Faucon himself is not a minority filmmaker but is a *pied noir*[19] from Algeria, whose previous two films *Dans La Vie* (2007) and *La Désintégration* (2011) also deal with issues of Islamophobia.

The female protagonists of *Fatima,* Fatima, Nesrine and Souad, are three very different women and the film portrays each of their daily struggles individually and in their particular contexts, as well as the tensions that arise amongst them and their surroundings. The film is about each of these women trying to find their place in society, where each of the worries that they have to deal with is born out of being an immigrant.

Fatima is a cleaner and she does everything she can to provide a good life for her daughters. She still holds traditional notions for women and their public demeanour, which clash with the way Souad wants to live her life. She scolds her youngest for exposing her shoulders for example, to which Souad pays no attention. However, Fatima is not just a cleaner; she is also a writer, her writing is in Arabic, shown in close-ups of her notebook as well as voice-overs. Indeed, the film is based on the collections of poems in diary form entitled *Prière à la Lune* of North-African immigrant Fatima Elayoubi. Fatima's writing is the only place where she can express herself fully. This is also where the audience gets a more intimate understanding of her.

Nesrine, the eldest, seizes the opportunity for free education provided in France to all its citizens in order to escape from discrimination and become an integrated member of French society. She studies medicine and feels an immense pressure to succeed in order to avoid being a disappointment to her mother's efforts. She does not take breaks or go partying with

---

[19] *Pieds Noir* refers to the European French settled in the three North-African French colonies of Tunisia, Algeria and Morocco.

her roommate, nor does she accept the flirtatious advances of a young man on the bus, insisting that she must get work done. At the same time, Nesrine also rebels; she calls out her father's double-standard approach towards women and smoking.

On the other hand, her 15-year-old sister Souad is defiant and rebellious and could not care less about school. She is ashamed of the work her mother does, with frequent outbursts at home, where she does not hold back from insulting her mother, calling her "a living rag". The more Souad is assimilated into French culture and distances herself from her Moroccan origins, the more she challenges her mother's authority and her traditions (Collins 2016).

Faucon met with Fatima Elayoubi and one of her daughters to discuss the diary on which the film is based. Faucon states that they discussed issues "about the conditions of her work, about the difficulty of being understood in French society and even at home. The theme of being invisible, both in the external world and also at home, of being out of work or unable to communicate" (Aguilar 2016). Indeed, both for this film and for *Dheepan*, the inability to speak French is a weight on the shoulders of the characters, which inevitably leads to a form of isolation. The importance of language is best described in the words of Frantz Fanon: "[t]o speak means to be in a position to use a certain syntax, to grasp the morphology of this or that language, but it means above all to assume a culture, to support the weight of a civilization" (Fanon 2008: 8). Not knowing a language leads to the impossibility of integration; for Fatima this is a handicap on a daily basis in terms of both her social relations and her relationship with her daughters. The scene where Fatima meets with Souad's school's principle reflects Fatima's difficulty in not being able to express and communicate about her daughter. Her linguistic disadvantage isolates her. Nonetheless, she does the best she can to learn French: she questions her daughters on the meaning of certain words and goes to French lessons. Furthermore, the gap between first- and second-generation immigrants is represented linguistically in that Fatima speaks to her daughters in Arabic, and they respond in French. Her inability to express her thoughts and feelings to them in a language that they will fully understand leads her to write in her diary where she pours her heart out.

The inherent everyday racism faced by visible minorities is represented in two scenes in the film: the first one is the opening scene, where Fatima, Nesrine and Nesrine's friend go to see an apartment to rent for the two girls. However, when the landlady comes and sees Fatima, she states that

80   Ş. F. ERENSOY

she has "forgotten the keys" to the apartment. Fatima is in the foreground of the frame, her headscarf clearly in focus. Her cultural difference is given from the outset of the film. This will be the driving factor of the film. She states "it's the headscarf; she kept staring".

The other scene is when Fatima begins working as a cleaner for a rich bourgeois family; she finds money in a pant pocket when doing laundry. She hands the money to her employer. It is insinuated that the money was put there on purpose to test the new immigrant employee. Whether these scenes are based on genuine misunderstanding or not, the tension and suspicion in both cases can be felt and the likelihood of similar situations happening on a regular basis for immigrants. This is also felt in the encounter Fatima has with a mother of one of Souad's classmates, where the mother recognises Fatima but wants to cut the conversation short.

Problems are not only encountered with the non-immigrant French citizens in the film. There seem also to be social pressures and classist prejudices amongst Fatima's own community. Their neighbours gossip about the family and resent Nesrine because they believe now that she has been accepted at medical school, she will look down on them. One neighbour is angry that Nesrine does not greet her as she passes her by on the street, but Nesrine is simply lost in her thoughts.

Fatima came out at a time when racial prejudice had increased against a backdrop of Islamist terror attacks and the rise of support for right-wing extremism. In this sense, it brings to the fore the daily struggles of citizens of immigrant descent, the inner-negotiations they have to undergo as well as the pressures they feel from the spaces surrounding them. Faucon's film counters prejudices in that it demonstrates that these citizens do what they can to contribute in a positive manner to their adoptive countries despite all the negotiations that they have to go through.

CONCLUSION: THE URGENCY OF A NEW CONCEPTION OF IDENTITY

Referring primarily to Audiard's *Dheepan*, an editorial by Stéphane Delorme in *Les Cahiers du Cinéma* states: "French cinema [...] shuts itself away in a world of images cut off from the real. At its worst this political vacuum barely conceals a cynical affirmation, a more or less brazen move to the right – from Audiard's war fantasies to flashy dramas" (Délorme 2015). According to Delorme, French cinema, just like French politics, does not deal with the foundation of the errors of the Republic; each attempt to do so, has brought out the underlying darkness of the apparent tolerance and open-mindedness that France likes to parade itself as having. This is especially the case in crisis situations, where polarising and exclusionary politics have been the immediate responses to problem solving. One of the longest lasting problems in France regarding the French *banlieue* prevails; reforms such as the allocation of supplementary funds to Priority Education Zones, where more government attention has been given to decrease drop-out rates from schools in French *banlieues* are demonstrative of steps taken to bridge the gap and feeling of alienation. Nonetheless, the effects of this type of reform are nullified by other measure such as the burkini ban on French beaches. Such measures aggravate the situation with visible minorities instead of addressing and acknowledging their lives and lifestyles, incorporating their realities in a new conception of Frenchness. More recently, Prime Minister Manual Valls proposed an amendment to the constitution after the 2015 attacks aimed to revoke the French citizenship of those dual citizens who had served sentences for crimes relating to terrorism. This type of approach does not prevent attacks from happening but relegates the 3.3 million people with dual nationality to the status of second-class citizens (Le Monde 2015).

Todd states that there are two options for France: a "confrontation with Islam, or an accommodation with it" (Todd 2015: 144). Although he believes that it seems like France has chosen the former, which will have catastrophic consequences for France, what needs to be done is to accept Islam as a reality of contemporary France instead of passing more laws that exclude its practitioners from public life. A new and more inclusive understanding of citizenship needs to be developed and accepted on a political and social level instead of holding on to values as if they were absolute. If the social fracture is not addressed, the impending violence will be inevitable. As Kassovitz's Hubert in *La Haine* states at the beginning of the film, "It's the story of a society in free fall and which repeats endlessly to reassure itself: so far all is well . . . Important is not the fall, but the landing." The landing for France seems to be near.

BIBLIOGRAPHY

Aguilar, Carlos. 2016. Losing Her Voice: In Philippe Faucon's Poignant Fatima, an Immigrant Faces Cultural Difference Even Within Family. *Moviemaker*. https://www.moviemaker.com/archives/interviews/philippe-faucon-cultural-difference-family-fatima/. Accessed 07 August 2017.

82   Ş. F. ERENSOY

Austin, Guy. 2009. *Contemporary French Cinema: An Introduction.* Manchester: Manchester University Press.

Balibar, Etienne. 2007. From Reason to Common Sense: Towards a Critique of Universalism. *Transversal.* http://eipcp.net/transversal/0607/balibar/en. Accessed 1 August 2017.

Bourdieu, Pierre. 2004. Preface. In *The Suffering of the Immigrant.* Ed. Sayad, Abdelmalek. Cambridge: Polity Press.

Bronner, Luc and Pascal Ceaux. (2005) Le bilan chiffré de la crise des banlieues. *Le Monde.* http://cettesemaine.info/spip/imprimersans.php3_id_article=264. html. Accessed 1 August 2017.

Canet, Raphael, Laurent Pech and Maura Stewart. 2015. France's Burning Issue: Understanding the Urban Riots of November 2005. In *Crowd Actions in Britain and France from the Middle Ages to the Modern World.* Ed. Davis, Michael, T. New York: Palgrave and Macmillan.

Carr, T. (1997). French Cinema and Post-Colonial Minorities. In *Post-Colonial Culture in France.* Ed. A.G. Hardgreaves and M. McKinney London, New York: Routledge.

Chevalier, Karine. 2016. Le Cinéma Français face à la Violence: du New French Extremism à une violence intériorisée. *Modern & Contemporary France,* 24 (4): 411–425.

Collins, Gillian. 2016. Fatima is a Tender Look at Making a Home in a New Land. *Seventh Row.* https://seventh-row.com/2016/03/09/fatima/. Accessed 22 August 2017.

Delorme, Stéphane. 2015 Vide Politique. *Les Cahiers du Cinéma.* https://www. cahiersducinema.com/produit/edito-714-septembre-2015/. Accessed 28 July 2017.

Dobson, Julia. 2017. Dis-Locations: Mapping the Banlieue. In *Filmurbia: Screening the Suburbs* Ed. Forrest, David, Graeme Harper and Jonathan Rayner. London: Palgrave Macmillan.

Doyle, Natalie J. 2011. Lessons from France: Populist Anxiety and Veiled fears of Islam. *Islam and Christian-Muslim Relations,* 22 (4): 475–489.

Ebert, R. (2016). Dheepan [online]. Roger Ebert. Available at: http://www.rog-erebert.com/reviews/dheepan-2016. Accessed 27 August 2017.

Echchaibi, Nabil. 2007. Republican Betrayal: Beur FM and the Suburban Riots in France. *Journal of Intercultural Studies,* 28 (3): 301–316.

Fanon, Frantz. 2008. *Black Skin White Masks.* London: Pluto Press.

Fassin, Didier. 2006. Riots in France and Silent Anthropologists. *Anthropology Today,* 22 (1): 1–13.

Gaspard, Françoise and Farhad Khosrokhavar. 1995. *Le Foulard et la République.* Paris: La Découverte.

Hayward, Susan. 2005. *French National Cinema.* London and New York: Routledge.

Higbee, Will. 2005a. The Return of the Political, or Designer Visions of the Exclusion? The Case for Mathieu Kassovitz's 'fracture sociale' Trilogy. *Studies in French Cinema*, 5 (2): 123–135.

Higbee, Will. 2005b. Towards a Multiplicity of Voices: French Cinema's Age of the Postmodern Part II—1992–2004. In *French National Cinema*. Ed. Hayward, Susan. London and New York: Routledge.

Koff, Harlan and Dominique Duprez. 2009. The 2005 Riots in France: The International Impact of Domestic Violence. *Journal of Ethnic and Migration Studies*, 35 (5): 713–730.

Le Figaro. 2016. Faut-il aller voir Fatima, César du meilleur film? http://www.lefigaro.fr/cinema/ceremonie-cesar/2016/02/27/03020-20160227ARTFIG00098-faut-il-aller-voir-fatima-cesar-du-meilleur-film.php. Accessed 22 August 2017.

Lehin, Barbara. 2005. Giving a Voice to the Ethnic Minorities in 1980s French and British Cinemas. *Studies in European Cinema*, 2 (3): 213–225.

Le Monde. 2015. Contre le Terrorisme, La Plus Grande Manifestation Jamais Recensée en France. http://www.lemonde.fr/societe/article/2015/01/11/la-france-dans-la-rue-pour-defendre-la-liberte_4553845_3224.html. Accessed 24 August 2017.

Mauger, Gérard. 2006. *L'émeute de Novembre. Une révolte Protopolitique.* Broissieux: Éditions du Croquant.

Meiner, Carsten. 2017. The Ghost of Grandeur: Home in French Cinema from Truffaut to Haneke. *Home Studies,* 14 (1): 7–24.

Milleliri, Carole. 2012. Le Cinéma de Banlieue: un genre instable. *Mise au Point.* https://map.revues.org/1003. Accessed 22 August 2017.

O'Malley, Sheila. 2016. Dheepan. *Roger Ebert.* http://www.rogerebert.com/reviews/dheepan-2016. Accessed 27 August 2017.

O'Shaughnessy, Martin. 2010. French Cinema and the Political. *Studies in French Cinema,* 10 (1): 39–56.

Pagesy, Hélène. 2016. César: Guillaume Gallienne «s'interroge» sur la victoire de Fatima. *Le Figaro.* http://www.lefigaro.fr/cinema/2016/03/07/03002-20160307ARTFIG00208-cesar-guillaume-gallienne-s-interroge-sur-la-victoire-de-fatima.php. Accessed 22 August 2017.

Palmer, Tim. 2011. *Brutal Intimacy: Analyzing Contemporary French Cinema* (Middletown: Wesleyan University Press)

Romney, Jonathan. 2016. Jacques Audiard: 'I wanted to give migrants a name, a shape...a violence of their own'. *The Guardian.* https://www.theguardian.com/film/2016/apr/03/jacques-audiard-interview-dheepan-prophet-rust-done-director. Accessed 2 August 2017.

Ross, Kristin. 1996. *Fast Cars, Clean Bodies: Decolonization and the Reordering of French Culture.* Cambridge, MA and London: The MIT Press.

84   Ş. F. ERENSOY

Roy, Oliver. 2013. Secularism and Islam: The Theological Predicament. *The International Spectator*, 48 (1): 5–19.

Shohat, Ella and Robert Stam. 1994. *Unthinking Eurocentrism: Multiculturalism and the Media*. London and New York: Routledge.

Silverman, Max. 1999. *Facing Postmodernity: Contemporary French Thought on Culture and Society*. London and New York: Routledge.

Tarr, Carrie. 1997. French Cinema and Post-Colonial Minorities. In *Post-Colonial Culture in France*. Ed. Hardgreaves, Alec, G. and Mark McKinney. London and New York: Routledge.

Tarr, Carrie. 2005. *Reframing Difference: Beur and Banlieue Filmmaking in France*. Manchester and New York: Manchester University Press.

Taylor, Charles. 2011. Why We Need a Radical Redefinition of Secularism. In *The Power of Religion in the Public Sphere*. Ed. Mendieta, Eduardo and Van Antwerpen, Jonathan. New York: Columbia University Press.

Todd, Emmanuel. 2015. *Who is Charlie? Xenophobia and the New Middle Class*. Cambridge: Polity Press.

Welch, Edward and John Perivolaris. 2016. The Place of the Republic: Space, Territory and Identity around and after Charlie Hebdo. *French Cultural Studies*, 27 (3): 279–292.

Zappi, Sylvia. 2015. En France, environ 3,3 millions de personnes ont deux nationalités. *Le Monde*. http://www.lemonde.fr/societe/article/2015/12/24/en-france-environ-3-3-millions-de-binationaux_4837454_3224.html. Accessed 1 September 2017.

CHAPTER 5

Documenting the *Charlie Hebdo* Tragedy

Hugo Frey

In 1991 the French filmmaker Bertrand Blier released his new work, *Merci La Vie*. Starring Charlotte Gainsbourg and Anouk Grinberg, it recounts the misadventures of two teenage girls as they live life to the full while on vacation at an unspecified location on the French coast. Almost impossible to summarise in any accurate detail, the work uses the hyper-paced format of a remix aesthetic, which at the time was associated with MTV rock videos, to narrate through flashback and flashforward the horrors of modern French history and the contemporary agonies of late-twentieth-century youth culture. On the one hand, the protagonists are plunged backwards in time into the world of the Nazi Occupation, while on the other hand, in the present day they are confronted by the menace of contracting AIDS. The former plot line is cleverly mixed up with substantial sequences where the girls accidentally encounter a film crew making a movie about the Occupation. Most memorably it is towards the end of the film that Blier depicts images associated with the Holocaust deportation trains. It is in this scene from the film that one character screams to the audience: why do we live in a time with both Nazis and AIDS—that cannot be fair or right! One should add that the many meta-levels within the work also directly reference back to Blier's first major *succès de scandale*—*Les Valseuses*

H. Frey (✉)
University of Chichester, Chichester, UK
e-mail: h.frey@chi.ac.uk

© The Author(s) 2018
J. Harvey (ed.), *Nationalism in Contemporary Western European Cinema*, Palgrave European Film and Media Studies,
https://doi.org/10.1007/978-3-319-73667-9_5

85

(1974). It was another anarchic road movie that featured the then relatively young male star protagonists, Gérard Depardieu and Patrick Dewaere.

Both *Les Valseuses* and *Merci la Vie* have been analysed as examples of films that exploit and reference ideas of the 'carnivalesque' (citing of course the work of Michel Bakhtin, see Harris 2001). Rightly so, since grotesque and even obscene humour play a major part in each film. In addition, Blier's strand of modern French cinema derives some of its more general tone from the anarchic world of café cabaret comedy. For example, Michel Leblanc who has a significant role in *Merci la Vie* began his career precisely in this milieu. Both films also owe a debt to the world of the French satirical comic strips of the late 1960s. Typically one thinks of the brutally horrible *Hara-Kiri* magazine covers that specialised in grotesque (obscene) photographs that mocked the standard notions of beauty associated with post-war consumer society (see Michallat 2007). Later, from the same milieu, there is *Charlie Hebdo*: the low circulation, cult reading, twisted-sister to the better-known satire weekly, *Le Canard Enchaîné*. *Charlie Hebdo*, unheard of outside of France until, first, its republication of the Danish cartoon depictions of the Prophet Mohammed in 2006 and, second, when on 7 January 2015 its offices were attacked, twelve people murdered, and French society plunged into near civil-war conditions (which continue to this day, the time of writing being autumn 2017). *Charlie Hebdo* for a few days after the same horrifying attack created a world-wide online media network with the slogan 'Je suis Charlie' but then only shortly afterwards disappeared back into the underground, returning to its raison d'être to poke fun at everything and anything, including itself.

This chapter does not propose a new history of the infamous satirical weekly newspaper, nor for that matter to debate the wider aesthetics of anarchy and carnivalesque humour so beloved of *Charlie*, Bertrand Blier and parts of the French literary intelligentsia, its anarcho-left and anarcho-right wings and some in between. Instead, its subject is the feature length documentary *L'Humour à Mort*, directed by Daniel Leconte and Emmanuel Leconte (2015). Made just months after the fatal attack on the staff at *Charlie*, it provides a day-by-day account of the events of January 2015, as well as contextualising the periodical's earlier defence of its right to publish the Danish cartoons. In addition, the documentary provides a palimpsestic tribute to the publication, the victims of the terrorist attack on its staff, as well as police and French Jewish victims killed during the same bloody week at the beginning of 2015 (including the attack on the Jewish supermarket that occurred in suburban Paris on 9 January 2015). The hypothesis that I will develop further is that the work is a strong example of a contemporary twenty-first-century national cinema for France. Following a standard definition of nation-film relations associated with many scholars, including Marc Ferro, this film holds up a mirror to society and adds its own voice to national political events. As I will explain further shortly herein it also argues for a broadly Republican secular vision of France, although it is also careful to underline that the terrorists murdered many different victims other than just the secular satirists. So, our example in this chapter is not that of a simplistic far right-wing work (some of which I have discussed before, see Frey 2014), nor for that matter is it a mass hit movie projecting a vision of France for domestic and international audiences. What is however at stake is the representation of crisis and national tragedy. That much is clear. I will also spend much of this chapter arguing that the work is greatly nuanced and a significant documentary film in its own right. My ground for this argument is twofold. Firstly, that the structuring of the work owes something to the fragmented and polyvalent narrative techniques of late-modern aesthetics of the remix (and as espoused in Blier's *Merci la vie*). Secondly, that *L'Humour à mort* is a telling micro-history that ably shows its viewers the horror of the experience of a contemporary terrorist attack. Implicitly responding to debates led by Georges Didi-Huberman (2004) on the relevance of depicting traumatic photographs from the Holocaust, Leconte and Leconte employ the documentary film to draw their viewers directly into the mortal space of the terror attack. Not much detail of that is spared from us as viewers.

Clearly this is a work of national cinema. How so? The film engages with a set of political circumstances that have dominated twenty-first-century France and offers a series of implied and explicit interpretations on the subject: this is a film for and about contemporary France. The general content of the documentary advocates a Republican national defence of *Charlie Hebdo*'s content and is therefore a work implicitly in favour of secularism, freedom of speech, and the French democratic values of 1789 as re-staged today. As I will return to later herein, there is also a selection of material from the January 2015 crisis that espouses a place for Muslim French citizens inside the Republican nation state and so one can identify that the work aims for inclusivity, without evaluation of the pros and cons of *Charlie Hebdo*'s use of caricature that as readers of this chapter will appreciated contain all manner of provocative imagery. Moreover,

88   H. FREY

L'Humour à mort contains reportage footage on the French public's mass demonstrations against terrorism and in favour of *Charlie Hebdo*, including in these passages of the film symbolically patriotic images of the capital city. Therefore, there is a clear expression of a defence of and pride in France in the face of the violent external threat of terrorism. Let me add, to be comprehensive, that the film also explores some of the intellectual and public discussion that followed the crisis. Here it underlines that some people (intellectuals, journalists) rather quickly equated the deliberately controversial content of *Charlie Hebdo* with the terrorists' motivations. The work implies quite strongly that such an approach perversely misunderstands the horror and nature of the attack. The film (while taking a clear political-intellectual line) does therefore mirror a popular national debate. In the spirit of academic analysis, one would also note that the film does not question underlying French social-economic realities, analyse the backdrop of a racist extreme right on the rise, nor for that matter discuss French foreign policy. These are not its concerns. In summary, it is pro-*Charlie Hebdo*, pro-Republican freedom of speech and secularist rights. It asserts a positive vision of these dispositions as well as the mass public demonstrations in their favour that followed the attacks. Whether one defines national cinema as a bundle of culturally specific cinematic themes, traits and emotions, or asserts that film can be used to communicate nationalist myths and narratives (see Hayward 2005; or Frey 2014), it is clear that the documentary is part of one kind of twenty-first-century nationalism in France. In addition, it fits soundly inside a strong tradition of historical documentary cinema that has been very important in France over the past fifty years, especially in works addressing the traumas of the Occupation and the Holocaust (notably in the cinema of Alain Resnais, Marcel Ophuls and Claude Lanzmann, respectively, see also Insdorf 2003).

Nonetheless, it is not a work of blunt propaganda. Instead it uses a compelling aesthetic structure to draw the reader into the subject. More specifically it deploys an editorial method indebted to the temporal shifts and multiple points of view associated with the video remix culture, already adroitly pioneered in Blier's late-1990s fictional works (though with less adrenalin than in the hyped-up *Merci la vie*). Thus, new and original footage of testimony from survivors of the January attack is sequenced next to historical film materials that allow the (deceased) victims of the terrorists to 'live again' on screen, to re-explain their motivations for their art and journalism, and to 'exist' just one more time as (photographed-videoed) human beings. Some of this archival material is similar to an earlier film by Leconte that had focussed on the original controversy of the Danish cartoons (*C'est dur d'être aimé par des cons,* 2008). Other sequences are derived from footage that gives a snapshot of the life and vibrancy of the *Charlie Hebdo* staff: notably their singing and joking around on a bus trip together. Similarly, a fun sequence showing the artist Charb (murdered in 2015) messing around in the paper's offices with his colleague Luz is also tellingly included and is very funny. In addition, there is also space for photographic reproduction of original *Charlie* caricatures. These include the original controversial cover art for the issue of *Charlie Hebdo* that reprinted the Danish cartoons; as well as the drafts and finished responses of works prepared for the first issue of the weekly that was published after the January 2015 murders.

In summary, the remix approach provides a multi-layered documentary that engages its audience. The montaging of images of deceased victims speaking to the camera (as if from the grave), alongside horrifying new details from the surviving witnesses of the attack, creates a visceral portrayal of the terrible events, while also demonstrably showing the life energy of the men and women whose lives were so tragically cut short by the terrorists. Rather cleverly the more comic footage (the films of the *Charlie Hebdo* team having fun) brings a lightness to the work (despite its subject) and gives time for the audience to take stock of what they are watching. The representation of drawn caricatures poses questions for the audience: how could so small, childish, plainly stupid, and crudely funny little drawings, be ever read by anyone with such murderous hostility? They also inevitably provide further (small) relief as the intrinsically crude humour of the cartoons lightens the mood from the direct representation of the attacks and their aftermath. The inclusion of the cartoons themselves is a forceful rhetoric of political defiance: remediating the original *Charlie Hebdo* vision onto film to counter any censorship.

Next, one should add that this palimpsestic-remix approach facilitates an openness to and recognition of the other victims who were murdered. Thus, woven in between the material on *Charlie Hebdo* there is a slow chronological charting of the murder of police and the anti-Semitic attack on the supermarket (Paris, 9 January 2015). Similarly, the film finds space to include extended extracts from an interview with the philosopher Elizabeth Badinter who asserts the importance of a defence of strong Republican values (a position she has often adopted in the past and that is shared by many intellectuals claiming a 'hard' Republican position).

To repeat, in *L'Humour à mort* instant contemporary history is documented through fragmentation, temporal shifts, multiple perspectives, and inserted authority statements. As in *Merci la vie*, historical time is circular and seemingly fluid, yet also profoundly tragic, because as audience-viewers we know that so many of the bright and funny lives we watch on screen in historical footage have been already callously wiped out. The aesthetic organisation of remix allows for some political subtly. Let me explain. What overt explicit commentary that is present (very present) is guarded and protected from sounding propagandistic by being always blended with the other multiple formats and subjects. Thus, certainly the film espouses a full defence of Charlie Hebdo and all of its works, but such a position is always also mediated alongside different and very powerful images and messages about: the suffering of individuals, the humour and banal reality of the ordinary life experience of working at the publication, the dignity of the family of the police victim (a Muslim), the basically stupid and funny banality of cartoon art which (by implication) absurdly has somehow led to the massacre. It also means that when Islamic terrorism is discussed in the film it is contextualised around these themes: further underlining its deep and disturbing otherness.

Nevertheless, *L'Humour à mort* is at its most powerful and relevant when operating as a documentary of testimony. For all the movement between different images and historical footage-materials in its remix aesthetic, it is here that the work forces viewers to engage and recognise the horror of the attack and as such becomes a significant work of documentary cinema for the twenty-first century, transcending the national-political context or the specifics of cartoons, religion, and stereotyping. Three of these interviews are from eyewitnesses of the attack on *Charlie Hebdo*—Riss, Coco, and Eric Portheault—and were filmed especially for the documentary presumably just a short time after the events themselves. The fourth sequence of testimony is from the family of murdered policeman, Ahmed Merabet, which is sourced from a press conference given in January 2015. In each case the combined power of the details of the interview with the visual representation of the emotion on the faces of the speakers establishes a unique, if entirely, upsetting form of cinematography. The material is remarkable and makes the film deserving of much greater recognition than it has yet received.

The first and in my opinion the most upsetting of these interviews is with the cartoonist Coco. She is positioned speaking to camera in an art studio/office and can appear to be simply talking naturally about her experience of the attack. Her words feel slowly paced. Coco recalls that she had been working at the *Charlie* offices but as she explains had left the building to find her daughter. As this everyday detail about ordinary life is recounted one cannot anticipate what will be disclosed next. In a calm and clear voice Coco continues to explain that it was on returning to the offices that she stumbled directly into the terrorist attack as it was just beginning. Very quickly, but again with absolute clarity in her voice, she explains that this coincidence meant that she was suddenly held at gun-point and forced to allow the attackers entry through the security door to the offices (using her security code at the point of a Kalashnikov machine gun). She describes in meticulous detail that the terrorists had shouted out their purpose and that they were searching to kill cartoonist Charb. She adds that she and Charb (who was killed) had recently been getting on so well and had become great office buddies. As she tells her story the camera gradually moves to a more consistent close-up framing of her face. Moreover, we can see that Coco begins to cry quite naturally. She wipes tears from her eyes. But her testimony carries on calmly, as she explains that she had opened the door and then recalls hearing the sound of gunfire. Coco describes how the sound of real gunshot is completely different to those in a film. This sequence of the documentary ends. It is a searing passage of cinema of which I know only very few, if any at all, equivalents.

The voices and images of Riss and Eric Portheault interchange on screen to take up the account of what they experienced inside the editorial offices during the raid. As with Coco's interview, the protagonists are framed mostly in mid-shot and are set in front of work like backdrops. Portheault provides further details of the horror. He states that he fell almost instantly to the ground and for one minute listened to the carnage around him. He recalls that he could see one of the assassins making a final killing before leaving the room; adding also that his dog, who was at work with him, moved to be next to his own prone body, lying across his eyes as if by implication to protect him from seeing the terrifying scene all around him. Riss describes similarly terrifying details but one may argue that his words are less important than the mise en scène of his face and body. The details of the attack are given but one is always more transfixed by the pale white skin of Riss's face and of his tired and still profoundly sad eyes. Here the words matter less than the clear physical manifestation of bereavement and sadness that is projected through the image of his body on the screen. The picturing of Riss generates a huge sense of audience empathy, as do the two other interviews described above.

92   H. FREY

The fourth sequence is different and a little shorter. It is a screening of contemporary journalistic film footage of a press conference given during the events themselves by the family of murdered policeman Merabet. Here words and images speak in unison as first Merabet's brother declares that he was a Muslim, Frenchman and Police Officer. This honouring of the victim continues by a very powerful assertion against all racists—Islamophobes and anti-Semites. It includes a declaration of the values of the Republic: Liberty, Equality, Fraternity. Another female family member speaks quietly of not recognising what images she had seen on a television showing the attack as it was happening. Neither man nor woman can continue speaking and the camera shows them collapse in despair. The screen fades to black before cutting to images of pro-*Charlie* mass demonstrations on the Place de la République.

None of this material is dealt with in a sensational or exploitative manner. The dignity and courage of the individuals speaking is allowed to shine through the screen and to mitigate (a little) of the horrific subject matter. It is also the case that the blending of these sequences with less harrowing visual images (protest rallies; historical footage of *Charlie* staff or cartoons) allows for some distancing from the horror, to repeat. I would argue that the directors' specific juxtaposition of individual testimonials with expansive panning shots of people, crowds, flags, Parisian monuments, is significant. Thus, the individuals' biographical stories are showcased but they are framed with images showing the mass support of the people. There is a visual rhythm at work: first interview recollection, then next portrayals of city streets and crowds, then returning again to a new sequence of more frightening and unique eyewitness testimony. This editorial approach communicates a consistent internal visual pattern inside the more fluid shape of the remix mode.

The treatment is a comparatively original approach in terms of the wider representational field around *Charlie Hebdo* and the attack. It seems from preliminary research that more commonly there is an indirect and more metaphorical strategy in play. For example, this is how *The New Yorker* magazine approached the subject in the first days after the attack when it devoted a cover to the subject. Therein the Americans blended images of an artist's pencil with the iconic shape of the Eiffel tower. In the world of cartooning itself there has been a preference to debate issues of stereotyping and free speech; and again, not to so strongly emphasise biographical details from the survivors. Grosso modo, these are the terms and frames of reference used in statements on the *Charlie* crisis and controversy from

Joe Sacco and Art Spiegelman, though clearly both men did fully appreciate how horrible a human price had been paid. One would also add that the first *Charlie* cover after the attacks created by Luz preferred irony, defiance, and satire: another direct representation of Mohammed now holding a 'Je suis Charlie' banner, shedding a tear, positioned under the headline originally in French, 'Everything is forgiven.' *L'Humour à mort* is therefore distinctive in its use of emotive first-person accounts of the tragedy. As I have been suggesting in this chapter, this documentary film places the witness-survivors on the screen and encourages the audience to confront the precise details of their accounts.

As aesthetic theorists know only too well showing the unshowable is always a complicated business. *L'Humour à mort* provides a fundamental piece of historical evidence on its subject matter that does take the viewer straight into the *Charlie Hebdo* offices on the day of carnage. It includes graphic detail on the technical details of the massacre and the camera shows us the individual survivors; capturing their horrifying recent memories. The faces, bodies, eyes, and tears of Coco, Riss, and Portheault display everything one needs to know about the worse possible experience of a terror attack in a contemporary European city. The work therefore circumvents many of the problems posed in debates that have occurred on, for example, the analogous subject of Holocaust representation. As described above, the material presented in the film is completely open and frank about the trauma that has occurred. There is no shying away from representing the scope and meaning of the terror attack. Nor on the other hand, is there any sensationalism or over-representation as has been sometimes critiqued in Holocaust representation. The classical, modest, framing, the combination of voice and image, the rhythmic interchange of testimony and crowd scenes, the matter of fact details, all function very elegantly. This is a commemorative and memorialising work that moreover inscribes the histories of the victims and witnesses onto a public consciousness via the medium of film. It is of course also a work of national testimony and one should not overlook this aspect when drawing our discussion to a close. As I have discussed in this chapter the work functions as a strong national Republican discourse, celebrating the freedoms of the *Charlie Hebdo* staff, and exploring the horrible events of the attacks as a national tragedy played out on the streets of Paris. None of this is xenophobic or confrontational. Instead, there is a matter of fact defence of a core tradition of French political values, schematised onto the documentary narrative necessary to recall the details of tragedy. On its own terms the film is a triumph and could and arguably should be widely appreciated, debated, and re-viewed.

Or so it would seem. The implied predictions of *Merci la vie* that an accelerated visual and popular media culture would mix up periods, conflate times, and generally cause representational chaos has to some extent come to pass (this is also a part of remix culture after all). Sadly, *L'Humour à Mort* is almost an entirely lost and forgotten film because of the constantly changing political landscape between 2015 and 2017 and the media representation of subsequent attacks and the associated French political responses to them. Thus, the documentary was initially planned to be released in French cinemas in the winter of 2015, approximately eleven months after the subject of the film. Its scheduled release date in France was December 2015 the high point of security alerts following the new and even more devastating attacks of 13 November 2015. This meant it was almost too dangerous and too complicated to be screened in cinemas; and audiences were not likely or willing to wish to view it in a public space. The content of the work was a national-Republican narrative (in part) and a work of witness and commemoration. The practical possibility for the film to succeed in the public sphere in winter 2015/2016 was however extremely limited. New horrors were blocking the theatrical representation of those from just months earlier. In an echo of some news media refusal to print or show any cartoons directly relating to the Danish or *Hebdo* caricatures, it seems that outside France one of the most remarkable documentary films of the twenty-first century has been marginalised again (perhaps also for understandable public safety reasons). However, a distribution company have released a DVD and the work is also no doubt available on the internet. This chapter has argued for a re-evaluation of this film as a ground-breaking work of contemporary testimony, and yes also as an example of contemporary French national cinema. For all the many images of different kinds included in the work after a viewing one cannot ever forget the voices or images of Coco, Riss, Portheault, and the Merhabet family. Whatever one's political opinions on the café-theatre culture of directors like Blier or publications like *Charlie*, these voices of witness merit full and firm recollection. The bravery of their statements is admirable and it is time that this film gained a greater scholarly and public recognition. Sorry to write, it is a document for and of our times that reminds us that today we have Nazis, AIDS, and psychopathic terrorists among our real and representational horrors. 'Merci la vie'—with apologies to Bertrand Blier.

BIBLIOGRAPHY

Didi-Huberman, Georges. 2004. *Images malgré tout*. Paris: Les Editions de Minuit.

Frey, Hugo. 2014. *Nationalism and the Cinema in France*. New York: Berghahn.

Harris, Sue. 2001. *Bertrand Blier*. Manchester: Manchester UP.

Hayward, Susan. 2005. *French National Cinema*. London: Routledge.

Insdorf, Annette. 2003. *Indelible Shadows: Film and the Holocaust*. Cambridge: Cambridge University Press.

Michallat, Wendy. 2007. Modern life is Still Rubbish. *Journal of European Studies*. 37 (3): 313–331.

CHAPTER 6

Diasporic Belgian Cinema: Transnational and Transcultural Approaches to Molenbeek and Matonge in *Black*

Jamie Steele

Since the terrorist attacks that took place in Paris (13 November 2015) and Brussels (23 March 2016), the Brussels suburb of Molenbeek and the diasporic communities of Belgium have been frequently analysed in European and Western media outlets. Two days before the tragic events in Paris, the (francophone) Belgian film *Black* (Adil El Arbi and Bilall Fallah 2015) was released to Belgian audiences. The film achieved critical valorisation after winning the Discovery prize at the Toronto international film festival, prior to its screening at film festivals in Belgium, namely the Ghent film festival (in Flanders) and the Festival International de Film Francophone (FIFF) in Namur (Wallonia) (Feuillère 2015). The contextual backdrop of terrorism and Islamic fundamentalism has led to a synchronic interpretation of *Black* as a potentially radical and subversive film. For instance, interviews with the two filmmakers adopted a greater level of topicality, with a stronger international and national spotlight received by Belgium's Moroccan diasporic community and Molenbeek. Crucially, francophone

J. Steele (✉)
Film and Screen Studies, Bath Spa University, Bath, UK
e-mail: j.steele@bathspa.ac.uk

© The Author(s) 2018
J. Harvey (ed.), *Nationalism in Contemporary Western European Cinema*, Palgrave European Film and Media Studies,
https://doi.org/10.1007/978-3-319-73667-9_6

97

98   J. STEELE

Belgian film criticism and newspaper articles have placed little emphasis on the action unrolling in Molenbeek, instead focusing on the level of screen time afforded to Matonge—the largely Congolese-Belgian neighbourhood in Brussels.[1]

As *The Guardian* outlined, French cinemas refused to exhibit the film, along with *Made in France* (Nicolas Boukhrief 2015)—a film that dealt more directly with Islamic fundamentalism, extremism and disenfranchised youth—and *Salafistes* (François Margolin and Lemine Ould M. Salem, 2016) as a result of the terror attacks in Paris (Agence France Press 2015). *Black*, however, remained the only fictional feature film to be overlooked for cinematic distribution and exhibition in France, and the reasoning was primarily predicated on the film's setting in Molenbeek—the location of the terrorist cells—along with the violent subject matter (Ibid.). In the days leading up to the terror attack in Paris, Denis contended that *Black* was fiercely polemical with little political correctness (2015: 4), perhaps portending the bans and restrictions to follow on the film. Due to the 'current context' in the words of the distributor, Paname Distribution stated on 18 February 2016 that the film would not be released in cinemas in France. Belgium's linguistic neighbour represents a crucial film market for French-language Belgian films. According to the French newspaper *Le Figaro*, the film arrived only in small and little-known French cinemas on the 16 March 2016 (Gausserand 2016), and it received a delayed online release on 24 June 2016 (Paulet 2016). The film, therefore, received only a modicum of distribution in France. The limited distribution of the film is particularly problematic for this production, with the filmmakers noting that their filmmaking style is peculiarly cinematic (Bouras 2015).

Since the terror attacks in France and Belgium, the documentary *Molenbeek, génération radicale?* (José-Luis Peñafuerte and Chergui Kharroubi 2016) was filmed in the Brussels suburb in order to nuance

[1] Western media outlets in the UK, Australia, the USA and France have offered either sensationalist, specious or nuanced interpretations of the Brussels suburb, Molenbeek. In *The New York Times*, Cohen proposes that '[i]t is hard to resist the symbolism of the Islamic State establishing a base for its murderous designs in the so-called capital of Europe at a time when the European idea is weaker than at any time since the 1950s' in addition to foregrounding that '41 percent of the population of Molenbeek is Muslim' (Cohen 2016). After the two terror attacks, *L'Express* (2016) drew attention to the 'jihadi threat in Belgium', whilst Gendron (2015), in *Libération*, described Molenbeek as a site of an invisible presence of jihad, that is, that much of the radicalisation takes place online. Simon and Traynor nuance the generalised view of Molenbeek as a 'jihadi central', since the inhabitants of Molenbeek are attempting to change this specious interpretation (Simon 2016). Traynor's (2015) interviewees note the 'stigmatisation' of the community against the backdrop of the terrorist attacks and the Syrian war.

interpretations of the area's population. This is reminiscent of the critical and media attention experienced by the French *banlieues* in light of the riots in the 1990s and early 2000s. The televised debate in a local primary school, that bookended the documentary's screening on the francophone Belgian TV channel RTBF, recalls the TV series *Écran Témoin. Molenbeek, génération radicale?* provides an important intervention in terms of a balanced representation of the diasporic communities residing in Brussels' suburbs. This is set against the backdrop of 'deep social anxieties' linked to the growing Muslim population in Brussels (Fadil 2014: 315). It is precisely these inflections that have coalesced into a reading of films like *Black*, which unroll only fleetingly in Molenbeek. The location has become a discussion point, alongside the diasporic community and the 'ghettoising' principles that have impacted on this development and geographic concentration of a minority group.

CINEMATIC TRANSNATIONALISM AND DIASPORIC BELGIAN FILMMAKING

The notion of Belgian identity is multifaceted, particularly since

> (t)he abandoning of Belgium's neutrality [after WWII] has led to the influx of a great many people from a range of different countries, ethnic groups and social strata, each with their own legitimate identity. The large number of European civil servants adds a further foreign presence. (Spaas 2000: 8)

Despite the tradition of post-WWII migration, Belgian cinema's diasporic filmmakers have been largely overlooked in academic and scholarly consideration, except for Chantal Akerman and, to a lesser extent, Michel Khleifi. These two filmmakers, one of Jewish and the other of Christian Palestine origin, constitute case studies for Naficy's (2001) oft-cited concept of 'accented cinema'. Alternatively, Mosley highlights the fraught and tense relationships between the native and immigrant populations in francophone Belgian cinema in the 1990s, against the backdrop of increasing 'global labour mobility' and a lack of employment opportunities (Mosley 2002: 164).

Saeys presciently argues that second-generation diasporic filmmaking arrived around twenty years after the 'banlieue film's' emergence in France, observing that Belgium's first arrived after the millennium (2009: 351) with *Au delà de Gibraltar/ Beyond Gibraltar* (Mourad Boucif and Taylan Barman 2001). Beyond this transnational cinematic reference point, two newspaper articles in the press—one in *La Libre Belgique* and one in *Le Soir*

(Denis 2015: 4–5; Manche 2015: 4–5)—use the term 'beur' in order to refer to the filmmakers and the characters in *Black* of Moroccan heritage.[2] Denis (2015: 4) and Manche (2015: 4–5) both foreground the 'Black-Beur' dynamic of the film, which is clearly reminiscent of the Black-Beur-Blanc triptych of *La Haine*. The concept also emerges dialogically in the non-diegetic soundtrack, *Du plomb dans les ailes* (literal translation 'Lead in the Wings', however idiomatically it pertains to 'Weakened') by Belgian hip-hop group CNN199, accompanying the sequence in which Mavela and Marwan are arrested for separate petty crimes. However, it is salient to note that the Moroccan-Belgian characters avoid the use of the loaded term in the film. The use of '*beur*' furthers the dialogue between French filmmaking of the late 1980s and 1990s—in addition to requiring nuance. Whilst these terms are applied liberally in film criticism, it is important to acknowledge the rejection of the '*beur* filmmaker' and '*beur* cinema' labels by diasporic filmmakers, 'because these set them apart from "unmarked" practitioners and, explicitly or implicitly, identify them as (albeit authentic) voices who can and must speak (only) about and for their communities' (Berghahn and Sternberg 2010: 18).

Higbee and Lim's concept of 'critical transnationalism' provides a key critical approach in terms of deciphering diasporic filmmaking in Western European cinema. In so doing, the concept 'understands the potential for local, regional and diasporic film cultures to affect, subvert and transform national and transnational cinemas' (2010: 18). The 'flows and exchanges' (Ibid.), therefore, pertain to people and populations within the nation that may have allegiances and senses of identity that lie beyond the nation's borders. Within this problematising of the national cinema context, power relations emerge that articulate centre/margin, insider/outsider, local/global, and host/home binary oppositions (Higbee and Lim 2010: 9–10).

In the context of so-called 'world cities', Hannerz (1996) articulates the power dynamics in operation between populations in the city and diasporic communities. According to Hannerz:

> the cent[re]-to-periphery flow, at the cent[re] itself, whatever passes for a native culture frequently seems to view itself as beleaguered or invaded by the local representations of the people…These are the people of the cent[re] wanting the periphery to go away from their doorstep, or at least to show up there only discreetly, to perform essential services. (Hannerz 1996: 134)

---

[2] See Bosséno (1992) for an outline of 'beur filmmaking' in the context of French cinema in the early 1990s.

In cinematic terms, Naficy interprets diasporas in relation to 'a long-term sense of ethnic consciousness and distinctiveness, which is consolidated by the periodic hostility of either the original home or the host societies towards them' (2001: 4). This hostility, therefore, plays a role in the formation of the collective along ethnic lines due to a lack of integration within the 'internal diversity'.

The 'non-places' of the malls and the historic centre remain closed-off for the film's enunciating subjects, whereas the public spaces of Matonge and Molenbeek offer a controlled form of socialisation for its subjects. As a result, 'transnational cinema is most "at home" in the in-between spaces of culture, in other words, between the local and the global, it decisively problematizes the investment in cultural purity and separatism' (Ezra and Rowden 2006: 4). The exploration and analysis of interstitial spaces is, therefore, key in unlocking references beyond national borders. It also allows for a nuanced interpretation of individuals whose sense of identity is not neatly pigeonholed and challenges the rather myopic perceptions of national homogeneity. A group sense of belonging is constructed in a local context, with the neighbourhoods of Molenbeek and Matonge providing a starting point for forms of allegiance. The representation of the districts highlights key themes of social marginality and social polarisation amongst the diasporic communities in Belgium, as well as addressing the continued sentiments of 'ghettoisation'.

In the conclusion to Orlando's analysis of *Les barons* (Nabil Ben Yadir 2009), the scholar posits that the film works to move beyond 'postcolonial paradigms' to offer an interpretation of a 'worldly' and de-centred Frenchness where diverse and integrated communities are the dominant and normative mode (2014: 177). However, these strict lines between Moroccan and Congolese ethnic groups and white Belgians does not place *Black* within the context of an evolving theoretical debate on a de-centred 'cinéma-monde' (Gott and Schilt forthcoming). The pastiche of US gangsta rap and popular music in *Black*'s set-pieces transcend Belgian nationalism, forming new senses of belonging for excluded communities through a dialogue with the local and the global. By including the musical set-pieces 'Problèmes' and 'Back to Black', *Black* conforms to the hip-hop and rap genre's patriarchal concerns, creating a fetishistic look on the female body and a voyeuristic perception of the two districts and articulating the characters' hybrid identities. The foregrounding of hip-hop culture in the margins connects the film with its counterparts in the USA and France to offer new forms of group identity.

COMPETING NATIONALISMS, EXCLUDED COMMUNITIES AND HIP-HOP QUOTATIONS

Language lies at the foundation of Belgian nationalism. Mosley, drawing his ideas from the oft-cited sources of Anderson (1991) and Gellner (1983), posits that 'the proponents of Belgian nationalism sought to manufacture as appropriate a cultural identity through language and more specifically through the production of literary texts', and this leads to a 'bourgeois' perception (2001: 17). The elitist and bourgeois forms of Belgian nationalism were primarily configured in French, within which 'the Flemish people long remained a purely latent force' (ibid.: 17) (effectively, historically sidelined). The nationalist split predicated on linguistic grounds leaves two competing national identities according to regions and linguistic communities. Hayward posits that within new Western nationalisms and cultures 'there has been a foregrounding of the margins of nation-space of which so-called marginal cinema is but one manifestation' (2000: 94). The argument is later furthered with reference to the flexibility of the nation as a construct, offering that '[b]ecause the fact that nations are invented and fictional means that they can be re-defined and re-appropriated by actors – in other words, a re-possessing of the nation by excluded groups is possible' (Hayward 2000: 99). From this premise, new Western nationalisms work through fragmentation and understanding notions of group identity on a local and regional level (Elsaesser 2005: 116–117); and those who have been historically, and are presently, excluded. Moreover, for Elsaesser, region, religion and lifestyle generate allegiances and forms of community outside and within the state boundaries of Western Europe (Elsaesser 2005: 117). In Belgium, this is evidenced in this case by Flanders' increasing claims for separatism and at the level of the sub-state in political terms.

Firstly, Flanders is politically considered right-leaning, whereas the francophone populations are generally viewed as Socialist and leftist (Cerulus 2015). The political turn to the Right has subsequently seen the exclusion of the francophone Socialists from the national Belgian government for the first time since 1988 (Ibid.). Since the terrorist attacks in France (and later Belgium) and the revealing of the terrorist cells in Molenbeek, the New Flemish Alliance (N-VA), a conservative Flemish-separatist group led by Bart De Wever, have gained an increased role in the national Belgian political structures, thereby 'pushing Belgium to the [political] Right' (Cerulus 2015).[3] Both the 'extremist party Flemish interest (*Vlaams Belang*) and the separatist party New Flemish Alliance [...] represent the Flemish Movement politically and advocate for an independent and monolingual Dutch Flemish state that includes the capital of Brussels' (Verheul 2016: 322). The interior minister Jan Jambon, another outright right-wing politician, outlined the requirement to 'clean up' Molenbeek (Cerulus 2015) with the 'Plan Canal' project (Belga 2016) in discourse that pertains to issues of stigmatisation. Much of the discourse surrounding these policies, mandates and events concerned the question of immigration. The question of Western European nationalism is marked by a political turn to the Right, which has been gradually building towards its peak at the time of the 2015–2016 terrorist attacks. The year 2016 has become a watershed, with increased levels of fear in the context of the perceived Other amongst a rise in terror attacks in Western Europe and the USA. As a result, a far-right ideology has gained greater traction in the media and popular consciousness, witnessing the election of Republican Donald Trump in the USA (with policies including the construction of a wall between the USA and Mexico), the UK's decision to leave the European Union (amongst strong support from UKIP [United Kingdom Independence Party]) in 2016, and Marine Le Pen of the Front National receiving the second-largest percentage of the French presidential votes in 2017.

In 2014, whilst analysing the Belgian film *Les barons*, Orlando (2014) sees an increasing liberalism in a political and ideological sense in Europe, beyond right-wing ideas of cultural homogeneity. For Orlando, these 'hardline ideas about nationhood and nationalism...seem incongruous in today's multicultural societies' (2014: 164). Instead, Hayward posits that national identities are pluricultural rather than multicultural, since separation arises in the context of competing nationalisms (2000: 94). In *The Guardian*, Adil El Arbi and Billal Fallah discuss the racism and prejudice that they suffered during their teenage years, suggesting that it is even worse now than in 1995 when Kassovitz produced *La Haine* (Rose 2016), particularly since 9/11 and the subsequent paroxysm of terrorism in cities across the globe. This is further articulated by sociologists Demart and

---

[3] Bart De Wever has increasingly used loaded discourse that exacerbates the climate of fear around the terror attacks in Europe. De Wever described the attacks in Paris as 'Europe's 9/11...It changes public opinion. And just like we have seen in the United States, you'll now see new laws being voted across Europe' (Cerulus 2015).

104   J. STEELE

Robert, who interpret the representations in *Black* as 'stigmatised, minoritised and raced', with the representation of gang violence—formed along ethnic lines and ethnic difference—as a backward step, 'taking us back by 20 years' (2015: 50).

Secondly, in terms of the diasporic communities, the hip-hop allusions and African-American cultural appropriation for the Congolese, and to a lesser extent the Moroccan-Belgian community in Belgium, connect with wider discourses of black nationalism. This form of nationalism is not contained within geo-political boundaries, since Androutsopoulos and Scholz posit that, for hip-hop and rap culture, 'appropriation is the productive use of an originally imported cultural pattern' (2003: 465). As Hardt and Negri contend, 'black nationalism names precisely the circuits of self-valorisation that constitute the community and allow for its relative self-determination and self-constitution' (2001: 108). However, through its 'homogeneity' and 'uniformity', it offers only 'de facto representatives of the whole' (Ibid.). Hip-hop, as a form of nationalism, is inclusive of certain strata of the community, who 'were either disillusioned by the racial hostilities brought on by the participation in the societal mainstream or dislocated from the centre of social and economic life altogether' (Watkins 2001: 381). The dislocation is epitomised in hip-hop and rap music by the disenfranchised and 'disadvantaged populations' of the USA's 'inner cities' and France's *banlieues* (Quittelier 2015). Instead, the use of hip-hop offers an alternative form of representation for excluded communities and for youth cultures.

It is precisely 'a new articulation of the nation' (Elsaesser 2005: 114) along local lines and smaller forms of community that the hip-hop allusions gain greater valence in *Black*, with a sense of collective and group identity forged in relation to their neighbourhood and district in the Belgian capital, Brussels. At the same time, the hip-hop iconography and sampled rhythms and beats, infused within *Black*, interact with both the local and the global. The relevance of hip-hop in Belgium to questions of Belgian nationalism is limited, primarily by virtue of rap music and hip-hop's limited popular appeal in the country, with the exception of Stromae [*verlan* for Maestro] (Mertens et al. 2013: 93). Instead, in this study, Congolese-Belgian hip-hop—to which Romano Daking's music in the film adheres—is more invested in post-colonial memory and challenging the obfuscation of Belgium's violent and fraught colonial history in Africa (Ibid.). To this end, hip-hop and rap music as a mode of expression offers a competing form of nationalism to excluded groups in contrast to a sense of Belgian national identity. El Arbi describes Belgian national identity as inherently 'artificial' (El Arbi 2017) and, therefore, returns to Mosley's (2001) initial problematic interpretation of Belgian nationalism. In the case of Belgian hip-hop, linguistic difference has left at least half of the nation 'marginalised' and 'silenced', with its articulation in French, as opposed to Dutch (Mertens et al. 2013).

As Brooks and Conroy posit, 'whereas hip-hop may continue to be associated with minority cultural expression, it exists now in global context and allows for the possibility of new kinds of cross national identity' (2011: 8). The Belgian hip-hop culture is nothing new, with Quittelier positing that 'it has existed in Brussels for more than 30 years' (Quittelier 2015). Its cultural development has existed in relation to its predecessors and contemporary articulations in the USA and its discernible presence in France in the 1980s and 1990s (Ibid.). As Mertens et al. assert, Belgian hip-hop, of a Congolese-Belgian inflection, re-affirms that '[s]ince national identities – the Belgian as well as the Congolese – are closed to these immigrants, hip-hop artists identify with the city and the districts that they live in' (Mertens et al. 2013: 96). The use of hip-hop enters into a pattern of shorthand references to urban life and youth subcultures that connect the local and the global whilst transgressing the national.

The allusions to hip-hop culture also resonate with films like *La Haine* (Mathieu Kassovitz 1995) in France and the representation of an 'international ghetto youth culture', inspired by 'American ghettos as the future world order: a growing underclass of *exclus*, in which "old-fashioned" divisions of class and race are irrelevant' (Vincendeau 2000: 324). Ezra and Rowden summarise *La Haine* as a film in which 'young second-generation immigrants from North Africa, West Africa, and Eastern Europe reject the traditional values of their families in order to embrace a "French" youth culture inspired by the global fashion for violent Hollywood films and rap music' (2006: 8). There is also a certain aestheticism and a 'polished look' to the film that both Higbee (2006: 70) and Vincendeau (2000: 316–319) recognise in *La Haine*, which emerges through cinephilic and intertextual allusions. For Spence, *La Haine*'s citation system in film is concomitant with hip-hop culture more generally, which demonstrates its 'reverence for and homages to past masters' (2017: 104) and is, therefore, full of 'borrowed material' (Ibid.: 109). The hip-hop culture evoked in *La Haine* is not unique to Kassovitz's film, since McNeill (2017) critically analyses the musical allusions and pop culture references in the French film *Girlhood/ Bande de Filles* (Céline Sciamma

106   J. STEELE

2014). McNeill (2017) frames her approach to the film as both cohering with the conventional gaze of the camera and rap music's patriarchal, male and 'normative' ideological concerns at the same time as 'queering' the diaspora and its female characters in the lip-syncing sequences.

BLACK (ADIL EL ARBI AND BILALL FALLAH 2015): GANGS AND STEREOTYPES

The primary point of difference between Mourad Boucif, Nabil Ben Yadir and the two filmmakers Adil El Arbi and Bilall Fallah concerns notions of community identity. The latter filmmakers grew up in the Northern Belgian region of Flanders, in the cities of Diegem (on the outskirts of Brussels) and Antwerp/Anvers, producing their first short film *Broeders/Brothers* (Adil El Arbi and Bilall Fallah 2011) and feature film *Image* (Adil El Arbi and Bilall Fallah 2014) in Dutch.[4] As a result, the first feature film was only circulated in Flanders and one cinema in Brussels, leaving the film 'totally absent from cinemas in Wallonia' (Van Dievort 2014). Filmmakers Mourad Boucif and Nabil Ben Yadir, however, grew up in and around Brussels in francophone immigrant communities (certainly miscegenated in the case of Boucif), whereas El Arbi and Fallah are considered 'outsiders'.

As Adil El Arbi and Billal Fallah note, Belgium currently has an issue with 'ghettoising' immigrant communities onto the margins of the city (Rose 2016)—as evidenced by the film's setting in both Molenbeek and Matonge. Steffens notes that the district of Matonge in Ixelles pertains to a neighbourhood in the capital of the Democratic Republic of Congo, Kinshasa (2007: 6). From this premise, the naming of the district is created in relation to the immigrant population living in the area, which, as Steffens observes, can have potentially xenophobic undertones (Ibid.). The issue of racism emerges within denunciative analyses of the film in francophone Belgian and French film criticism. Moreover, in Belgium, the notion of Flemish nationalism and recognition of the ethnic sub-grouping remains an important political question.

In *Black*, the notions of difference operate on four levels, between francophone Belgian, Flemish, Moroccan-Belgian and Congolese-Belgian senses of identity. Baumann posits that the articulation of language and

---

[4] There is also a distinct lack of consistency in newspaper reports concerning the filmmakers' origins in Belgium, and their linguistic identity (e.g., see Denis 2015: 4, which does not follow the dominant narrative).

linguistic plurality in the film serves as the only instance of cultural and national nuance (Baumann 2016: 49). The use of language primarily highlights the notion of a Belgian identity riven by linguistic allegiances and communities that extend beyond the French-Flemish divide (Rose 2016). Moreover, Flemish adopts increased importance in terms of articulating majority and minority positions. The dominance of French in the film is predicated on 'realism', since 'Flemish Dutch is the language of the rich, not the street' (El Arbi in Mastorou 2015). The film's linguistic shift is particularly salient since the books—on which the film is based—were not translated into French (Bouras 2014). A certain hierarchy is also established between the representation of ethnically white Belgian characters and diasporic Belgian characters. The former roles are primarily lensed in the context of the police. After Marwan and his brother's (Nassim) first arrest, the two white, Flemish policemen adopt an aggressive stance against the two young men. In this case, the policeman provides information in Dutch, with Nassim pleading for the use of French. Power dynamics are established between the two men arrested on linguistic grounds, positing an inferiority predicated upon linguistic and group identity. In *Les barons* (Nabil Ben Yadir 2009), Orlando contends that similar interactions are primarily articulated on linguistic rather than ethnic grounds, whilst still foregrounding political issues between the two/ three Belgian regions of Brussels-Wallonia and Flanders (2014: 173–174).

The image of a multi-ethnic Belgium—in a post-colonial context—is uneven in terms of its focus on interracial relationships and its diasporic communities. For instance, the Moroccan-Belgian characters are viewed in a more sympathetic light, as troubled teenagers from a disenfranchised background, who fall into petty crime and gang culture to form a sense of belonging and group identity. The gang culture steps away from the nation, offering the characters of Marwan and Mavela an alternative form of collective identity. El Arbi, perhaps revising an earlier position offered in Rose (2016), posits that

> *Black* highlights the fact that for those young people, they feel they do not belong in Belgium. They will never be Belgians, they will never be accepted. On the other hand, they will never be Moroccans either, drop them in their country of origin and they won't belong. So they are in between two worlds, looking for an identity. A gang is something clear, in a gang you have an identity (1080 or Black Bronx), you are something instead of nothing. (El Arbi 2017)[5]

---

[5] This particular emailed response by El Arbi (2017) resonated with his own interpretation offered in an interview with Rose (2016). However, the tone of the response in 2017 was less focused on the role of Islamic fundamentalism and Isis in this context.

108   J. STEELE

As El Arbi evokes, the sense of identity and solidarity emerges on a microcosmic level, within the confines of the small neighbourhoods and districts. These subcultures articulate a competing form of collectivity that nuances and works against the dominant nationalisms and ideologies expressed in politics and in the media. Marwan, in particular, seeks change in terms of social mobility (working as a mechanic), despite his brother's assertions that it is not possible due to his ethnicity. Denis proposes that the members of 1080 are more inclined to 'escape their milieu, their social determinism' (2015: 4). These aspirations facilitate a reading of the film that pertains to 'social realism' as opposed to a genre-based approach to which *Black* most closely adheres.

The Moroccan-Belgian community is not foregrounded to the same extent as the Congolese diaspora, despite the filmmakers' Moroccan-Belgian identity and heritage. There is a greater narrative focus and screen time afforded to Mavela and her gang, the Black Bronx. Differing from *Kamel*—in which women are distinctly absent (Royen 1997: 33)—*Black* focuses on the breakdown of a relationship between a mother and daughter and the hardships experienced by young women in Belgium's *banlieues*. The depiction of violence is heightened in the gang of the Congolese diaspora, particularly in terms of the representation of sexual violence against women, as this chapter explores in the following section. Demart and Robert are critical of *Black*'s racial stereotypes, which continue 'a postcolonial racism and threaten an already fragile social bond [between Belgium's different ethnic groups]' (2015: 50). Despite the lack of ethnic reference, the concluding image from the film provides evidence for this analysis, noting that 'Since 2002, 23 people have been killed in youth gang fights in Brussels.' The elision of poverty and delinquency with the ethnic groups in the film demonstrates that 'dystopian imaginaries of the city are often also deeply racialised' (Fadil 2014: 316). In particular, the film's articulation of ethnic difference through representations of space harks 'back to the colonial endeavor, which was organised around the necessity of spatially marking the differences between the self and the Other' (Ibid.). As a result, *Black* marks a return to the exploration of institutional racism and systemic discrimination articulated in the French *banlieue* films of the 1990s, contrasting radically with *Les barons*—also set in Molenbeek—which intended to show a positive depiction of the Moroccan-Belgian second-generation (Orlando 2014) or, in Ben Yadir's words, 'another image of Molenbeek' (Mouton 2013: 14).

BLACK AND SPATIAL DYNAMICS IN THE BRUSSELS BANLIEUE

In terms of a transnational cinephilic approach, *Black* has been compared to the French *banlieue* film *La Haine* in film criticism (Les Inrocks 2016; Robertson 2016; Rose 2016). In the Belgian version of the glossy, popular culture magazine *Elle*, the filmmakers even claim that they considered Dirk Bracke novels *Black* and *Back* as 'notre *La Haine*' (Fralon 2015) as well as citing Kassovitz's film as a key source of inspiration (Delpâture 2015).

Black is essentially structured through three musical set pieces, which provide the film with its impetus and drive forward. Thanouli's 'post-classical model' becomes instructive, nuancing a surface MTV-style or 'postmodern pyrotechnics' analysis (2006: 194). For Thanouli, 'the post-classical paradigm tries to capture the real in more contemporary terms by establishing a hypermediated realism that favours the expressive mode of hypermediacy (Bolter and Grusin 1999) and the use of intermedia, layering and intensified continuity' (Thanouli 2006: 186). Each sequence, or movement, condenses the action to fit the parameters of a tightly bound YouTube-style video, which - to adopt Thanouli's terms – 'manipulat[es] the spatial and temporal qualities of the image' (Ibid.). The first movement coincides with CNN119's *Du plomb dans les ailes*, which foregrounds Mavela and Marwan's first meeting as they both commit petty crimes in the City 2 shopping mall. The sequence elides the two *banlieues* with petty crime, with the non-diegetic track intensifying with its beats at the moment in which Mavela grabs the bottles of alcohol. The tight, proximate framing of the thefts alongside the non-diegetic tracks distances the individuals from their actions, articulating that they are paradigmatic examples of a wider social concern.

The second 'movement' pertains to Romano Daking's *Problèmes*, which operates as the Black Bronx gang's music of initiation and ritual. The diegetic music and hip-hop song, played through the gang's boombox, becomes symbiotic with the gang's rape of young women. The titular sequence includes the music alongside the screams of an unknown female, depicting the rape of first Loubna, as a symbolic act of gang violence against both women and the Moroccan-Belgian 1080 gang, and second Mavela, the young member of the Black Bronx. The differences in the two sexual violence sequences (Loubna and Mavela) is discernible, since the gang's rape of Mavela is articulated graphically. The continuity of the editing style further highlights the sheer violence of the scene, with Mavela's washing the blood away in a shower.

Within the influences of these hip-hop aesthetics, an expression of post-colonial trauma rises to the surface in its most raw form. The title of Mambu's (2015) article 'Why Mavela and not Loubna' attests to why the difference is drawn by the filmmakers to not show the rape of Loubna but to graphically depict Mavela in the same circumstance. For Mambu, the ethnically Congolese-Belgian women are conceived as 'victim-objects' in which 'the black female body has always attracted looks, even when put in a position of repulsion...it [the colonial subject] did not lack in its description of its contents in its photographs and writings, thus contributing to an erotic imagination that appeals to Western fantasies' (Mambu 2015). Demart and Robert adopt the same position, articulating that 'the collective rape of the young Arab girl [Loubna] is translated with a certain modesty...the camera erotises the rape of the young, Black girl' (2015: 50), primarily through fetishizing close-ups and tight, proximate framing. At this point, the camera adopts a voyeuristic position (Mambu 2015), objectifying Mavela. It adopts an imperialistic and colonialist view of her body, which is forcibly rendered passive and punished for her agency. In Orlando's analysis of *Les barons*, the scholar contends that 'the interstices of the hyphen' as a strand of 'schizophrenic identities' are caught between two poles (2014: 177). In this instance, Mavela's enforced subjugation articulates the male gang members' 'schizophrenic' mindset of the colonialist position on indigenous populations (in this case Belgium's extremely violent colonial rule of the Congo), re-acting and projecting symbolic historical colonial abuses in the present in Belgium.

The remix of Amy Winehouse's *Back to Black*, as the third movement, epitomises this stylistic feature, and resonates with Kassovitz's use of *Nique la Police/ Non, je ne regrette rien* by DJ Cut Killer in *La Haine*. Whereas Cut Killer's remix is articulated in French, re-appropriating NWA's original, this version of *Back to Black* retains the use of English despite the re-writing of the song by Flemish singers Oscar and the Wolf and Tsar B. Oscar and the Wolf's cover is syncretic, complementing the film through its infusion of jazz, with its African-American origins, the use of English lyrics, and Tsar B's vocals reflect the artist's 'feeding on world music' (Aïnouz 2016). The song evokes hip-hop's allusions to 'past masters' as well as pastiching popular culture. In the context of postmodernity, Jameson (1991) foregrounds the presence of the pastiche as part of a wider system of frequent allusions, borrowings, and recyclings. As the singer further posits, 'When I sing, I do not use the entire Western range, but instead [I use] the Arab system, which has a lot more notes' (Aïnouz

2016). These descriptions of the film's selected music dialogically echo Berghahn's assertion that 'soundtracks of diasporic youth films…consist of Western and World music, underscoring the cultural hybridity of the protagonists' (2010: 249). The non-diegetic music, in this case, is concomitant with the action, the spaces and the identities of the individuals included on screen. The hybridity of the sound mix evokes the cultural hybridity expressed through the characters' lack of national belonging. This is particularly the case of the inclusion of Marwan driving alone alongside the canal that acts as a symbolic border between the centre of Brussels and the Molenbeek periphery (Fig. 6.1). The discernible pause between the end of the non-diegetic *Back-to-Black* and the long shot of the canal echoes the end of a music video, which similarly appears during the 'Girlhood' theme in the contemporaneous French film *Girlhood* (McNeill 2017: 5).

The 'Back-to-Black' sequence marks a rapid descent for Mavela, following her rape, into a world saturated by drugs, physical, psychological and sexual violence, and crime. However, whilst the sequence focuses on Mavela and her decline, the pastiche of Amy Winehouse's song re-joins the phallocentric and patriarchal concern of hip-hop. The opening line of the song evidences this, stating 'He left no time to regret, kept his dick wet'. The camera's gaze on Mavela—in the two musical set-pieces of *Problèmes* and 'Back to Black' is inherently male and pre-occupied with re-asserting a dominant patriarchal positioning, which is echoed by the provocative lyrics of Romano Daking (and his local version of US gangsta

Fig. 6.1 The brief pause on the canal after the 'Back to Black' sequence, a border between Molenbeek and Brussels' centre

rap) as well as Oscar and the Wolf's pastiched 'Back to Black'. Daking's *Problèmes* is invested with terminology that pertains to the circulation of capital—which is posited through criminal activities—with a male-driven gang mentality. McNeill posits that in the case of *Bande de filles* the camera's gaze and the lyrics of the 'Wop' music sequence re-affirm 'rap's objectification of women' (2017: 9), which suggests that the sequences are primarily male-orientated and (hetero-)normative in terms of their mass appeal and ideological positioning (McNeill 2017: 13).

As with the lead protagonist Kamel in *Kamel*, the snorting of cocaine functions as the initiating factor that instigates his/her decline. Drug-taking and delinquency represent thematic signifiers for disenfranchisement and a spatial vortex that originates in the city's peripheries. *Black* and *La Haine* feature striking parallels in terms of how the sequences commence. In *La Haine*, Hubert, representing a generalised sub-Saharan African diaspora in France, cuts and prepares marijuana before rolling and smoking a joint in his bedroom. This recalls the opening to the sequence in *Black* in which a line of cocaine is cut and then snorted by Mavela. The representation of the Moroccan diaspora is reduced at this point, with Marwan operating as a counter-point and symbolic of multiracial Belgium and Brussels. The shots of Marwan fleetingly capture his journey around the city as he searches for Mavela, articulating his intention to eschew gang violence and petty crime as an alternative economy. His hope and search are counter-balanced by exaggerated moments of violence between Mavela, her gang and an Arabic shopkeeper and Mavela's unprovoked attacks on passers-by.

In a francophone Belgian context, cinematic reference points, similar to those of *La Haine*, highlight the differences within a variegated diasporic filmmaking environment. For instance, Boucif and Barman in *Kamel* and *Au delà de Gibraltar* create a transnational stylistic dialogue with Ken Loach (Goodfellow 2002: 26), whereas in the case of *Black*, the two filmmakers draw on similar reference points, showing a greater affinity with post-classical Hollywood filmmaking, the 'hood' film, and independent American filmmaking from the 1980s and the 1990s. El Arbi notes that when they were growing up and honing their filmmaking craft, the filmmakers were not interested in the films of the Dardenne brothers (fellow Belgian filmmakers), but were instead preoccupied with the work of Spike Lee, Martin Scorsese, Steven Spielberg, Michael Mann and Quentin Tarantino (Bouras 2015). Berghahn proposes that the notion of 'the "hood" is not directly transferable to the French banlieue...the ghettocentric and its use of hip-hop and rap music has had a discernible influence' (2010: 237). As a result, *Black* operates within the interstices of 'generic templates' and 'aesthetic strategies' (Berghahn and Sternberg 2010) emerging from the USA and the *banlieue* film in France. Stylistic filiation is composed of a 'genre style of filmmaking: accelerations and explosive action scenes, dramatic slow motion, passionate lovemaking scenes without artifice, and the energetic casting of non-professionals' (Mambu 2015). This style of filmmaking is concomitant with the 'action genre' (Bouras 2015). By drawing heavily on the semantic and syntactic, to adopt Altman's (1984) terms from genre theory, of the gangster genre, Baumann contends that *Black* references a series of clichés from the genre, leading to the conclusion that it is a '*mauvais polar*' [a bad thriller] in a denunciative analysis (2015: 49). The lack of a coherent genre appellation applied to the film attests to its generic fluidity.

Spatial dynamics engender a further nuanced understanding and interpretation of social marginalisation and social polarisation, which operate as two key thematic concerns. The representation of Molenbeek in *Black* is limited to the brief shots of the Belgian youths of Moroccan descent gathered in public spaces and the brief scene in which the group throw Molotov cocktails at a police car in Molenbeek. In the case of the Moroccan diaspora, the first generation is overlooked in the narrative, with the youths making no reference to their parents, their cultural heritage or the 'homeland'. As a result, the film adheres more closely to theories of diasporic cinema than to migrant cinema. The Molenbeek apartments—in which Marwan and his elder brother Nassim reside—are not included, eschewing an analysis of a mise en scène that may evoke Naficy's (2001) typologies of claustrophobia and loneliness. The binary opposition, underpinning a structuralist approach to genre criticism, between the 'claustrophobic home vs. the "cool places" where youths hang out' (Berghahn 2010: 250) is discernibly absent, focusing instead solely on the latter notion, the streets and 'non-places'. This also coheres with Vincendeau's (2000: 313) interpretation of *La Haine*'s mise en scène and on-location shooting, which is 'decontextualised' and, therefore, 'lacks sociological depth'. *Black*'s mise en scène, therefore, contrasts with Boucif and Barman's *Kamel*, which offers an authentic 'gaze' into the dated and cramped Molenbeek apartments and stairwells, which recalls Dridi's construction of apartments

Fig. 6.2 Marwan escapes from the historic centre with the stolen handbag beneath the Palais de Justice

laden with tactile objects, creating a nostalgic connection to the 'homeland', in *Le Panier*, the multicultural district of Marseilles in *Bye-Bye*.[6]

For instance, *Black*'s opening sequence sketches out the film's spatial dynamics, outlining and ossifying a centre-periphery model that maps onto the city's geography. The sequence incorporates the three primary spaces, articulating a balance between the perceived centre and the *banlieues* of Molenbeek and Matonge on the city's margins. The characters' entry into the centre is, however, an alienating experience, leading to their arrests, since they operate as spaces of petty crime. Moreover, Marwan's theft of an ethnically white, Belgian lady's handbag from her car emphasises the perverse side of one of Brussels' most well-known cinematic backdrops from the elevated point of the Palais de Justice. The phone booth sequence in the Brussels-based comedy *Dikkenek* (Olivier Van Hoofstadt 2006) is the most obvious and memorable example. The hierarchal construction of space comes to the fore, with Marwan travelling in a (physically) downward direction from the 'centre' to the margins of Molenbeek. The evocation of power dynamics, of an insider/outsider dynamic is exposed spatially. The street elevator at Palais de Justice, therefore, operates as a physical and symbolic border, since it is the point at which the Flemish passer-by stops his pursuit of Marwan (Fig. 6.2). Drawing on the documentary *Molenbeek*,

[6] Higbee (2001: 56) offers a nuanced and considered close reading of the mise-en-scène of the 'miscegenated' and 'multi-ethnic' Le Panier district in Marseilles. Tarr (2005: 85) cites Higbee's analysis of space in the endnotes to her approach to *Bye-Bye* as a banlieue film, and further considers the 'claustrophobic spaces' of the apartments in the district (Tarr 2005: 81).

génération radicale?, it posits that tourists remain in the city's historic centre, visiting landmarks such as the Palais de Justice, the Grand Place and the Bourse [Stock Exchange], but never venture into the suburbs. This is equally implied by Marwan's comment to the police, on patrol in Molenbeek, that 'foreigners' were involved in the theft, attesting to Molenbeek's population as perennial suspects. The term, in particular, makes a knowing reference to Brussels' transnational composition, which falls between the two categories outlined by Hannerz of an 'managerial and entrepreneurial class' and 'Third World populations' viewed primarily as 'labour migrants' (1996: 128–132). The 'centre' remains the hub for the cosmopolitan elite—tourists, businessmen, Eurocrats—whereas the excluded diasporic communities are restricted to the urban peripheries.

Whereas the opening theft sequence coheres with intensified continuity editing (Bordwell 2002)—a form of editing in line with post-classical Hollywood action films—the introduction to Molenbeek adopts a style and tone that evokes post-war European art cinema. In Molenbeek, El Arbi and Fallah opt for a long take with fluid and nervous camera movement, occurring for 85 seconds. Although El Arbi and Fallah ludically articulate their eschewal of European auteurs at film school, the use of the camera in *Black*'s set-up creates this reference point. As Marwan returns to the suburb from the centre by car, the camera continues with the horizontal direction initiated by the movement of the car. Shohat and Stam contend that '(t)he diverse directionality of the scripts of different languages – that fact that Hebrew and Arabic are read "horizontally" from right to left...can inflect camera movements over script' (1985: 36). During the spectator's first introduction to Molenbeek, the horizontal movement from right-to-left as the camera enters the district populated largely by Moroccan-Belgian subjects is evocative of and 'inflects' the direction of Arabic writing. Although the enunciating subjects speak only in French, the movement of the camera frames the public space of Molenbeek through a direction that interacts with the characters' cultural hybridity, that is, Moroccan-Belgian. The presence of written Arabic also emerges in the promotional material for Mourad Boucif and Taylan Barman's *Au delà de Gibraltar*, which includes the language between the framing of the Moroccan-Belgian Karim and the native Belgian Sophie. To this end, the use of written language functions as a form of (cultural) difference, forming a symbolic boundary. The camera movement—which glides at a fast-pace—also evokes the excitement and adrenaline rush that the youth are experiencing as delinquents, introduced to the spectator *in*

116   J. STEELE

medias res. The first image draws attention to a rock, clasped in Marwan's hand, and the three Adidas stripes down the side of his tracksuit bottoms. Immediately, the dialogue with *La Haine* is instigated through the inclusion of 'hip-hop iconography' in the form of branded fashion (Higbee 2006: 77).

The introduction to Molenbeek coheres with what Higbee (2001: 55) describes as a 'discursive chain', in which the suburb is collapsed alongside the theme of delinquency. The set-up, therefore, demonstrates a tight unity of action, which encourages such a reading, and contrasts with the developed and nuanced set-ups of the social realist *Kamel*, which hints at, but does not reveal, substance abuse until half-way through the film. It is, from this point, that the film has received denunciative responses, since it does little to de-bunk Molenbeek's associations with crime and delinquency. The shift in location in *Black* from one margin in Molenbeek to Matonge is articulated through a sound bridge, shifting from the strings of North-African beats evoked non-diegetically, to the Anglo-American style rap music, originating diegetically from a boombox, of the Black Bronx gang on a basketball court. Through the dialectical composition of editing, the two spaces are differentiated along ethnic lines, resonating with Berghahn's 'ghettocentric imagination' (2010: 237). Molenbeek becomes shorthand for the Moroccan-Belgian community, and Matonge for the Congolese diaspora. The 'internal diversity' of each of the suburbs is overlooked according to this premise. The choice of hip-hop music is, thus, concomitant with the surrounding location and its enunciating subjects. The articulated mise en scène pays lip-service to films such as *Boyz n' the Hood* (John Singleton 1991) and *Do the right thing* (Spike Lee 1989), since the representation of the two suburbs is reminiscent of the, as Higbee argues in the case of *La Haine*, 'racially segregated ghettos of urban America' (Higbee 2006: 83). For El Arbi, these brief allusions articulate a sense of 'not belonging' that 'connects the struggling neighbourhoods of France, Belgium, The Netherlands and the USA' (El Arbi 2017). Similar to hip-hop's previously discussed homages and allusions, *Black*'s references to the aforementioned US films through the inclusion of American-style basketball courts in Matonge in the opening sequence operate as a simple quotation and shorthand for black, urban life that is marginalised from the dominant forms of society and nation (as represented by the police). As a result, the form of quotation serves to articulate a new sense of belonging and collective formed primarily at the local level, particularly for excluded groups, that reaches out to global discourses for purposes of allegiance.

Black's 'Non-places' and 'Centre-periphery Models'

Black is generally preoccupied with the city's 'non-places', which contrasts with discursive debates around the film invested in the depiction of Molenbeek. For Feuillère (2015), the Brussels metro operates as a 'neutral space' for the two gangs. They are not invested with the aforementioned ghettoising principles, as represented by the Molenbeek and Matonge districts. The notion of a perceived 'neutral space' can be interpreted as misleading, since it connotes a space where tolerance between the different ethnic groups is possible. The church clearly offers this possibility for Marwan and Mavela, operating as an in-between and clandestine meeting space where they can express their love for one another. Instead, the 'non-places' are locations where the city's 'internal diversity', to adopt Hannerz's terms, is represented, but, as Orlando foregrounds, it is a space where 'cross-cultural exchange' between ethnically white and immigrant communities does not take place (2014: 173). Hardt and Negri (2001) similarly consider these spaces. In this case, the 'urban landscape is shifting from the modern focus on the common square and the public encounter and the public encounter to the closed spaces of malls, freeways, and gated communities' (Hardt and Negri 2001: 188). The malls prevent the socialisation of the subjects, resulting in themes of alienation and isolation. As a result, Ezra and Rowden outline the significance of interstitial locations and Augé's 'non-places', such as airports, highways, malls and hotels, that 'problematise national or cultural identity' (2006: 8). In *Black*, the Brussels metro, Bruxelles-Nord/Brussels North train station, and the City 2 Brussels shopping mall represent these prominent 'non-places'.

By drawing on familiar and easily recognisable spaces (in an international context), these 'non-places' also pertain to the film's universalising aspect. Whilst these places and locations are identified for the purposes of this chapter, they do not function as regional or local anchoring devices for the action. In so doing, they could be easily substituted in different national contexts. The use of the City 2 shopping mall as the backdrop for the concurrent thefts, by Marwan, Nassim and Mavela, becomes readable only to locals and spectators who understand the location outside the confines of the film. Although both representatives of the two diasporic communities are within the shopping mall concurrently—collapsing space and time through the use of parallel editing—they do not 'interact' or potentially 'socialise' (drawing terms from Hardt and Negri 2001:

188) with the dominant, white ethnic Belgian community prevented through representations of control, such as the police. The enunciating subjects are drawn to these public spaces to obtain forms of capital, since these spaces 'are increasingly becoming privatised' (Hardt and Negri 2001: 188), yet the subjects are held at a distance from a sense of community through limited group interactions and their own limited means (i.e. capital through theft).

The 'City 2' shopping mall sequence also positions the enunciating subjects within a local-global context, based in a shopping mall in Brussels but able to purchase/steal circulated goods—pertaining to capital—from across the globe. The objects obtained by Marwan and his brother Nassim pertain to an Americanising and universalising tendency, purchasing caps emblazoned with NYC, Pittsburgh Steelers and Chicago Bears (two NFL teams) and Batman logos, and Nike trainers. The sequences that unroll on the Brussels metro further evidence this dialogue with the USA. Names and locations of the Brussels stations, such as Heysel, are glimpsed in the background, but the violence occurring in a predominantly plain and nondescript subterranean setting evokes the New York subway system.

As *Black*'s final sequence suggests, the stations constitute the locations within which violence erupts and unfolds between the two diasporic groups, in this case the Brussels-North train station. The film's dénouement—which deviates from the two original source texts (Bouras 2015)—collapses into the context of Hollywood-style filmmaking, culminating in a 'Mexican stand-off', between the character 'X' and Marwan of the two rival gangs. This also coheres with Kassovitz's ending of *La Haine*, borrowing from 'the international noir territory of Scorsese, Tarantino, Woo et al.' (Vincendeau 2000: 323). Manche posits that the final sequence is quintessentially '*à la* Scorsese' (2015: 4–5). The use of slow motion at the moment of X's gunshot at the much younger, innocent-looking and weaponless Marwan echoes Hong Kong director John Woo's extended 'stand-offs' in Hollywood cinema of the late-1990s, particularly *Face/Off* (John Woo 1997). The final shot perfectly captures the sentiments of Belgium's minorities, and their sense of belonging and 'integration'. The aerial shot encompassing the arrests of representatives of the two diasporic groups as well as the Romeo-and-Juliette-style suicidal deaths of the two lead characters emphasises a distinct lack of hope and the need for change in contemporary Brussels. The filmmakers perfectly capture the plight of the two major ethnic groups in Belgium, on a microcosmic level in Brussels and its suburbs, and the failings of a desire for 'internal diversity'. The collective punishment—by death or by arrest—is evocative of the two diasporic communities' place in the Belgian nation. It represents a failure of 'integration', re-affirming the antiquated ghettoising policies of the 1960s.

CONCLUSION

Black's dénouement provides an instructive way of concluding this chapter, since it epitomises Hayward's previously explored notion of the 'pluricultural' (2000: 94) in terms of broaching nationalisms in Western Europe. It represents the futile hope of a multicultural understanding of Belgian nationalism, as it reinforces the separation between excluded groups. Working through approaches to cinema and nationalism, Hayward (2000) and Elsaesser (2005) offer the potential for competing allegiances and collective identities to be formed by excluded groups. It is from this premise that *Black*, its musical set-pieces and representations of 'non-places', transcends regionalism and nationalism in a contemporary Belgian context. The *'Du plomb dans les ailes'*, *'Problèmes'* and *'Back to Black'* sequences stand apart and articulate the enunicating subjects' exclusion from dominant modes of society and Belgian culture as well as operating within a re-articulation of group belonging that is formed within a distinctly local context. Focusing on these sequences, *Black*'s representation of the Moroccan-Belgian and Congolese-Belgian communities coheres with the 'silenced voices, hidden and forbidden histories, and emerging identities' that constitute 'cinemas at the periphery' (Iordanova et al. 2010: 13). These collective identities 'emerge' through 'intertextual appropriation' (Iordanova et al. 2010: 13), resonating with the hip-hop iconography and aesthetics of international traditions of filmmaking in the French *banlieues* and US ghettos. The interaction between the local and the global, in terms of music, aesthetics and iconography, form the basis of emerging collective identities that offer an alternative for diasporic communities in a Western European context.

BIBLIOGRAPHY

Agence France-Presse. 2016. Brussels gang film pulled from French cinemas. *The Guardian*. https://www.theguardian.com/world/2016/feb/19/brussels-gang-film-black-pulled-french-cinemas-paris-attacks. Accessed 25 March 2016.

Aïnouz, Abigail. 2016. Les Inrocks – Tsar B, nouvelle reine du r'n'b belge'. *Les Inrockuptibles*. http://www.lesinrocks.com/2016/10/28/musique/tsar-b-nouvelle-reine-du-rnb-belge-11875817/. Accessed 10 August 2017.

120   J. STEELE

Altman, Rick. 1984. A semantic/syntactic approach to film genre. In *Film theory & criticism*. Ed. L. Braudy and M. Cohen. Oxford: Oxford University Press.

Anderson, Benedict. 1991. *Imagined Communities: reflections on the origins and the spread of nationalism*. London and New York: Verso.

Androutsopoulos, Jannis and Arno Scholz. 2003. Spaghetti Funk appropriations of hip hop culture and rap music in Europe, *Popular Music and Society*, 26 (4): 463–479.

Baumann, Fabien. 2016. Black [Review]. *Positif*, 661, March 2016: 48–49.

Belga. 2016. Jambon: "57 individus menaçant l'Etat identifés à Molenbeek". *La Libre Belgique*. http://www.lalibre.be/actu/belgique/jambon-57-individus-menacant-l-etat-identifies-a-molenbeek-57ece055cd70e9985fe7273d. Accessed 13 August 2017.

Berghahn, Daniela. 2010. Coming of age in "the Hood": the diasporic youth film and questions of genre. In *European cinema in motion: migrant and diasporic film in contemporary Europe*. Ed. Berghahn, Daniela and Claudia Sternberg. Basingstoke: Palgrave Macmillan.

Berghahn, Daniela and Claudia Sternberg. 2010. Locating migrant and diasporic cinema in contemporary Europe. In *European cinema in motion: migrant and diasporic film in contemporary Europe*. Ed. Berghahn, Daniela and Claudia Sternberg. Basingstoke: Palgrave Macmillan.

Bolter, Jay David and Grusin, Richard. 1999. *Remediation: Understanding new media*. Cambridge, MA: MIT Press.

Bordwell, David. 2002. Intensified continuity: visual style in contemporary American cinema. *Film Quarterly*, 55 (3), Spring: 16–28.

Bosséno, Christian. 1992. The case of beur film. In *Popular European cinema*. Ed. Dyer, Richard, and Ginette Vincendeau. London: Routledge.

Bouras, Dmitra. 2014. Quand les enfants de l'immigration s'invitent derrière la camera. *La Libre Belgique*. 10 September 2014.

Bouras, Dmitra. 2015. Tournage de "Black" de Bilall Fallah & Adil El Arbi', *Cinergie.be*, http://www.cinergie.be/webzine/tournage_black_bilall_fallah_adil_el_arbi. Accessed 5 July 2017.

Brooks, Siobhan and Conroy, Thomas. 2011. Hip-hop culture in a global context: interdisciplinary and cross-categorical investigation. *American Behavioral Scientist*, 55 (1): 3–8.

Cerulus, Laurens. 2015. Belgium's Mr. Right. *Politico.eu*, http://www.politico.eu/article/belgium-bart-de-wever-government-flemish-nationalism-n-va-migration-terrorism/. Accessed 13 August 2017.

Cohen, Roger. 2016. The Islamic State of Molenbeek. *The New York Times*. https://www.nytimes.com/2016/04/12/opinion/the-islamic-state-of-molenbeek.html. Accessed 11 November 2017.

Delpâture, Gorian. 2015. L'interview de Bilall Fallah, et d'Adil El Arbi, les réalisateurs de Black'. *RTBF*. https://www.rtbf.be/culture/cinema/detail_l-

interview-de-bilall-fallah-et-d-adil-el-arbi-les-realisateurs-de-black?id=
9132362. Accessed 10 July 2017.

Denis, F. 2015. Black & Beur. *La Libre Belgique*, 10 November 2015: 4–5.

Demart, S. and Robert, M-T. 2015. Le film "Black": un cocktail de racisme post-colonial! *La Libre Belgique*. 24 November 2015: 50.

El Arbi, Adil. 2017. *Interview with Dr. Jamie Steele (email)*. 5 September 2017.

Elsaesser, Thomas. 2005. *European cinema: face to face with Hollywood*: Amsterdam University Press.

Express, L'. 2017. La menace djihadiste en Belgique. *L'Express*. https://www.lexpress.fr/actualite/monde/europe/operation-antiterroriste-en-belgique_1641263.html. Accessed 11 November 2017.

Ezra, Elizabeth and Terry Rowden. 2006. What is transnational cinema?. In *Transnational cinema: the film reader*. Ed. Ezra, Elizabeth and Terry Rowden. London: Routledge.

Fadil, Nadia. 2014. Brussels as a landscape of fear: containing "Otherness". In *Islamic movements of Europe*. Ed. Peter, Frank and Rafael Ortega. London: I.B. Tauris.

Feuillère, Anne. 2015. Black de Bilall Fallah and Adil El Arbi'. *Cinergie.be*. http://www.cinergie.be/webzine/black_de_billal_fallah_et_adil_el_arbi. Accessed 5 July 2017.

Fralon, Elsa. 2015. Black: Adil El Arbi et Bilall Fallah se confient sur le film. *Elle*. http://www.elle.be/fr/102669-black-adil-el-arbi-et-bilall-fallah-se-confient-sur-le-film.html. Accessed 10 July 2017.

Gellner, Ernest. 1983. *Nations and nationalism*. Malden and Oxford: Blackwell.

Gausserand, Hugo-Pierre. 2016. Black, film belge sur les banlieues, ne sortira pas en France. *Le Figaro*. http://www.lefigaro.fr/cinema/2016/02/18/03002-20160218ARTFIG00091--black-film-belge-sur-les-banlieues-ne-sortira-pas-en-france.php. Accessed 15 July 2017.

Gendron, Gillaume. 2015. A Molenbeek, les fantômes du jihad. *La Libération*. http://www.liberation.fr/france/2015/11/17/a-molenbeek-les-fantomes-du-jihad_1414230. Accessed 11 November 2017.

Goodfellow, M. 2002. Beyond the rock. *The Bulletin*, March 14 2002: 26.

Gott, Michael and Thibault Schilt. Forthcoming. *Cinéma-monde: de-centred perspectives on Global Filmmaking in French*. Edinburgh: Edinburgh University Press.

Hannerz, Ulf. 1996. *Transnational connections*, London and New York: Routledge.

Hardt, Michael and Antonio Negri. 2001. *Empire* Cambridge and London: Harvard University Press.

Hayward, Susan. 2000. Framing national cinemas. In *Cinema and nation*. Ed. Hjort, Mette and Mackenzie, Scott. London: Routledge.

122   J. STEELE

Higbee, Will. 2001. Hybridity, space and the right to belong: Maghrebi-French identity at the crossroads in Karim Dridi's *Bye-Bye*. In *France on Film: reflections on popular culture*. Ed. Mazdon, Lucy. London: Wallflower Press.

Higbee, Will. 2006. *Mathieu Kassovitz*. Manchester: Manchester University Press.

Higbee, Will. 2007. Beyond the (trans)national: towards a cinema of transvergence in postcolonial and diasporic francophone cinema(s). *Studies in French Cinema*, 7:2: 79–91.

Higbee, Will and Song Hwee Lim. 2010. Concepts of transnational cinema: towards a critical transnationalism in film studies. *Transnational Cinemas*, 1 (1): 7–21.

Inrocks, Les. 2016. Les Inrocks – Black: "La Haine" dans la banlieue de Bruxelles. *Les Inrockuptibles*. http://www.lesinrocks.com/2016/06/24/cinema/black-haine-banlieue-de-bruxelles-11849306/. Accessed 10 July 2017.

Iordanova, Dina, David Martin-Jones and Belen Vidal. 2010. Introduction: a peripheral view of world cinema. In *Cinema at the periphery*. Ed. Iordanova, Dina, David Martin-Jones and Belen Vidal. Detroit: Wayne State University Press, 1–19.

Jameson, Fredric. 1991. *Postmodernism, or the cultural logic of late Capitalism*. Durham: Duke University Press.

Mambu, Djia. 2015. Black: Pourquoi Mavela et pas Loubna? *Africultures*. http://africultures.com/black-pourquoi-mavela-et-pas-loubna-13266/. Accessed 5 July 2017.

Manche, Phillipe. 2015. Black, un Roméo et Juilette dans le Bruxelles des bandes urbaines. *Le Soir*, 10 November 2015: 4–5.

Mastorou, Elli. 2015. Notre référence pour ce film? La cité de Dieu. *Metro*. 10 November 2015.

McNeill, Isabelle. 2017. 'Shine Bright like a Diamond': music, performance and digitextuality in Céline Sciamma's Bande de Filles (2014). *Studies in French Cinema*.

Mertens, Jamina, Wouter Goedertier, Idesbald Goddeeris and Dominique De Brabantier. 2013. A new floor for the silenced?: congolese hip-hop in Belgium. *Social Transformations*, 1(1): 87–113.

Mosley, Philip. 2001. *Split screen: Belgian cinema and cultural identity*. Albany: State University of New York Press.

Mosley, Philip. 2002. Anxiety, memory, and place in Belgian cinema. *Yale French Studies*, 102: 160–175.

Mouton, Olivier. 2013. En Belgique aussi, il est temps de marcher contre le racism. *Le Vif/ L'Express*, 48. 29 November 2013: 11–14.

Naficy, Hamid. 2001. *An accented cinema: exilic and diasporic filmmaking*. Princeton: Princeton University Press.

Orlando, Valérie K. 2014. Being-in-the-world in the global age: marginal spaces as alternative places in the Belgian-Moroccan transnational cityscape of *Les Barons*. *African Studies Review*, 57 (2): 163–181.

DIASPORIC BELGIAN CINEMA: TRANSNATIONAL AND TRANSCULTURAL... **123**

Paulet, Alicia. 2016. 4Black: tourner à Molenbeek, le film jugé trop noir pour les salles. *Le Figaro.* http://www.lefigaro.fr/cinema/2016/06/23/03002-20160623ARTFIG00167-black-tourne-a-molenbeek-le-film-juge-trop-noir-pour-les-salles.php. Accessed 15 July 2017.

Quittelier, Benoit. 2015. Hip-hop in Brussels: has breakdance left the ghetto? *Brussels Studies,* 84. http://brussels.revues.org/1273. Accessed 11 November 2017.

Robertson, Erin. 2016. Moroccan-Belgian Duo's breakout Indie film black exposing Belgium's cultural divide is now streaming. *OkayAfrica.com.* http://www.okayafrica.com/in-brief/morrocan-belgian-duo-indie-film-black-now-streaming/. Accessed 10 August 2017.

Rose, Steve. 2016. From Molenbeek to Hollywood – why Belgian thriller Black is the new La haine. *The Guardian.* https://www.theguardian.com/film/2016/aug/11/from-molenbeek-to-hollywood-why-belgian-thriller-black-is-the-new-la-haine. Accessed 5 July 2017.

Royen, Marie-Cecile. 1997. Filmer contre la came. *Le Vif/ L'Express,* 12 December 1997: 32–33.

Saeys, A. 2009. Imag(in)ing the global city. Postnational filmmaking in Brussels and Amsterdam. Paper presented to *The 4th International Conference of the International Forum on Urbanism (IfoU).* Amsterdam/Delift, 2009. Accessed 16 August 2017.

Shohat, Ella and Robert Stam. 1985. The cinema after babel: language, difference and power. *Screen,* 26 (3-4): 35–58.

Simon, Evan. 2016. Molenbeek: An Immigrant Community Tries to Shake Its Jihadi Reputation. *ABC News,* March 19 2016. http://abcnews.go.com/International/molenbeek-immigrant-community-shake-jihadi-reputation/story?id=35555590. Accessed 11 November 2017.

Sonuma.be. 2017. L'Écran Témoin. *Sonuma.be.* http://www.sonuma.be/collection/ecran-temoin-l. Accessed 11 August 2017.

Spaas, Lieve. 2000. *The Francophone film: a struggle for identity.* Manchester: Manchester University Press.

Spence, Steve. 2017. Hip-hop aesthetics and La haine. *Liquid Blackness,* 4 (7).

Steffens, Sven. 2007. Urban popular place names past and present: the case of Molenbeek-Saint-Jean/ Saint-Jans-Molenbeek. Trans. Gabrielle Leyden. *Brussels Studies,* 9. http://brussels.revues.org/453. Accessed 5 July 2017.

Tarr, Carrie. 2005. *Reframing difference: Beur and Banlieue filmmaking in France.* Manchester: Manchester University Press.

Thanouli, Eleftheria. 2006. Post-classical narration: a new paradigm in contemporary cinema. *New Review in Film and Television,* 4(3): 183-196.

Traynor, Ian. 2015. Molenbeek: the Brussels borough becoming known as Europe's jihadi central. *The Guardian.* https://www.theguardian.com/world/2015/nov/15/molenbeek-the-brussels-borough-in-the-spotlight-after-paris-attacks. Accessed 11 November 2017.

Van Dievort, Charles. 2014. La personalité. *La Libre Belgique*, 23 December 2014.

Verheul, Jaap. 2016. Out of many, one : the dual monolingualism of contemporary Flemish cinema. In *The multilingual screen: new reflections on cinema and linguistic difference*. Ed. Mamula, Tijana and Lisa Patti. New York: Bloomsbury.

Vincendeau, Ginette. 2000. Designs on the Banlieue: Matthieu Kassovitz's *La Haine* (1995). In *French Film: texts and contexts*. Ed. Hayward, Susan and Ginette Vincendeau, G. Abingdon; New York: Routledge.

Watkins, S. Craig. 2001. A nation of millions: hip-hop culture and the legacy of black nationalism. *The Communication Review*, 4(3): 373–398.

CHAPTER 7

The Freedom to Make Racial Jokes: Satires on Nationalism and Multicultural Comedies in Dutch Cinema

Peter Verstraten

Three days before the Dutch elections on 15 March 2017, *De oplossing?*, a film directed by Sander Francken, was screened twice at LAB111, a small arthouse theatre in Amsterdam. The film had first been shown in 1983 at the Nederlandse Filmdagen, the most important festival for Dutch cinema. The jury had decided to award it the main prize, the Golden Calf, but the film, it turned out, did not meet the competition's formal requirements. *De oplossing?* was cofinanced by the Anne Frank Stichting, but its board, wanting to use the 65-minute film for educational purposes in secondary schools, objected to a regular release. Due to this obstruction, the jury could not give *De oplossing?* any awards. The film was shown in classrooms until the mid-1990s and although more than 300,000 pupils have seen Francken's movie, it is no more than a minor footnote in Dutch film history.

De oplossing? is nonetheless worth mentioning, because of the reason given for the screening thirty-four years after it was made. It was shown

---

P. Verstraten (✉)
Film and Literary Studies, Leiden University, Leiden, The Netherlands
e-mail: p.w.j.verstraten@hum.leidenuniv.nl

© The Author(s) 2018
J. Harvey (ed.), *Nationalism in Contemporary Western European Cinema*, Palgrave European Film and Media Studies,
https://doi.org/10.1007/978-3-319-73667-9_7

125

before the 2017 elections because no Dutch feature has addressed the theme of eerie nationalism as explicitly as this 1983 film had. In Francken's picture, a new political party blames a financial crisis on the arrival of 'hordes of foreigners' and the five employees of a garage on the brink of bankruptcy come under the spell of this rhetoric. Unabatedly didactic in its aim, *De oplossing?* reveals the shortsightedness of the mechanics, making an unambiguous plea to resist the logic of the scapegoat.[1] The film was screened at the eve of the 2017 election because its warning was regarded as being even more relevant then than it was in 1983, since polls had predicted that Geert Wilders' PVV, with its anti-immigrant agenda, could become the largest political party in the Netherlands.[2]

Asked why there are hardly any Dutch films like *De oplossing?* in this era of increasing nationalist sentiments, Francken's answer was tactful, as if he wished not to offend any of his colleagues: because it takes time to produce a film, he said, the medium is not very adept at responding to topical debates (quoted in Dijksterhuis). Overwhelmingly, indeed, most contemporary Dutch films are not concerned with current issues, and one of Holland's most prolific directors, Alex van Warmerdam has even claimed that he wants to avoid social themes at all costs.[3] In this chapter I aim to examine those attempts that do rework and/or contest the influence of a politics informed by nationalist fervour. These attempts take the form of satires, multicultural comedies, or dramas about the second generation 'new Dutch'.

WALHALLA AS A FAILED FILM SATIRE

In his study on the limits of tolerance, Ian Buruma observes that in the twentieth century people in the Netherlands were usually described as phlegmatic and forbearing—by 'lazy foreign journalists'—he is quick to

---

[1] *De oplossing?* was made in 1983, the year of a notorious murder by stabbing of a 15-year-old-black boy by a 16-year-old skinhead. The crime was presented as being racially motivated in the media, but the film *Skin* (Hanro Smitsman 2008) downplays this motivation twenty-five years later. As the film suggests, the kid became a skinhead only as a reaction to unfortunate personal circumstances: his Jewish father was still marked by Holocaust experiences and his mother had just died from cancer. The stabbing followed obnoxious behaviour, and the victim's 'skin' was irrelevant.

[2] The PVV became the second largest party.

[3] Don't let me be misunderstood: some interesting Dutch feature films have been made this century, but they are not related to current political subjects at all: *Guernsey, Zwartboek, Nothing Personal, Ober, Borgman, Aanmodderfakker, Gluckauf, Beyond Sleep*, to name a few.

add (Buruma 2006: 10). Dutch tolerance was not so much ingrained in the national character as it was, basically, the pragmatic consequence of a lack of clear hierarchy among groups, according to historian James Kennedy. The Netherlands was a country that never had one leading group, but consisted of several minorities: Catholics, (orthodox) Protestants, liberals, socialists. This resulted in a 'politically quiescent society, with a live-and-let-live mentality' that always had room for other 'pillarised' associations, ranging from tiny religious groups to homosexuals (Kennedy and Zwemer 2010: 261).

This mentality, which invigorated the myth of Dutch tolerance, had a flipside, however. With the advent of rebellious movements in the mid-1960s and early 1970s that defied the bourgeois with ludic actions, disorderly conduct, and the making of specific claims (e.g., advocating free childcare), the authorities reacted to the uproar and the demands by smiling politely, Kennedy argues in his *Nieuw Babylon in aanbouw*. This politeness is a good example of 'repressive tolerance' in practice: the best way to keep existing power structures intact is to allow certain superficial changes (Kennedy 1995: 144). This authorities' display of strategic forbearance reduced the 'motivation for vigorous political and social protest' (Kennedy and Zwemer 2010: 261).

Dutch politicians had and still have the habit of negotiating compromises, and over the years this resulted in several achievements, based on a policy of acquiescence: it was not illegal to use recreational drugs; the red-light district in Amsterdam turned into a tourist attraction; abortion was first tolerated, then in 1984 was legalised, albeit under strict conditions; support for gay rights was popular enough to be manifested in an annual Canal Parade in Amsterdam every August. The first of these parades occurred during the period of the country's first 'purple' government, which took power in 1994 and consisted of a coalition between liberals and social-democrats and contained none of the confessional parties. Buruma notes that all these developments led to 'an air of satisfaction, even smugness, a self-congratulatory notion of living in the finest, freest, most progressive, most decent, most perfectly evolved playground of multicultural utopianism' (2006: 11).

Philomena Essed convincingly argued in a 1991 study that Dutch culture is pierced with various kinds of 'everyday racism' (by way of discouragement of minorities, overemphasis on differences, jokes, et

128 P. VERSTRATEN

cetera);[4] nonetheless, many Dutch, as Buruma's quote suggests, live according to a self-fashioned idea of their indulgence towards others. To underscore this idea of a 'typically Dutch tolerance,' it was often pointed out that the one substantial nationalist, anti-immigrant party was marginal in parliament: in the 1994 election the Centrum Democraten reached their all-time high when they garnered 2.4% of the votes, but the party was to lose their seats four years later. In hindsight one can observe that *Walhalla*, Eddy Terstall's second feature film, released in 1995, was the one Dutch film that responded in this era to a modest rise of the radical right.

Critics unanimously considered *Walhalla* a courageous project—for a Dutch director, that is, considering Dutch films were held in low esteem in those years. Movie attendance for products of the national cinema had reached a nadir, which critics said was due to 'navel-gazing' directors who had restricted their pictures to explorations of their personal preoccupations. Though practically all reviewers agreed that Terstall deserved credit for addressing a potentially hot-button social issue, they were almost unanimously dissatisfied with how he had handled a racial conflict in a fictive town on the border between the Netherlands and Belgium. In *Walhalla*, the local council obstructs plans for the building of the furniture palace Walhalla on a dilapidated square, which was being used as a playground by Moroccan kids. An opportunistic property developer bets that the support of the right-wing party will help him bring his scheme to fruition. In order to make the party respectable, he blackmails a bulky socialist politician, who frequents the local bordello to enjoy S&M games, into taking up its leadership. Party sympathisers commit acts for which Moroccans are held responsible, such as besmirching a tombstone with Quranic texts, in order to further incite anti-foreigner sentiment and fear. A skinhead kicks a Moroccan teenager to death because he erroneously thinks that the teen has misused his feeble-minded twin sister. In the end, the right-wing party wins the local elections and Walhalla is about to be built.

---

[4] Essed gives an example of an 'active tolerance of racism.' When a waiter refuses to serve the one black person in a restaurant, the white Dutch feel inhibited from confronting the situation: 'the group *failed to take responsibility* as Whites to speak out against racism' (Essed 1991, p. 278). In this case, the 'norm of tolerance legitimizes nonaction against racism.' Due to this 'it is none of my business' attitude of the group, the offender is supported in his racist practice (ibid.: 277).

Terstall's *Walhalla*, a box-office failure, met with vehement criticism in the press. The case is nonetheless instructive, because the harsh comments directed towards it are related to doubts about the effectiveness of making such a political movie. Terstall claimed that he had wanted to warn the audience about the rise of the right, which in 1995 was more acute in the Flemish part of Belgium than in the Netherlands. By showing the ridiculousness of neo-Nazis rather than highlighting their maliciousness, Terstall assumed that viewers would dis-identify with them. By isolating segments from reality, such as a bizarre speech proposing the banning of 'negro fruit' such as papaya and mango (based on an actual debate among the right-wing Vlaams Blok in Belgium), he thought that the film would deflate fascist tendencies in the Low Countries. Maybe this stance is naïve, Terstall admitted, but as long as his film provokes discussion, he would not mind being a sitting target (Van Ieperen 1995: 107).

Despite this readiness to be a fall guy, Terstall would certainly not have expected that his caricatured sketch of right-wing sympathisers would unleash what was basically a vitriolic response. When the columnist Max Pam was in a theatre viewing the film, he observed that though the Moroccans are portrayed as hard-working citizens and the skinheads as noisy nitwits, the audience became so petulant that many viewers started to audibly encourage the aggressive whites. Terstall's intention might have been to make viewers laugh at the skinheads, but alas, as Pam noted, there was laughing with them instead: 'Are you in favour of neo-Nazis? Go see this film,' he concluded wryly. If Terstall's naïve attempt to be critical through satire missed the mark, this was partly because the right-wing party in the Netherlands was thought to be a negligible force. Critics despised *Walhalla* because they believed that it was better to ignore these silly, aggressive people than to ridicule them, for any attention risked the prospect that some would end up favouring them.[5] Arguments about a lack of urgency for a film such as *Walhalla* can also imply, however, that the Dutch dearly wanted to avoid any acknowledgement of the dark impulses that might pervade their 'typically' lenient mentality.

---

[5] Another example which shows that the strategy of dis-identification can work counter-productively: Koot and Bie, two of Holland's most appreciated satirists in the history of Dutch television, regularly played the extreme right-wing characters Jacobse and Van Es in the early 1980s, but their act with absurdist slogans became so popular that they decided to stage the death of the characters. It troubled them that viewers started to take the silly non-sense seriously.

SATIRE ON PIM FORTUYN

These dark impulses were addressed obliquely in a famous essay by sociologist Paul Scheffer in January 2000. He warned in 'The Multicultural Tragedy' that the 'old' method of peaceful coexistence, which characterised the pillarisation, would not be sufficient in a country where a growing number of immigrants were not offered viable prospects. The seeming tolerance of the Dutch, Scheffer argued, could also be taken as a startling indifference towards their fellow citizens. Their overriding attitude towards the non-Western newcomers might be summed up as: 'I tolerate your presence, but do not interfere with my stuff.' The immigrants' integration and that of their children were further problematised because of 'white flight': the native-born Dutch tended to send their kids to schools with few if any pupils of Turkish or Moroccan descent. Especially the second-generation children of immigrants came to regard themselves as victims of this policy of 'coexistence without interacting.' Although the basic assumptions of this 'multicultural tragedy' were widely contested, it became a popular catchphrase to advocate the idea that an unbridgeable divide separates the Dutch from the newcomers and their children.

From September 2001 onwards, in the aftermath of 9/11, Pim Fortuyn, aged fifty-three, suddenly had momentum. He was worried that the newcomers, especially the practicing Muslims among them, might express their frustration at the Dutch way of living and its hard-earned luxuries. It piqued him that their presence in the Netherlands might mean that 'we' would have to reprise the emancipation struggles of women and gays all over again. His attitude was exemplary of a tendency among Dutch people, in the words of Buruma, to suffer from the sour mood of *verongelijktheid*, 'to be wronged, not by an individual so much as by the world at large' (Buruma 2006: 15–16). The Dutch started wondering: *What did we do to deserve such intolerant people, signified by the women's headscarves, coming to join our little paradise of tolerance where we celebrate sexualised bodies at the Canal Parade?* From this perspective, the Muslims, Buruma writes, are regarded as 'the spoilsports, unwelcome crashers at the party' (2006: 127).

A dandy who wore pinstripe suits, Fortuyn became the object of mimicry because of his frequent use of the English expression 'It's a bloody shame!' in a high-pitched voice. He excelled in outrageous claims and provocative retorts: 'I do not hate Moroccan guys, on the contrary, I like to fuck them' (in dark rooms, that is). The bolder his statements, the greater his success in the polls. Any attempt by his political opponents to damage his reputation only increased his fame. When it was revealed that 'Professor Pim' unjustly gave the impression that he could legitimately use the title of 'professor,' his supporters' reaction ran along the lines of 'this is a vile tactic to discredit our beloved candidate.' After Fortuyn was banned as the party leader of Leefbaar Nederland in February 2002 due to controversial statements, such as 'the Islam is a retarded culture,' he founded his own political organization: LPF (Lijst Pim Fortuyn). Nine days after he was fatally shot in the head by an animal-rights activist, his brand-new party got no less than 26 out of 150 seats on Election day, 15 May 2002. The totally inexperienced politicians of LPF performed very poorly in both government and parliament, and after eighty-seven days the new cabinet had collapsed.

That the LPF had become a laughing stock was due to the party's decapitation, according to its voters. Fortuyn's supporters hypothesised that had Pim not been murdered, the LPF would not have been set adrift: its collapse only strengthened the profile of its former leader. The LPF's swift decline left a vacuum that was ultimately filled by Geert Wilders, a member of parliament who, after a split from the VVD in September 2004, started his own group. Wilders' PVV became a party to reckon with, particularly after a Muslim extremist's brutal murder of filmmaker Theo van Gogh on 2 November 2004 incited fears of Islamic immigrants. The genie would not go back in the bottle.

A quick glance at this thumbnail sketch might suggest that Holland had been transformed overnight from a liberal country, run by a purple government until 2002, into a xenophobic one. The point is rather that the drawbacks of the presumed tolerance of the Dutch—such as Essed's examples of not consciously intended 'everyday racism' or publications by journalist Anil Ramdas—have not always had due respect in the public domain. An item on the VPRO programme *Waskracht!*, broadcast in March 2002 on Dutch national television, can be considered as a satiric acknowledgement of the claims by Essed and Ramdas that a substantial degree of intolerance had been lurking underneath even during the country's heyday of tolerance. The show's gimmick was that a Dutch-Iranian journalist, Bahram Sadeghi, in a suit as impeccable as what Fortuyn might wear, went to see the notorious Hans Janmaat to offer a make-over. Janmaat used to be the leader of the Centrum Democraten, and during his political career, he was either ignored by the media or given a bad press. He seemed all too happy to cooperate, apparently believing that he was being taken seriously.

132   P. VERSTRATEN

Newly groomed in clothes, he was made into a lookalike for Fortuyn. The satire cut both ways: it implied that Janmaat was not getting his ideas across because of his unattractive physical presentation. Dutch people might lend an ear to right-wing anti-immigrant messages, but only, it seemed, if the speaker were a flamboyant type with rhetorical talent. Janmaat fell short on both counts, and thus his political programme flopped in the 1980s and 1990s. Still play-acting, Sadeghi offered his services as a media trainer to revive Janmaat's career.[6] Important here to note is whereas Janmaat could think that the item was contributing to the rehabilitation of his reputation, it was, in fact, using him to vilify Fortuyn, as if the latter were the natural successor to the former: old wine in new bottles. Fortuyn could strike a chord among his supporters because they had the inclination to harbour racist ideas all along: this was the purport of the *Waskracht!* item. These ideas had always been there, they were merely dormant—and all that was required was the proper 'prince' to kiss them awake.

Two Terstall Movies: *Simon* and *Vox Populi*

Terstall's career did not get off to a particularly good start—his debut feature *Transit* (1992) had not fared well either—but the low-budget films he made after *Walhalla* were met with more sympathetic reviews. His seventh feature film, the comedy-drama *Simon* (2004) received a number of awards, among others a Golden Calf for Best Picture in the Netherlands. Released internationally, it is still the highest-rated Dutch fiction feature on IMDb, with an eight rating. Terstall's tragi-comedy was the first instalment of a trilogy on Dutch society, addressing, in the director's own words, spiritual life (*Simon*), private life (*Sextet* 2006) and official life (*Vox Populi* 2008), respectively.

In *Simon*, the gay dentist Camiel is almost run over by a car in October 2002. The driver is the he-man Simon, the proverbial 'rough diamond,' whom the dentist had befriended in the summer of 1988. Worlds apart, they nonetheless kept seeing each other for a while because Simon was the supplier of soft drugs for Camiel. Significantly, the many flashback scenes in Terstall's film are shot in saturated colours, and 1988 is remembered because that was the year when the national soccer team won the European

---

[6] It was Janmaat's latest public appearance before he died on 9 June 2002, one month after Fortuyn.

THE FREEDOM TO MAKE RACIAL JOKES: SATIRES ON NATIONALISM... 133

Championship and its victory was enthusiastically celebrated all over the Netherlands, as is shown in *Simon*. This year marked the origin of 'Orange madness,' when huge crowds gathered publically to watch the football games. By contrast, the colours in Autumn 2002 are gloomy, and within the first minute of their renewed acquaintance, Simon has told Camiel (with 'typical' Dutch directness), 'I have cancer. That's life.'

With Simon at the point of dying in 2002, and given the film's gloomy colour scheme, it would seem that the vision presented here is of a Holland in decline as the new millennium gets underway. But there is another side of the coin, as Terstall explained himself. Because there had been a so-called purple ministry without any denominational parties between 1994 and 2002, some liberal agreements had been approved or were continued, as with the policy of turning a blind eye on the recreational use of soft drugs. Because the Netherlands was the first country to legalise gay marriage (it did so in 2001), Camiel and his partner Bram use the opportunity to have a wedding at short notice so that Simon could be the best man. And an active form of euthanasia had become possible, under strict conditions, on account of a law passed by the Dutch parliament in 2001. Since Simon does not want to become a vegetable, he chooses the day of his death, at a time when he is still relatively mobile.

In addition to its combination of black humour and feel-good tragedy (Simon's death is meant to be a happy farewell), *Simon* received accolades because it addressed socially relevant issues of, to paraphrase Terstall, a 'spiritual' nature. In comparison to other countries, he claimed, the Netherlands is some kind of Disneyland, because of its passage of liberal legislation regarding gay marriage, euthanasia, and soft drugs. These achievements, realised by a secular Dutch administration, had come under threat according to Terstall, since the Christian Democrats were back in government after the May 2002 elections. His *Simon* can be considered a 'veiled pamphlet for a libertine society,' in which citizens are 'open, curious, and extroverted' (Terstall, quoted in Busch 2004). Whereas the bleak caricature *Walhalla* depicted a dystopian future at a time when right-wing movements were still marginal in the Netherlands, *Simon* represents a quite utopian sketch of an almost bygone Holland. In calling *Simon* a 'relatively naïve 10 September'-movie, Terstall indicates that he meant his film, with its emphasis upon liberal rules, to be an antidote towards growing scepticism about Dutch tolerance (Terstall in Cornelissen 2011: 84). Terstall did not want to contribute to the heated debates that had been unleashed since Fortuyn's rant against Islam. That is to say, not yet, for the last film of the trilogy, *Vox Populi* (2008), is a critique of a populist strategy to favour the prejudices of ordinary people over one's moral values.

Jos Fransen is the political leader of the Red-Green party, whose 'idealistic' programme is at odds with the ambitions of the rising populist newcomers in the 'Go Holland Go' Party. Because his daughter Zoë falls in love with Sjef, Jos becomes acquainted with the latter's father, Nico de Klerk, a big-mouthed plebeian. Nico distrusts the elite, for they look down upon the common people. He is also suspicious of Muslim men who wear the djellaba, or 'alibaba,' as he calls their garment. Jos integrates some of Nico's statements into his public performances and interviews. His party's popularity increases considerably, but according to his colleagues he is betraying his principles. For his part, Jos himself euphemistically calls his new discoveries 'progressive insight.' Despite favourable polls, Jos' fate is sealed when a hidden camera and microphone capture him telling a racist joke about Muslims, which he had heard from Nico's son-in-law, who is a man who eagerly feeds him, Rasputin-like, foul opinions. According to the prime minister, Jos has gone beyond 'flirting with the underbelly' of society. Ultimately needing bodyguards to ensure his safety, he steps down as leader of the Red-Green Party.

On the basis of Jos' edifying farewell speech (you should not give the people what they want), it is clear that a politician should not sell out his social agenda: moral principles are preferable to instant popularity. Vanity being one of Jos' weaknesses, he could not resist the lure of short-term success. But while the serious bottom line may favour politicians who show steadfastness, the film nonetheless privileges the plebeian characters who manipulate the politician to advocate vile opinions. Terstall himself was aware of the discrepancy, he explained on the extra features on the DVD. The viewer is supposed to agree with the position of the politicians who are firm in their principles, but the viewer tends to sympathise with Nico and his son-in-law, for the latter are the most memorable characters and they are given the best one-liners. On the same extra features, Ton Kas, who plays Nico, states that in general the lower-class fiddlers are more humorous than the righteous people: One cannot reproach them for a lack of *joie de vivre*. Hence *Vox Populi*, however anti-populist its 'message,' would be forgettable without its cheerful common folk characters. Moreover, Terstall's film is shot without much ado—*Vox Populi* employs much handheld camerawork, copying the hectic feel of the work of political (television) journalists. Formally, this makes the (charm of the) film as direct as the talk of its lower-class characters.

Progressive Racism

To Terstall's credit, he appears conscious of the fact that the actual effect of a film like his *Vox Populi* can contradict its intended message. A gap between message and effect is an inherent 'risk' of any form of communication, but comedy and satire are more prone to it than other genres.[7] In the case of his regrettable *Walhalla*, Terstall himself had experienced the pitfalls of humour and satire more than he would have liked. At the same time, there is always a way out when someone makes a witty remark that can be taken as an insult. If the joker is taken aback by the bad-tempered reply of his target, his usual excuse is that it was a mere attempt to get a rise out of him: don't react so touchily, I was only kidding and did not mean to tread on your toes.

The title hero of Terstall's *Simon* employs the brutal sort of humour that sceptics of a multicultural society often use in the Netherlands. Simon excels in making politically incorrect jokes, which include many homophobic remarks. Though gay himself, Camiel laughs at them because he understands that Simon isn't trying to humiliate him: 'guacamole fag,' for example, is meant as a term of endearment rather than an offensive slight. This interpretation is representative of a train of thought that posits if we really take freedom of speech seriously, then one is permitted to say anything. Complaining about his ex-girlfriend's many lovers, Simon says: 'First a Jew, then a gay, then a black brother. Just a Turk and a dyke, and she will get the Nobel Prize.' Since a guy like Simon makes jokes about everyone, making sexual and ethnic minorities the target of comic scorn is proof for him that these groups have been accepted in society. From this perspective, a politically incorrect joke even functions as an emancipatory tool and a token of tolerance. A Dutch man would say: we poke fun at you (whether you are Jewish, Chinese, gay, lesbian, etc.) just like I joke about my native-born, heterosexual compatriots, and thus we are all equals.

The phrase 'progressive racism' has been used to describe the situation when a joker disavows that his remarks about an ethnic other come from a privileged position. The white Dutchman casts an exchange of insults as a gift to the minority group: I give you the opportunity to make jokes about me, but then I am also permitted to ridicule you. This gift is a poisoned chalice, however, for it affords the whites the luxury of further

---

[7] It was with good reason that Sigmund Freud examined jokes and humour in relation to, respectively, the unconscious and the superego.

136   P. VERSTRATEN

occupying space. In the words of Sara Ahmed, 'the progressive racist would expect the other to be willing to be the butt of the joke by receiving that joke *as* an expression of solidarity' (Ahmed 2016). Thereupon, the white Dutchman acts on this expectation by making fun, as a first move, of the other. Humour is abused here as an instrument to circumvent censorship of politically incorrect remarks. Due to this mechanism of progressive racism, (black) humour and satire, long rooted in Dutch culture,[8] have become predominant vehicles for expressing discontent with multiculturalism.

No one used the instrument of brutal jokes about immigrants as distinctly as the filmmaker and columnist Theo van Gogh, a provocative jester par excellence who incessantly offended Muslims, until one of them killed him.[9] Following Van Gogh's murder, eighteen directors made the compilation film *Allerzielen* [*All Souls*] (2005) to memorialise him. Insofar as the tone of the seventeen segments is one of anger, this is subdued, for time and again it is expressed in the form of mockery. If, in the first story, Van Gogh, sword in his breast, cannot speak his mind in the afterlife, then, he demands, the guards should open the gates so he can go back to the Netherlands. In another segment, 'Greetings from Holland,' a Turkish-born Muslim and a Moroccan-born Muslim quarrel about a trash bag on the pavement. On hearing the news that a filmmaker has been killed by a man of Moroccan descent, the Turkish-born man is relieved that he does not have to barricade his house like his neighbour now must. But a white Dutch man throws the trash bag through his window, anyway. One might say that the Dutchman is the butt of the joke here, because of his lack of judgement, but that is beside the point. The Dutchman simply does not care about the distinction between these immigrants: whether from Turkey or from Morocco, a Muslim is a Muslim. And thus, the Turkish-born man is the actual butt of the joke, for he is punished for his naïveté.

---

[8] As regards the predominance of humour in the Netherlands, one can think of Johan Huizinga's canonical study *Homo ludens* (1938), of the many film comedies that became huge big box-office hits, such as *Fanfare* (Bert Haanstra, 1958), *Wat zien ik!?* (Paul Verhoeven, 1971), *Flodder* (Dick Maas, 1986), but also of a strong and vivid tradition of cabaret performers (Toon Hermans, Freek de Jonge, Hans Teeuwen, Brigitte Kaandorp, Najib Amhali).

[9] Even though Van Gogh's columns had angered Muslims, the direct cause for the murder by Muhammed B. was the fact that Van Gogh had agreed to direct the anti-Islam short film *Submission* (2004), scripted by Ayaan Hirsi Ali.

THE FREEDOM TO MAKE RACIAL JOKES: SATIRES ON NATIONALISM... 137

Taken together, these two segments from the compilation film are emblematic of a cinematic reply to Scheffer's 'multicultural tragedy': the gap is presented in the form of humour. The first segment from *Allerzielen* expresses a comic reverence towards the idea of a 'Holland' where one is accustomed to speaking out about anything. The second sketch illustrates that what seems like a form of ironic Dutch self-regard is in fact a joke at the expense of, in this case, a Turkish-born man. This contribution to *Allerzielen* can be taken as an early example of a new sub-genre in Dutch cinema: the 'multicultural comedy.' Starting with *Shouf shouf habibi!/ Hush, Hush Baby!* (Albert ter Heerdt 2004) and the equally successful *Het schnitzelparadijs/ Schnitzel Paradise* (Martin Koolhoven 2005), several comedies were released in a relatively short time span as a reaction to the rise of right-wing populism: *Dunya & Desie* (Dana Nechushtan 2008), *Alibi* (Johan Nijenhuis 2008), *Gangsterboys* (Paul Ruven 2010), *Pizza Maffia* (Tim Oliehoek 2011), *De president* (Erik de Bruyn 2011), *Snackbar* (Meral Uslu 2012), *Alleen maar nette mensen/ Only Decent People* (Lodewijk Crijns 2012), *Valentino* (Remy van Heugten 2013), and *De Masters* (Ruud Schuurman 2015). In the least significant of these films, divergent racial commonplaces are quite randomly juxtaposed: in *Alleen maar nette mensen*, a serious remark about the history of slavery is immediately downplayed by a tongue-in-cheek reference to the womanizing and/or lazy 'nature' of black men. These strategically ambiguous films affirm as well as contradict cultural ideas, basically for the sake of laughter. But if anything can be ridiculed, then there is no way to adopt a truly critical perspective, and, as I have claimed in evoking the concept of 'progressive racism,' this mechanism ultimately privileges the force of whiteness.

In the best of these multicultural comedies (*Shouf shouf habibi!*, *Het schnitzelparadijs*) it becomes clear how the 'new Dutch' are sandwiched between cultures. The plot of *Shouf shouf habibi!*, cowritten by the main actor, the Dutch-Moroccan Mimoun Oaïssa, is structured around certain incidents that activate typical clichés about Moroccan immigrants and the Dutch alike. The Dutch follow a by-the-clock mentality and are ruled by a strict sense of exactitude—eight o'clock means eight o'clock, not a minute later—to which the protagonist Abus cannot adapt. Significantly, *Shouf shouf habibi!* is advertised as an 'oerhollandse'—meaning 'primal Dutch'—comedy, in which the young men of Moroccan descent despise their 'brothers' who have made Dutch customs and habits their own. The humour resides in their contempt being a cover-up for their own missteps: better to be labelled 'bad Moroccans' than to become an indistinct 'half Dutchie.'

138 P. VERSTRATEN

Entertaining as it is, this form of comedy has, in its display of ethnic stereotypes, some pitfalls. First, even if it questions stereotypes through an exaggeration of the norm, stereotypes can never be fully exorcised: reproducing and/or recalling them risks affirming them. Second, this type of comedy tends to privilege effect over aesthetics, and laughter, over critical reflection. The pace of such movies leaves little room for contemplation, since one is always keen to get to the next joke. Nonetheless, comedies—even plain ones—always have the potential to address issues of social significance, which can either be too complicated or too controversial. *Shouf shouf habibi!* took the form of a self-mocking display of clichés about and by Moroccan immigrant characters. This comedy articulates how they are split between the mentality of their non-Dutch background and the tireless punctuality of Dutch people. Though the film has no pretentions of offering a clear-cut analysis, *Shouf shouf habibi!* suggests that people like Abus are caught in an impasse. None of their options are very favourable, for, indeed, Dutch society is organised so strictly that newcomers and their children have little to no space for integration. Instead of whining about this unfortunate situation, *Shouf shouf habibi!* humorously confronts its viewers with the difficult, if not impossible, position of the second generation, of those sandwiched between cultures and their competing claims. And in the turbulent year 2004, such comic acknowledgement was as good as it was going to get.[10]

THE BRIGHT AND DARK SIDES OF DUTCH-MOROCCANS: *RABAT* AND *WOLF*

In the wake of the early multicultural comedies' success, the low-budget (150,000 euro) film *Rabat* (Jim Taihuttu and Victor D. Ponten 2011) was perhaps the most eye-catching of titles, if only thanks to the famous speech given by Nasrdin Dchar upon receiving a Golden Calf for best actor at the Netherlands Film Festival. *Rabat* is a road movie with many comic interludes, and for the final denouement, it makes hilarious use of the perception that the Netherlands is a licentious country. The Dutch-Moroccan Nadir is expected to drive his father's old cab from Amsterdam to Rabat, and though his father has told him not to take 'that Tunisian and that clown' with him, Zakaria and Abdel join him on his journey. Whereas

---

[10] Owing to the success of the film, *Shouf shouf!* was turned into a television series that ran for three seasons.

the serious Nadir has recently completed an economics degree, his two friends take life very easily. For Zakaria, only the present counts; his basic occupations are, in the accusatory terms of Nadir, 'smoking, drinking, waking up from a hangover.' Abdel is not much different, although he is always talking about his 'business plan.' Currently, he is still working in what Abdel euphemistically calls the 'restaurant' of his uncle, selling kebabs, but he claims he has a 'unique concept.' He presumes that his two friends have already agreed to be a part of the project, but it turns out that Nadir has had his doubts. In the film's crucial beach scene, when the three friends put their camaraderie to the test, Nadir reproaches Abdel that his business consists of 'talking for two years' and of designing logos, which took about half an hour. 'Your plan is an excuse for doing nothing. All the time we discuss it, you don't have to do anything else. Admit, you're a loser.'

In the film's first half, Nadir is positioned as its moral anchor, and his father's recommendation to travel without friends makes sense. In the eyes of his friends, he loses this position, because Nadir had kept silent that the car he has to bring to Rabat is in fact a wedding gift for his own arranged marriage. Nadir himself, however, becomes far less certain of the worth of this 'mission' set up by his father once he meets the French girl Julie, a shoplifter as fond of *The Godfather* as he is. By contrast, the girl who has been selected as his bride has not even seen Coppola's movie. Moreover, she confesses to him that she, too, is going along with the marriage only to please her parents. Back at her place, he tells the girl's father and her brothers about his spectacular business plan. He shows them a piece of paper with the logos designed by Abdel: Kebab Sutra. Dutch people are only interested in two things: sex and food. His plan is thus to hit two birds with one stone by having topless women serve the kebab meals. The restaurant's interior will be a combination of the Arabian nights and modern design; its menu will consist of dishes with names like Kebab 69, Kebab on the Beach, Kebab Happy End. Nadir pictures Holland as a shameless country where immoral values reign, and from the perspective of Yasmine's family, it must really seem like Sodom and Gomorrah. One might expect that Nadir's portrayal of the Netherlands might offend *Rabat*'s Dutch viewers, but the effect is rather the opposite. Holland can be presented as an undisciplined country only in the eyes of foreigners who stick to their traditional customs. They, the homebred Moroccans, cannot see the Dutch achievements as tokens of a progressive liberalism. The fact that 'our' (western) liberal principles come across as lawless is

140   P. VERSTRATEN

their shortcoming and only proves that we are more advanced and broad-minded than they are. At the same time, the joke on the various kebab dishes implies that Abdel and, by extension, Nadir, are perhaps more Dutch than they had realised. After the trip, the three assimilated Arabs will each go their own way: Zakaria will leave for Tunisia, Abdel will finally start a restaurant, and Nadir will choose *Godfather* aficionado Julie over the arranged bride.

Reflecting upon the accolades for *Rabat* among both the critics and the public, director Taihuttu realised that Nadir is too likeable a character.[11] 'If your daughter brings home a foreigner,' he said in an interview, 'every mother would hope it would be him' (Donkers and Kleijwegt 2014). Insofar as Dutch people might consider Nadir to be the sympathetic exception to the 'rule' that many Moroccan men are troublemakers, *Rabat* might obfuscate rather than clarify the problems of the multicultural society. *Wolf* (Jim Taihuttu 2013) represents the 'dark side' of sunny, colourful *Rabat*. Shot in black and white, the film opens with a scene shot from inside a shop-window at night. Majid and his friend Adil are in doubt whether to steal the black Asprilla motorcycle or the grey one. Once they have decided, the window is smashed before our very eyes. The scene is emblematic of Majid's existence, marked by petty crime and hanging around with his friends. He is on bad terms with his father; his older brother is the 'good' son, but he is terminally ill; his younger brother is too young to speak up. Majid is given the opportunity to work at a flower auction to help him integrate into mainstream Dutch society, but he looks down upon this work. He has one particular talent, though: when he visits a kickboxing school, he breaks his opponent's jaw in a test fight. He is too undisciplined, however, to build himself a career in sports. His trainer gets mad when he keeps on hitting after the referee has ended the match; he behaves brutally toward his Dutch girlfriend Tessa, and even more violently against anyone who dates her.

But the worst is yet to come. The Turkish Hakan, head of a criminal organization, is interested in Majid because of his strength. Hired as a security guard, Majid has to pull a gun during a deal. He starts using cocaine as a means to release his tension. A big match in the ring potentially awaits him, but he neglects his trainer's demand that he train twice a day. His trainer tells him: 'Well, walk away again. Do what you can do best,

---

[11] In 2012 Diederick Koopal's *De marathon* received the Audience Award at the Netherlands Film Festival: the Moroccan characters in this comedy are hugely sympathetic.

disappear,' and adds in a dismissive tone: 'Your father and brother will be proud.' When his braggart pal Adil suggests to his friends that they rob an armoured car, Majid, knowing that the plan has been concocted by Hakan, does not want to participate until Adil says: 'I told those Turks you're in as well.' In the heist Adil kills two men, but his friend Vleermuis is fatally wounded. They make money, but the loot is not as big as expected. Majid, downcast about Vleermuis' death, decides to keep a low profile for a while, but then Adil seduces Tessa, who is furious and hits him. When Majid informs about Adil's black eye, the latter says he interfered when 'that filthy Turk' Baris, one of Hakan's gang members, was flirting with Tessa. Predictably, Majid's revenge induces more violence: on his way to the dressing room for a kickboxing match, he is seriously hurt by Baris and his friends. Hakan says: 'If you go down in the second round, we will forget about this.' When he sees after the first round that his father and his younger brother are among the audience, he forgets about the deal and knocks out his opponent in the second round. We see Majid in close-up in the dressing room, recovering from the physical effort. The door opens— end of movie.

When viewed in an international context, Taihuttu's *Wolf* is not a ground-breaking film. It recalls the sense of frustration evident in Mathieu Kassovitz's *La Haine* (1995), also shot in black and white and set in a poor urban area; it is reminiscent of several Martin Scorsese pictures, recalling the street mentality of *Mean Streets* (1973), the boxing scenes in the black-and-white *Raging Bull* (1980), and the tracking shots forward behind the back of the protagonist in *Goodfellas* (1990). The confrontations between a young Arab and a gangster boss seem to be inspired by *Un prophète* (Jacques Audiard 2009). A Dutch film like *Wolf,* however, was unheard of in Holland, because, as Taihuttu himself explained, Dutch distributers are not inclined to invest money in a film that is a 'checklist for politically incorrect movie-making' (quoted in Linssen 2013): shot in black and white, containing nasty violent scenes, paced slowly at times, and taking at its subject non-sympathetic foreigners who appear hopeless (underscored by the choice of black and white). And the one character who has the chance to improve his position does not succeed, leaving it as a matter of debate whether he fails because of his environment or his own lack of backbone, or perhaps both.

A Counterargument to Easy Explanations

Insofar as current socio-political issues are addressed in Dutch cinema, both humour and irony are privileged over a 'serious' tone of engagement. I have described 'progressive racism' as a main tendency in Dutch films that focus on multiculturalism, implying that those claiming to speak on behalf of the common people believe that treating others as equals means that everyone should agree that those others are legitimate targets of comic scorn. Freedom of speech is then redefined as the freedom to tell 'dirty' (racial) jokes. We see this in the case of foul-mouthed characters like Simon, like Nico from *Vox Populi*, or like the five friends in the huge box-office hit *New Kids Turbo* (Steffen Haars and Flip van der Kuil 2010) who derive their identities from the small village where they live. By claiming time and again 'we are from Maaskantje,' they want to resist being infected by the effects of globalization and multiculturalism.

In the case of the new subgenre of the multicultural comedy, I argued that in adopting a pleasing tone, these films with their overt predilection for wisecracks risk falling prey to 'progressive racism' as well. As a consequence, they leave the roots of the discomfort towards the multicultural society in Dutch cinema largely unaddressed, though *Shouf shouf habibi!* deserves the benefit of the doubt.

The most convincing films to cope with the rise of nationalism are those pictures that aim to put representations about the 'new Dutch' in perspective. In addition to the two films by Taihuttu that present in-depth studies of second generation characters, some recent tentative steps can be observed. The arthouse film *The Paradise Suite* (Joost van Ginkel 2015), which won a Golden Calf for Best Dutch picture, offers a mosaic of six immigrant residents in Amsterdam from different backgrounds, whose lives intertwine at certain key moments. *Layla M.* (Mijke de Jong 2016), the Dutch entry for the Academy Awards 2018, is about a young Muslim woman from Amsterdam who becomes a radical to the dismay of her parents. When she leaves for the Middle East after her marriage to a jihadist, she is confronted with the negative consequences of her choice. Since De Jong prefers close-to-the-skin shots of her characters, the film invites its viewers to have empathy with the troubled protagonists. I mentioned at the start that there is no film, except for *De oplossing?*, that explicitly warns against the rise of nationalism. Films with a clear political message are perhaps not very effective, for they may provoke abrasive comments in the era of Twitter. I also mentioned that filmmakers may think it better to

THE FREEDOM TO MAKE RACIAL JOKES: SATIRES ON NATIONALISM... 143

ignore populist appeals than to satirise them, as illustrated by both the failure of *Walhalla* and Terstall's doubt about the tone of his *Vox Populi*. Hence, one had better wish that the eventual successors to films like *Wolf*, *The Paradise Suite*, and *Layla M*. will attract a larger audience so they can serve as counterarguments to easy explanations and solutions.

BIBLIOGRAPHY

Ahmed, Sara. 2016. Progressive racism. *feministkilljoys.com*. https://feministkill-joys.com/2016/05/30/progressive-racism/. Accessed 4 October 2017.

Buruma, Ian. 2006. *Murder in Amsterdam: The Death of Theo Van Gogh and the Limits of Tolerance*. New York: Penguin.

Busch, Gerhard. 2004. De stiekeme pamfletten van Eddy Terstall. *cinema.nl*. https://www.vpro.nl/cinema/leses/artikelen/interviews/2004/De-stiekeme-pamfletten-van-Eddy-Terstall.html. Accessed 6 October 2017.

Cornelissen, Flora. 2011. *Vox Terstall*. Universiteit Utrecht: MA Thesis Film- en Televisiewetenschappen.

Dijksterhuis, Edo. 2017. *De oplossing?* na 34 jaar toch nog in bioscoop. *De Filmkrant*. http://www.filmkrant.nl/nieuws_2017/15218. Accessed 29 September 2017.

Donkers, Sander and David Kleijwegt. 2014. De honger van Jim Taihuttu. *Vrij Nederland*. https://www.vn.nl/de-honger-van-jim-taihuttu/. Accessed 29 September 2017.

Essed, Philomena. 1991. *Understanding Everyday Racism: An Interdisciplinary Theory*. Newbury Park: Sage.

Kennedy, James. 1995. *Nieuw Babylon in aanbouw: Nederland in de jaren zestig*. Amsterdam: Boom.

Kennedy, James C. and Jan P. Zwemer. 2010. Religion in the modern Netherlands and the problems of pluralism. *BMGN – Low Countries Historical Review*, 125 (2–3): 237–68.

Linssen, Dana. 2013. Checklist tegen politiek-correct filmmaken: Jim Taihuttu in zwart-wit. *De Filmkrant* 357. http://www.filmkrant.nl/TS_september_2013/9820. Accessed 29 September 2017.

Pam, Max. 1995. Walhalla. *NRC Handelsblad* 16 June.

Scheffer, Paul. 2000. Het multiculturele drama. *NRC Handelsblad*. 29 January. http://retro.nrc.nl/W2/Lab/Multicultureel/scheffer.html. Accessed 4 October 2017.

Van Ieperen, Ad. 1995. Eddy Terstall schaamt zich nergens voor. *Vrij Nederland*. 17 June: 106–107.

CHAPTER 8

Building Bridges: Fatih Akin and the Cinema of Intercultural Dialogue

Owen Evans

Shocking incidents in Cologne, Berlin and Hamburg, three of Germany's most multicultural cities, in the past two years have heaped enormous pressure on Chancellor Angela Merkel after she allowed over a million refugees into Germany as the EU's migration crisis unfolded in the summer of 2015. Following this bold humanitarian decision, albeit one criticised for her perceived lack of consultation, it is often forgotten that Merkel believed the country's multicultural policies to have 'utterly failed' just five years earlier.

> At the start of the 60s we invited the *Gastarbeiter* [guest-workers] to Germany. We kidded ourselves for a while that they wouldn't stay, that one day they'd go home. That isn't what happened. And of course the tendency was to say: let's be 'multikulti' and live next to each other and enjoy being together, [but] this concept has failed, failed utterly. (Angela Merkel, German Chancellor in Connolly 2010)

Recent violent events made the issues of immigration and inner security central to the German Election in September 2017, with multicultural

---

O. Evans (✉)
Media Department, Edge Hill University, Ormskirk, UK
e-mail: evanso@edgehill.ac.uk

© The Author(s) 2018   145
J. Harvey (ed.), *Nationalism in Contemporary Western European Cinema*, Palgrave European Film and Media Studies,
https://doi.org/10.1007/978-3-319-73667-9_8

146   O. EVANS

tensions in the country running higher than for some time. In tandem with the populist anti-immigration Pegida movement protesting in Germany against a supposedly dangerous 'Islamisation of the West', the *Alternative für Deutschland* (AfD), a party originally founded in 2013 to challenge Germany's handling of the Eurozone crisis, subsequently sharpened its focus on immigration, winning seats in nine of the country's sixteen regional parliaments in the process. Subsequently, the party achieved disturbing, yet spectacular, success in the General Election, securing 12.6% of the vote and just over ninety seats in the *Bundestag*, becoming the third largest party and shaking the German Establishment. The AfD won twice as many votes in the eastern *Länder* than in the west, but also benefited from widespread disaffection with the government's immigration policy across Germany. Since the violent attacks on asylum-seekers in the early 1990s in Hoyerswerda and Rostock in the east, and Mölln and Solingen in the west, Germany has continued to struggle with certain pockets of neo-Nazi activity. Nevertheless, the advent of populist movements like Pegida and the AfD has stirred more overt xenophobia in public. *Der Spiegel* editor Dialika Neufeld recently noted how 'everyday life in many areas has become dangerous' (Neufeld 2017: 59) for ethnic minorities in Germany.[1] She highlights the increase in racially motivated attacks by extreme right-wing individuals across Germany with 23,555 cases in the past year, the highest number of reported incidents since records began:

> 1190 of these criminal acts related to incidents of racially motivated violence, grievous bodily harm, arson, and deprivation of liberty, which represented a rise of 300 per cent compared to 2010. In 2016 a third of Germans believed the country to be in danger of losing its national identity due to the rise in the immigrant population. 12 per cent were of the opinion that Germans were naturally superior to other nationalities, according to a study conducted by the University of Leipzig, which surveys political views across the country at regular intervals. That makes me nervous. It reminds me of how things used to be. (Neufeld 2017: 59)

Perhaps, in hindsight, Merkel's pronouncement, later echoed by former Prime Minister David Cameron in 2011 in the UK context, might seem prescient, in some quarters at least, as the AfD's electoral success might intimate. That the coalition discussions subsequently broke down in late November 2017 between the CDU, CSU, the Greens and

---

[1] All translations from the original German in this chapter are my own.

BUILDING BRIDGES: FATIH AKIN AND THE CINEMA OF INTERCULTURAL... 147

Liberals—the so-called 'Jamaica' Coalition, principally over disagreements about migration policy—merely underlines the problems the rise of the AfD has provoked. For now at least, Germany faces an uncertain future.

Following this renewed surge in nationalist sentiment, German director Fatih Akin's film have never seemed more relevant, or necessary, than they do now, as counterpoints to the prevailing atmosphere of ethnic tension. Akin's work has been widely revered on the A-list film festival circuit for many years since the Golden Bear-winning success of *Gegen die Wand/Head On* (2003) raised his profile significantly, following his early, mildly successful genre films, *Kurz und Schmerzlos/Short, Sharp Shock* (1998), *Im Juli/In July* (2000) and *Solino* (2001). He has adroitly negotiated a path that allows his films to appeal to diverse artistic, critical and popular audiences, making him one of the most engaging contemporary European filmmakers. The son of Turkish immigrants to Hamburg, though importantly considering himself German, Akin has frequently engaged cinematically with his Turkish heritage, including two documentaries about his parents' homeland: *Crossing the Bridge: The Sound of Istanbul* (2006) and *Müll im Garten Eden/Polluting Paradise* (2012). Consequently, many academics have focused on the perceived transnational inflections within his work.

Some scholars have highlighted the inherent problems with the concept of transnationalism. Steven Vertovec notes criticism of its 'analytical fuzziness, overuse, and lack of historical grounding' (2003: 641–42), while Briggs et al. describe it as a 'much abused word', pondering rhetorically its synonymity with globalisation or internationalism: 'If only the proliferating meanings could be sufficiently contained that we could all agree on a single naming system – if only, in fact, processes within and across nations were so easily divided into good and bad, left and right' (2008: 625). Therein lies the problem: it is too often poorly contextualised and used to promote a universalist framework that overlooks specific historical, geo-political or cultural milieus. Briggs et al. highlight its particular value in reiterating 'the importance of making the nation and nationalism an explicit question, and how the nation's ideologies and institutions are in play in countless obvious and not obvious ways in diverse struggles, symbols, institutions, and identities' (2008: 644). They stress:

> The nation itself has to be a question – not untrue and therefore trivial, but an ideology that changes over time, and whose precise elaboration at any point has profound effects on wars, economies, cultures, the movements of people, and relations of domination. (2008: 628)

148   O. EVANS

Transnationalism is significant by describing global interconnectedness and flows of people, capital, and cultures, while interrogating the national. In posing questions of the nation and nationalism, it is understandable how the transnational label is so frequently applied to Akin's oeuvre.

Vertovec valorises transnationalism in a different context, namely migration studies, finding Caroline Brettel's definition particularly insightful:

> As a theoretical construct about immigrant life and identity, transnationalism aptly suits the study of population movements in a world where improved modes of transportation as well as the images that are transmitted by means of modern telecommunications have shortened the social distance between sending and receiving countries. (Brettel in Vertovec 2003: 642)

Vertovec underlines how transnationalism captures the specific experience and consequences of migration, nevertheless a broader tendency exists to frame it as an always positive dynamic, especially when used without appropriate contextualisation. As events of 2015 underscore, and its direct impact upon the 2017 German Election, the shortening of social distance between countries in and of itself is not always unproblematic. The tragic loss of life in the Mediterranean and the ongoing tensions within the EU about how to tackle the situation cast a long shadow.

Akin scholarship tends to consider the perceived transnational dimension of his work as inherently positive. Randall Halle identifies a 'transnational normalcy' (2008: 167) where characters possess a 'strong foundation of existence in both places' (2008: 168), and Sabine Hake and Barbara Mennel interpret his films as representations of how multiple simultaneous affiliations unsettle links between 'home, belonging and cultural citizenship' (2012: 9) in positive ways. Akin himself has remarked: 'All of my characters are searching for something. They are searching for a better life' (Brockmann 2010: 485). The present chapter argues that Akin's films militate against any perception of a transient, variegated existence of multiple simultaneous affiliations as in any way normal or aspirational. As Hamid Naficy observes of 'accented cinema': '"Loneliness is an inevitable outcome of transnationality, and it finds its way into the desolate structures of feeling and lonely diegetic characters"' (Naficy in Ezra and Rowden 2006: 7). Establishing the better life Akin's characters seek, we argue, depends on building social capital situated within an ethnically diverse community, founded on establishing common ground and shared identities between cultural groups.

Akin's work importantly poses 'explicit question[s]' about Germany, whilst concurrently exploring the sense of loss that Ezra and Rowden identify as the motor of transnational cinema's narratives. Drawing on the work of Ted Cantle, British expert in intercultural relations and advocate of interculturalism, we argue that Akin be seen as the purveyor of a new cinema of intercultural dialogue, which reinforces optimism that robust intercultural identities *can* be forged within ethnically mixed societies. As Vertovec and Brettel imply, transnationalism has created ever more multi-culturally diverse societies. Nevertheless, we argue that the concept is unsuited to describe, or explain, what happens, or what needs to happen, *next* within those societies. Transnationalism explores neither the means of integration nor community cohesion. Conversely, interculturalism focuses *precisely* on those mechanisms for fostering dialogue and interaction between cultures *within* that multicultural context. In other words, it deals with the consequences of transnational flows. In the present context, if Akin's earlier work focuses primarily on mapping the sense of loss and loneliness his characters feel, his later films demonstrate opportunities for social capital to grow through intercultural dialogue.

An intercultural identity conceivably allows people to feel more rooted, rather than itinerant or liminal, to feel a sense of belonging hitherto deemed ephemeral or illusory, and to develop greater respect and under-standing for others. It does not preclude mobility and opportunities to travel, of course; such opportunities necessarily foster much richer inter-cultural dialogues, but the aspiration is to develop stronger social connec-tions within a community. Interculturalism works therefore to overcome the loneliness Naficy suggests transnationality creates. Akin's films pro-pose a model of cosmopolitanism, which, as Kwame Anthony Appiah pos-its, 'begins with the simple idea that in human community, as in national communities, we need to develop habits of coexistence: conversation in its older meaning, of living together, association' (2007: xvii). It is in such communities that nationalist forces can be resisted, where cosmopolitan values can flourish, and where, in the German context, intercultural dia-logue can refute Merkel's belief in a failed multiculturalism, while combat-ing the disturbing rise in overt xenophobia that Neufeld describes.

We maintain that Akin's voice is badly needed in Germany. His films simultaneously conjure and advocate spaces depicting a 'shared society' (Cantle 2012: 88), where dialogue between cultures can and *does* take place, within which challenges posed by globalisation, be they social, eco-nomic, or cultural, are surmountable. Akin's films evoke spaces recalling

150 O. EVANS

Homi Bhabha's 'third space', spaces that 'provide the terrain for elaborating strategies of selfhood – singular and communal – that initiate new signs of identity, and innovative sites of collaboration, and contestation, in the act of defining the idea of society itself' (1994: 1–2). Akin's work not only interrogates the German nation, but also challenges the rise of Western nationalist forces more broadly, which wilfully ignore the inevitable consequences of the way 'all Western economies are now characterised by some degree of "super" or "hyper" diversity' (Cantle 2012: 5).

In 2001, Ted Cantle, founder of the Institute of Community Cohesion, was asked by then Home Secretary David Blunkett to investigate the causes of violent ethnic disturbances that had shaken several towns across northern England. His most recent work focuses on the changing face of society under the increasing influence of globalisation. Cantle posits that 'multiculturalism is now much more complex and community relations are multifaceted, no longer simply revolving around majority/minority visible distinctions' (2012: 5). Nevertheless, he disagrees that multiculturalism has failed. On the contrary, he emphasises how the tide of globalisation cannot be reversed, that societies will inevitably become ever more multicultural. What are no longer fit for purpose in an era of super diversity, however, are the *policies* of multiculturalism that have created 'culturally and spatially distinct communities' (2012: 65), living alongside one another but with few, if any, meaningful points of contact. As well-meaning as UK multicultural policies were, originally devised in the 1960s to tackle Britain's first dramatic rise in racial tensions, they have, Cantle suggests, tended to create a society where different communities lead 'parallel lives' and a 'reluctance to promote interaction between them and the consequent fear and misunderstanding of the "other"' (Cantle 2012: 57) exist. A new mechanism, an intercultural framework, is required to build bridges between these communities to overcome the resultant 'plural monoculturalism' (Cantle 2012: 14).

Although Cantle focuses principally on Britain, the broader applicability of his thinking is axiomatic. Moreover, the elements he stresses in outlining why interculturalism is an important progression for generating better community cohesion chime with the specific themes and representations in Akin's films, which, we argue, attempt to represent how bridges can be built between discrete communities. As Cantle outlines:

> The concept of interculturalism is more about the creation of a culture of openness which effectively challenges the identity politics and entrenchment

BUILDING BRIDGES: FATIH AKIN AND THE CINEMA OF INTERCULTURAL... 151

of separate communities, based upon any notion of 'otherness'. But, it is also a dynamic process in which there will be some tensions and conflicts, as a necessary part of societal change in which people are able to positively envision ideas for multicultural and multifaith societies and where diversity and globalisation are recognised as permanent features of society, to be embraced, rather than feared. (2012: 142–3)

Interculturalism demands a new understanding of what comprises personal and collective identity, 'in particular, the development of common bonds on the basis of a more universal conception of humankind, replacing multiculturalist conceptions of primordial and "natural" distinctiveness and cultural fixity' (Cantle 2012: 143). All of Akin's films can be read through this intercultural lens. By celebrating rich, naturally occurring cultural interactions, usually in a German setting, they challenge the so-called German *Leitkultur*, a controversial term coined politically by conservative politician Friedrich Merz in 2000 to denote a dominant German culture akin to the 'cultural fixity' Cantle observes. Understandably, the *Leitkultur* concept has been hotly debated anew after the 2015 refugee crisis. A new cinema of intercultural dialogue will play an important role in that debate, especially following the AfD's electoral success in 2017.

TOWARDS A CINEMA OF INTERCULTURAL DIALOGUE

Mine Eren posits that the films *In July* and *Head On* 'question the possibility of simultaneous transnationalism and rootedness' (2012: 175). *In July* presents an idealised, if charming, celebration of pan-European mobility befitting its tone as a romantic comedy-cum-road movie. However, Akin's films generally underscore the potentially destructive forces at work for characters who inhabit what Deniz Göktürk, adapting Bhabha, calls a 'transnational third space' created by migration (Fenner 2012: 60). We argue, though, that while characters in Akin's earlier films might not always succeed in finding a better life, there is nevertheless hope that they might. Any sense of failure is mitigated in various ways, most usually by a personal epiphany about where one truly belongs. After *Head On*, although his protagonists encounter personal difficulties, even tragedy, the films are imbued with a stronger optimism that personal and communal belonging *is* possible, founded on nascent intercultural dialogue. The endings are often open, yet hint at a more optimistic narrative outside the frame. In *Head On*, having finally consummated their love, Cahit and

Sibell, the married couple of convenience, appear more robust emotionally and psychologically for their separate lives ahead. In *Soul Kitchen*, restaurateur Zinos has found new love in his newly solvent restaurant. In *Tschick/Goodbye Berlin* (2016), through his friendship with his enigmatic Russian-German classmate Tschick, who sometimes appears redolent of an exotic imaginary friend, and his first sexual awakening with the equally mysterious vagrant Isa, Maik has newfound self-esteem and resilience to cope with his deeply dysfunctional family. Finally, in *Auf der anderen Seite/ The Edge of Heaven* (2007), our principal case study, previously damaged parent–child relationships are in the process of repair.

Despite optimistic outcomes, Akin never downplays ethnic tensions. *Short, Sharp, Shock*, with its obvious indebtedness to early Scorsese and Tarantino with a twist of Mathieu Kassovitz's *La Haine* (1995) included for good measure, culminates in the violent deaths of two of the three protagonists, who have become embroiled in underworld activities. Significantly, Turkish-German Gabriel survives, although forced to flee to Turkey and sacrifice his German lover, Alice. In *Head On*, the physical, emotional and psychological damage inflicted on the protagonists stems from the loneliness transnationality inflicts. Akin's most recent film, *Aus dem Nichts/In the Fade* (2017), premiered in Cannes in May 2017, and recounts the revenge story of a German woman whose Kurdish husband and son are murdered in a neo-Nazi attack, the contemporary relevance of which is reinforced by the rise in hate crimes in Germany. Nevertheless, *The Edge of Heaven*, *Soul Kitchen* and *Goodbye Berlin* celebrate an alternative mode of existence grounded in the creation of bridging and bonding social capital within space and place, and possibilities of new ways of building community that erase, rather than reinforce, otherness, and are not predicated on national belonging. Many of the characters *do* find themselves with possibilities of attaining better lives, by forging new, or rebuilding existing, relationships. It does not derive from multiple affiliations oscillating between countries, but in small communities, by finding ways to integrate into local spaces that incorporate diverse, mutually enriching cultures; or kinship founded on new interactions between, often marginalised, individuals, who acquire a sense of belonging and greater self-efficacy within broader communities or networks.

In *Short, Sharp Shock*, the common bonds linking the protagonists—the Serbian Bobby, the Greek Costa and the Turk Gabriel—are central to the narrative. Although implicated in the underworld, they are well integrated socially to the extent that their ethnicity, albeit deliberately foregrounded in the Tarantino-esque opening sequence, is rarely significant. Their relationships are multicultural—Bobby and Gabriel love the same German woman, while Costa is dating Gabriel's sister—and presented as wholly natural in a city like Hamburg, which happily embraces its diversity in all of Akin's films set there. It is particularly significant that Costa, a Greek, is dating Idil, a Turk, in view of the tensions historically between both nations; the lovers here symbolise rapprochement. In many ways, Akin's debut anticipates the later comedy *Soul Kitchen*, which centres on the titular restaurant, run by the Greek Zinos, played by Adam Bousdoukos, who plays Costa in the earlier film. The restaurant is home to a diverse intercultural clientele of colourful characters, who might be outsiders anywhere else but here. Asked in interview if he considered himself German or Turkish, Akin replied that he was a Hamburger: 'That's a compromise, but it's relevant. My social circle comprises diverse cultures, and something completely new is developing. I call it Hamburg' (Akin 2011: 197). Intriguingly, Akin's metaphorical use of Hamburg echoes Bhabha's 'third space' in which cultural hybridity 'enables other positions to emerge' (Rutherford 1990: 211).

Akin's films are underpinned by humanist principles celebrating the virtues of exploring, and developing, common cause, and thus generally highlight universal human concerns. His position evokes Frantz Fanon, who professed to be '[battling] for the creation of a human world – that is a world of reciprocal recognitions' (cited in Bhabha 1994: 8). In *Polluting Paradise*, which documents the building of a controversial landfill site above his grandfather's home village of Çamburnu on the Black Sea, the disastrous impact upon the livelihood of the locals and their environment resonates with worldwide concerns about the way that the self-interest of global business, with the connivance of local political opportunism, can ride roughshod over the concerns of ordinary people. When the villagers angrily confront environment ministry officials, after effluent has escaped the plant and seeped into the water supply, which naturally endangers the tea crops, the camera captures the scene with a series of long takes that allow us to reflect upon the universality of such concerns globally. Their anger is easy to understand, and sympathise with.

Akin's concern for the villagers' plight in *Polluting Paradise* is personal, but he connects it to the wider world. A Hamburger he may call himself, rather than Turkish or German, but in many respects his films invite us to recognise, and embrace, the reality of a society characterised by super diversity and global interconnection. They acknowledge a

154   O. EVANS

universal interconnectedness that should be embraced at local, regional, national or international level. His films trace a journey from parallel lives to more integrated and open existences, and imagine or celebrate the virtues of an enriching dialogue and interaction between cultures, wherever they may be situated. They highlight the common ground that exists between them, whether it be political, socio-economic or cultural. Importantly, that dialogue does not preclude disagreement, so his films can be seen to depict 'innovative sites of collaboration, *and* contestation' (Bhabha 1994: 1, my emphasis). Without doubt, *In July* is his most idealised representation of intercultural dialogue, tracing trainee teacher Daniel's odyssey across Europe in pursuit of true love. He believes it to be embodied by a young Turkish woman, Melek, before realising his feelings for travelling companion, the German hippy Juli. Daniel's improbable journey to find love on the banks of the Bosporus is largely unhindered by national borders, but not without obstacles—he is at various times robbed, drugged and arrested—yet the film is an endearing intercultural fairy-tale. Initially rather conservative and materialistic, Daniel is transformed through his experiences, the different cultures, and various interactions with people along the way, such as the Siren Luna, as well as Juli herself, in ways that, the film implies in conclusion, have enriched and changed his life forever.

Goodbye Berlin, the first film Akin has directed from another's source material, namely Wolfgang Herrndorf's novel, is also the first project he did not produce. Nevertheless, the theme of disparate characters coming together bears his hallmark. We are presented with a touching coming-of-age tale, which echoes *In July*'s fairy-tale road-movie qualities. However, in the execution it is a much more effective story of an intercultural connection emerging, told from an adolescent perspective, at a time when German society has been interrogating itself about its multicultural identity. In Akin's now more experienced hands, the film beguiles initially, evoking a mixture of *Ferris Bueller's Day Off* (Hughes, 1986) and *Go Trabi Go* (Timm, 1990). Despite his initial antipathy towards new kid in town, Tschick, a Russian-German whose Asiatic appearance marks him as very clearly 'other', an *Assi*— German slang for asocial—as the class call him, rich misfit Maik, himself dubbed 'Psycho' by his peers, embarks on a road trip in a stolen Lada. A metaphorical journey ensues through the east German landscape, ostensibly en route to Tschick's grandfather in Wallachia, a region in Romania: appropriately for the narrative, the German idiom *mitten in der Walachei* translates as 'in the middle of nowhere'. The trip not only brings the two teenage misfits closer together through a series of picaresque escapades and a cassette recording of Richard Clayderman's 'Ballad for Adeline', but also into contact with a series of other marginalised, eccentric characters, such as the group of aristocrats on bikes (*Adel auf Radel*) who cycle from stately home to stately home, and by contrast, the large family in the slightly ramshackle provincial village with cobbled streets, who earn their dessert by answering general knowledge questions.

The film underscores how interculturalism recognises that '"difference" is not just confined to minorities, nor defined by "race"' (Cantle 2012: 82), but all forms of 'othering'. Intercultural dialogue thus seeks to find ways to challenge the 'prejudice, discrimination, hate crimes, community tensions and conflicts' that reflect the 'many dimensions of difference' (Cantle 2012: 168). Tschick, who teases Maik throughout about being gay and masquerades as being attracted by all the girls in their class, ultimately comes out as gay himself, in a touching scene as Maik bandages his friend's injured foot. In a voice over, in hindsight Maik professes not to be surprised, and it has no bearing on their relationship, where once it might have. Meanwhile Tschick, ostracised as 'other' earlier, is initially antagonistic towards the homeless Isa, ironically calling *her* an *Assi*, before eventually warming to their new travelling companion as the three frolic in the reservoir in the Harz. The simple act of spending time together enables these outsiders, initially hostile to one another, to learn to appreciate their differences, finding the ties that bind them together. As Appiah puts it: 'People are different…and there is much to learn from our differences' (2007: xiii).

The youngsters epitomise intercultural dialogue's potential to find, or at least explore the possibility of, a shared identity and sense of belonging. All are marginalised and do not appear to have stable family support. Maik's mother, with whom he is admittedly close, is an alcoholic, while his father has a younger mistress and leaves Maik alone with 200 euro to take her away 'on business' for two weeks; Tschick only ever mentions his grandfather in the context of his desire to visit Wallachia; and Isa eventually departs in search of her half-sister in Prague. Moreover, as befits the rites-of-passage narrative, the boys question their sexuality, and Maik experiences his first sexual awakening with Isa at the reservoir. When the two boys lie on the ground beneath the wind turbine in the countryside, gazing up at the stars and pondering if there are two aliens somewhere in the galaxy just like them, escaping on a similar trip, their friendship is sealed. The scene is echoed later when Maik, Tschick and Isa climb up to the hilltop ruin in the Harz mountains and resolve that no matter what befalls them in the future, they will rendezvous at this same spot fifty years hence. That Tschick carves their initials and the date into the rock, as others have before them, symbolically seals their bond. It is the last time we see the three together. Isa leaves for Prague shortly thereafter, borrowing the money she needs for her fare from Maik, and following the film's climactic accident, Tschick flees into the night to avoid being put in a home, but now in possession of Maik's expensive jacket, Tschick's admiration for which brought them together in the first place. Although Maik is alone again at the end, like Daniel in *In July* he has been transformed by the experience. His unrequited passion at the film's outset for the most popular girl in his class is unrequited no longer. But now he is utterly indifferent towards her, wondering only where his friend is.

Whilst Cantle acknowledges that understanding and empathy for the 'other' can be generated to some extent through film and literature, he suggests nevertheless that 'meaningful interchanges are difficult to develop – and sustain – at an indirect and remote level' (2012: 131). However, in light of the nationalist turn in Western Europe and a growing support for right-wing populist ideologies, there is surely a need to model intercultural dialogue in some way, and highlight its potential to engineer change, while simultaneously reflecting how truly diverse modern societies are. Film and media have the capacity to fulfil this function. In this context of establishing a model of intercultural dialogue, one might argue that the settings conjured by Akin are cinematically heterotopic in nature, in that they establish spaces that enact intercultural dialogue.

In his critical analysis of Foucault's inchoate concept, Peter Johnson describes heterotopia as 'spaces of, and for, the imagination' (2013: 798), spaces that, in Foucault's eyes, somehow reflect and simultaneously contest the space we live in, thus facilitating a change in perspective: 'It is the space in which we are "drawn outside ourselves"' (Johnson 2006: 78). By conjuring heterotopic spaces on screen for people to be drawn out of themselves, Akin's oeuvre provides a fresh perspective on Germany and celebrates its postwar multicultural nature, and the enrichment its ethnic diversity brings. *Solino*, for example, which is based on the true story of Germany's first pizzeria, underlines that Germany has long been a land of migration, a point echoed in *Soul Kitchen*, not only by the composition of the clientele, or the range of food that the gypsy chef Shayn prepares, but also, as Roger Hillman and Vivian Silvey (2012) observe, through the film's diegetic and non-diegetic music. The enrichment that cross-cultural exchange brings to communities also underpins *Crossing the Bridge*, which explores the conflation of myriad musical styles and forms in Istanbul, ranging from Western-inflected rock and indie music via hip hop and electronica to gypsy music from the east. Alexander Hacke of eclectic industrial German band Einstürzende Neubauten, whose own work has been heavily influenced inter alia by world music, narrates the film with cosmopolitan delight. Although the film's specific focus is Istanbul, the universal significance of such intercultural dialogue, and Akin's belief in its positive value, is implicit.

The way in which the spaces of interaction at the core of Akin's films operate, aligns with Cantle's advocacy of 'contact theory' as key in the development of intercultural dialogue. Developed in the 1950s by Allport, whose 'hypothesis was that bringing together the members of different groups, getting them working towards common goals on an equal footing, would lead to intergroup prejudice being reduced' (Cantle 2012: 145), contact theory has subsequently shown that:

> contact between groups does bring about positive (or at least less negative) attitudes, reduces prejudice and builds lasting friendships. The creation of intergroup friendships is seen as more important than simple cooperation. (Cantle 2012: 145)

'Intergroup friendships' are central to Akin's films. As he puts it, 'that is Hamburg', which we see in *Short, Sharp, Shock* and *Head On*. But it is also Istanbul in *Crossing the Bridge* and *Edge of Heaven*, or Duisburg in *Solino*. Or Berlin and provincial eastern Germany in *Goodbye Berlin*. Even in *The Cut*, arguably Akin's weakest film, the Armenian Christian protagonist, Nazareth, who narrowly survives the genocide that claims most of his family and friends, is aided by a network of people from other ethnic groups and nationalities in his quest to locate his twin daughters, an odyssey that takes him, rather implausibly, from Armenia via Turkey and Cuba to the USA.

The celebration of positive interactions in Akin's films does not preclude the representation of the problems and obstacles that exist. On the contrary, in holding up a mirror to Germany to remind it of its positive traditions as a land of migration, Akin also reflects upon the problems globalisation has caused, compared to when he was younger:

158 O. EVANS

> Germany was a different country then. I was born in an era, when we were *Gastarbeiter.* Today we are immigrants, but there seem to have been fewer problems with integration than today. Perhaps that's because of the media. When we were little children, there were three television channels, naturally all in German, two Turkish newspapers and Radio Cologne, that broadcast thirty minutes in Turkish, then came the Greeks. Today, there are Turkish internet sites, you can get hold of every Turkish newspaper, and satellite television. The result is a global ghettoization. In those days, you were challenged much more to integrate; today you don't even have to speak German any longer. (Akin 2011: 14)

Akin's identification of a 'global ghettoization' echoes what Cantle calls the 'paradox of diversity', whereby 'the more diverse societies have become and the more people have been exposed to difference and become accustomed to it, the more they seem to retreat into their own identity' (2012: 14). Such a retreat might help to explain the broader nationalist turn in Germany and the rise in support for the AfD.

Head On provides the clearest representation of the problems plural monoculturalism causes in Akin's work. Sibel's highly conservative and fundamentalist family suffocate her to such an extent that she makes several suicide attempts. They eventually disown her when Cahit, by now her husband, commits the manslaughter of one of Sibel's German lovers. All of which reinforces Akin's films' focus on relationships, and the spaces where different cultures interact, but also where they do not. Once she overcomes her self-destructive urges, Sibel escapes, making a new life for herself with a Turkish husband and child in Turkey. Nevertheless, her story underlines Akin's aspiration to create narratives that show the potentially destructive nature of 'global ghettoisation', the possibility of loneliness and isolation, and the attendant need to collapse the cultural boundaries between communities living parallel lives, and the generational tensions that exist within them.

The Edge of Heaven

The epitome of successful intercultural dialogue in his oeuvre, which addresses both the problems inherent within, and the potential of, super diverse societies, is *The Edge of Heaven,* winner of the Best Screenplay award at Cannes in 2007, where it premiered in competition. The second part of the so-called 'love, death and the devil' trilogy, the film responds

BUILDING BRIDGES: FATIH AKIN AND THE CINEMA OF INTERCULTURAL... 159

to aspects of the narrative both in *Head On* and *Crossing the Bridge*, with which it has much in common. By virtue of its nuanced characterisation and the sensitive focus on intercultural dialogue, *The Edge of Heaven* remains his most convincing and engaging film hitherto.

Margaret Littler has argued convincingly about the 'transformative cultural potential of minority writing in Germany' (2007: 178), specifically the work of Turkish-German writers, by drawing on Deleuze and Guattari's notion of 'minor literature'. In their own analysis of Kafka's work, the philosophers talk of the way minor literature 'deterritorialises' language, making it 'vibrate with a new intensity' (Deleuze and Guattari 1986: 19). By freeing language from its origins in a particular identity, history or geographical location, they argue affect is produced that enables multiple new identifications. Consequently, Littler suggests, minority literature in German 'gesture[s] towards new possibilities of community' and 'imagine[s] identities yet to come' (2007: 179). It is axiomatic how Littler's thesis can be related to Turkish-German cinema in general, and Akin's cinema specifically, as possessing its own transformative potential for modelling new modes of communal interaction.

Littler's thesis, which focuses on minor literature's capacity to creatively reimagine community formation, anticipates Ranjit Sondhi's belief that interculturalism can '"create a new living language"' (Sondhi in Cantle 2012: 152) in order to generate:

> 'the space and opportunity and inclination for two different entities to know a little more about how to reassure and interest the other while also avoiding those things that might insult or alarm them, thus minimising the potential obstacles to the transaction. But it is more than just a tool of communication – it is a process of mutual learning and joint growth.' (Sondhi in Cantle 2012: 152)

In creating what we propose as a cinema of intercultural dialogue, Akin depicts just such a 'new living language' in action, a minor cinematic language to convey a 'space and opportunity and inclination' for different cultures to come together. It underpins each film, but it is in *The Edge of Heaven* that we see a more concerted effort to illustrate some of the obstacles to, but also most crucially the opportunities arising from, the intercultural transaction Sondhi and Cantle posit. Akin does not ignore that the 'intercultural city is not always an easy place to be' (Cantle 2012: 147), since, as Bhabha underlines, the 'third space' is a site of contestation as much as communication.

160   O. EVANS

In *The Edge of Heaven* language is deterritorialised in that each of the six characters at some point inhabits a language that is not their own or with which they are not entirely comfortable. This deterritorialisation is especially evident when Ali, Yeter and Nejat have supper on Ali's balcony and the conversation ebbs and flows between German and Turkish, or the scenes between Lotte, Ayten and Susanne, where English is the lingua franca. It is also reflected in the different nuances of the film's contrasting titles in German, Turkish and English, reflecting the problems languages can pose and the different, not always complementary, perspectives that inhere within them.[2] The pivotal Nejat, arguably a cipher for Akin himself, is the possible exception in this respect, although he too suffers a deterritorialisation of sorts, when he displays unfamiliarity with his indigenous culture. Stopping at a petrol station en route to the Black Sea, he admits his ignorance of popular singer Kazim Koyuncu. Akin himself spoke of the 'insurmountable divide' in terms of 'language, mentality and social environment' (2011: 53) separating him from his parents' homeland when he was younger, only gradually appropriating more of his indigenous culture with each new film he has made in Turkey.

One could argue that the linguistic deterritorialisation in *The Edge of Heaven* is compensated for by a 'reterritorialisation of sense', which Deleuze and Guattari deem both cultural and physical (1986: 20). Akin uses cinematic language in the film's first two sections to underline the problems that parallel lives can cause, but the concluding section then demonstrates how the deterritorialisation of language can create a new language, a reterritorialised means of intercultural dialogue, imbued with a spiritual quality perhaps, that can bring people together in a newly imagined community founded on common bonds, an absence of prejudice and a Fanonian 'reciprocal recognition' (Bhabha 1994: 8). But what cinema can also do is represent, and create, a heterotopic space where that new language, and new community, can thrive. In other words, it can create a badly needed 'vision of a shared society and mixed communities' (Cantle 2012: 174). In the German bookshop in Istanbul, therefore, which Nejat, the Professor of German of Turkish extraction, eventually buys from the homesick German proprietor, Akin presents a concrete *cultural milieu* in and around which that new community can be built, where social capital can be generated. These Bhabhaist 'third spaces' in his later films emerge

---

[2] The titles are *Auf der anderen Seite*, *The Edge of Heaven* and *Yasamin Kiyisinda* (On the Shore of Life).

BUILDING BRIDGES: FATIH AKIN AND THE CINEMA OF INTERCULTURAL... 161

as rallying points for diasporic souls, public places where human beings can interact, irrespective of ethnicity, age or gender, where essentialising labels are eschewed and otherness is elided and presented instead as 'a potentially positive experience that can bring creative...advantage to society as a whole' (Cantle 2012: 152). In Akin's later films, we find liminal spaces where new possibilities for an intercultural community and the generation of social capital are located: the aforementioned bookshop in *The Edge of Heaven*, the restaurant in *Soul Kitchen*, and even the soap factory in *The Cut* (2014) or the Lada in *Goodbye Berlin*.

Narratively and stylistically, *The Edge of Heaven* exposes the extent to which transnationally itinerant figures are emotionally damaged by that experience. Thus Akin appears to counter the suggestion that this mode of existence is necessarily desirable or beneficial. Akin the filmmaker, celebrated at international film festivals, might arguably be cited as an epitome of what Halle calls a 'transnational inhabitant' (2008: 164), but by his own admission, the director has only very belatedly been able to feel more at home in Turkey. His position is a much more privileged one than that of his characters. Akin is blessed by the agency that derives from a successful global film career, but it is a mistake to equate the transnational auteur with his characters, who often appear deracinated in potentially harmful, or disorientating, ways. *The Edge of Heaven* advocates instead a rooted interculturalism.

The film tells three densely interwoven stories connecting three pairs of characters, father and son Nejat and Ali, mother and daughter Jeter and Ayten, and mother and daughter Susanne and Lotte, where, in each case, the parent–child relationship is strained in some way. Nejat, the German professor in Hamburg, lives with his father in Bremen, but often seems embarrassed by Ali, a former *Gastarbeiter*, especially when he invites Jeter, a prostitute, with whom Ali has slept, to live with them as his paid companion. Jeter, for her part, has not heard from her daughter, Ayten, for a long time, believing that she is studying in Turkey. In fact, Ayten belongs to a supposed terrorist group, and believes her mother to be working in a shoe shop in Bremen. Susanne and Lotte's bond is equally conflicted, seemingly because the once hippy mother, who hitchhiked to India via Istanbul as a young woman, has become conservative in middle age and unable to tolerate the same traits in her daughter. There are hints, too, of Susanne's unease about Lotte's sexuality, which becomes evident when her daughter falls in love with Ayten, who has fled the authorities in Turkey to come to find her mother. The intergenerational tensions

162   O. EVANS

between each group of characters might also be understood within the film's broader intercultural context as a whole, founded as they are in each case on different cultural positions and perceptions. As such, the film further develops the theme of Sibel's rebellion in *Head On*, albeit in more nuanced ways.

The narrative structure is tautly and carefully composed into three sections—'Yeter's Death', 'Lotte's Death', and 'Edge of Heaven'—incorporating parallels, echoes and repetitions, which serve to highlight how each character lacks agency, effectively trapped and prey to potentially destructive forces they cannot escape because of their isolation. Indeed, the first two sections of the film are replete with moments where characters, who seek one another, never quite meet. For example, Nejat endeavours to locate Ayten in Istanbul, after his father accidentally kills her mother in a drunken argument. In the process, he encounters Lotte, who is searching for her lover. In order to protect Ayten, Lotte gives a false name of the woman she is looking for, little realising that they both seek the same person. In the film's opening section, we see a student asleep in Nejat's lecture on Goethe, only later discovering that it is Ayten, who has just arrived illegally in Germany and has nowhere to stay. But the film's most poignant example of the emotionally damaging ramifications of a transnational existence, occurs when Jeter and Ayten pass within metres of one another, while both are travelling to Bremen, the latter (in Lotte's car) searching for the former (in a tram), wholly oblivious to their proximity. It is clear to the viewer that a failure, or inability, to communicate openly is at the root of each tragedy.

Moments of happiness or fulfilment are ephemeral for these characters, reflecting the loneliness Naficy ascribes to transnationality. Ali and Jeter share some tender moments of companionship, over and above their commodified intercourse in Bremen's red-light district, but their attempts to forge a conventional relationship founder fatally on the old man's alcoholism. Ali is imprisoned for manslaughter and later deported to Turkey. Similarly, Lotte and Ayten are shown enjoying a passionately hedonistic, yet fleeting, evening together in a pulsating Hamburg nightclub, before Ayten, too, is later deported when her plea for asylum is rejected, ostensibly on the grounds that Turkey's application to join the EU will guarantee the young political activist's life is not endangered. Lotte then sets out, against her mother's wishes, to find where her lover is imprisoned in Turkey. By contrast, Nejat and Susanne appear to be loners: the latter divorced, and the former teased by his father for not having a woman in his life. Hanna Schygulla imbues Susanne with a world-weary melancholy, which culminates in the overwhelming outpouring of grief in an Istanbul hotel room at the loss of her daughter, a montage sequence all the more affecting for being filmed from a fixed high-angle position that cinematically forces the viewer to intrude voyeuristically on her anguish. When both loners first meet in the hotel bar, Susanne asks Nejat how he recognised her. 'You're the saddest person in here,' he says. When Nejat first travels to Istanbul and is offered a place to stay, he assures his cousin that he likes his solitude, and disowns his father for killing Jeter. 'Someone who commits murder cannot be my father', he says, without any apparent sense of loss or regret, being more concerned to find Ayten and support her ongoing studies in order to expiate his father's guilt by proxy.

The characters' inherent loneliness in the first two sections is reinforced stylistically by the cinematography. The film is shot and edited in a very sedate way, with a predominance of long shots underlining the static nature of the camera, and thus forming an ironic counterpoint to the supposed benefits of transnational mobility. In carefully composed frames, the characters are often presented as trapped, hemmed in by their surroundings, an aesthetic redolent of Fassbinder's films, in turn influenced by Sirkian melodrama, where the dense mise en scène often suffocates. In *The Edge of Heaven*, the framing of characters in this way underlines their lack of agency, how their apparent mobility does not necessarily bring any sense of freedom. On the contrary, they are isolated, vulnerable, and prey to destructive, and even fatal, forces they cannot ultimately escape by themselves.

Crucially, having initially shown potential new relationships founder on circumstance—Lotte and Ayten, Ali and Jeter, and even hints that Jeter could become a surrogate mother for Nejat—the film then offers hopeful glimpses that cross-cultural support networks can be developed. In this respect, Akin diverges from Fassbinder's resolutely pessimistic outlook on relationships and society. *The Edge of Heaven* suggests that new possibilities for community, as Littler puts it, do exist, based on an intercultural dialogue that also has the potential to heal generational conflict. It posits that a space is required that can bring disparate, diasporic souls together, a space to help generate social capital through newly conceived interpersonal relationships founded on mutual concerns and a respect for difference. In *The Edge of Heaven*, that space is the German bookshop that Nejat stumbles upon. It becomes the base for his search for Ayten; it is where he meets Lotte; and then subsequently it is where Susanne contacts

164   O. EVANS

him. She ends up lodging with Nejat, just like her daughter, while she finishes the job Lotte started by helping Ayten rebuild her life. Thus, the tiny bookshop brings the disparate narrative threads together. It becomes the spiritual home, as it were, of a nascent intercultural community and a 'new kind of living language' (Cantle 2012: 152). In the subsequent *Soul Kitchen*, such a community and language already exist and thrive in Hamburg thanks to its inherent cultural hybridity.

The concluding section of *The Edge of Heaven* envisions intercultural bonds being forged between people, at a simple human level that transcends all forms of alterity, and thus holds within them the potential to create a shared society through dialogue and interaction. The mutual loss of Lotte reconciles Susanne and Ayten, the former effectively becoming a surrogate mother for the latter. Indeed, for Nejat, who was raised by his father after losing his mother as a baby, Susanne similarly adopts a pseudo-maternal role, helping him realise his haste in ostracising Ali. As he has supported her during her grief, so she now helps him come to terms with his own when, during the festival of *Bayram*, a Turkish national holiday celebrating the story of Ibrahim/Abraham, they discuss the story shared between the Islamic and Christian faiths in which a father's love for his son is tested. In the context of Akin's film as the epitome of a cinema of intercultural dialogue, *Bayram* is an effective reminder of the importance of emphasising what is shared culturally, rather than what divides.

At the film's climax, the cinematic space opens up for the characters, reflecting a greater sense of freedom, a broader perspective, and the elimination of prejudice. When discussing *Bayram*, Nejat and Susanne are captured in medium shot in front of the door frame, rather than through it and at a distance, and then more emphatically in close up, one of the first times this type of shot is used in the entire film. The sequence's final shot is of both characters framed against the open window with sunlight streaming in, underscoring how Akin's greater optimism that a better life is attainable infuses the scene. Nejat's subsequent journey to the Black Sea coast in search of his father is rendered with long, flowing travelling shots and sweeping pans that not only capture the beauty of Turkey, but also signify the more positive mood. The film culminates in the only extreme close up, of Nejat's face on the beach, followed by a long take over which the credits roll, as he sits on the beach waiting for his father's return, the diegetic sound of the water lapping on the shore is the sole thing we hear. Tellingly, the frame is open now, hinting at the reconciliation ahead, which simultaneously mirrors the burgeoning bond between surrogate mother and daughter, Susanne and Ayten, formerly antagonists now united in loss. When they meet again in the bookshop, it is rendered initially in the type of framing long shot so typical of the film, before the camera moves closer until they embrace, symbolising the rupture of the suffocating frame and the growing bond between them.

These moments encapsulate Akin's belief in intercultural dialogue's capacity to unite people and erode plural monoculturalist attitudes, and thereby to militate powerfully against both a sense of transnational contingency, and the populist and nationalist forces within German society.

CONCLUSION

As a filmmaker, Fatih Akin is motivated by a desire to demonstrate what Muir has called a 'new discourse around shared identity' (Muir in Cantle 2012:76). He describes *Soul Kitchen* as a film about '*Heimat*, but not one that is geographically determined, so much as a spiritual condition in the head and the heart' (2012: 202). It is an apposite description of each of his films, however, which focus on protagonists looking for somewhere to belong, for a home, but not one predicated on national boundaries. Even if Tschick ostensibly takes Maik on a fruitless odyssey in a stolen Lada through provincial eastern Germany to try to locate Wallachia, it is simply a means to an end, to carve out time and space and an opportunity for two outsiders to forge friendship. *In July* depicts Daniel's spiritual voyage of a self-discovery, which just happens to take him across Europe to Istanbul to find what was already in front of him in Germany. This is the spiritual *Heimat* Akin is talking about. Although Halle has proposed Akin as the 'first filmmaker to put forward images that truly imagine the possibility of life as a transnational inhabitant' proposing 'a new form of habitation' (2008: 164) that is grounded in the 'characters' strong foundation of existence in both places' (2008: 168), is that really what *Solino, Head On* or *The Edge of Heaven* tell us? In truth, Akin's films suggest that his view of home is not predicated on a national or transnational basis: it is principally where the heart is, in family, friendship, companionship, and in conversation 'in its older meaning of living together' (Appiah 2007: xvii). His films explore how individuals, and groups, from different cultural or ethnic backgrounds find ways to co-exist and connect using the 'new kind of living language' Sondhi describes. It is a mode of communication we see emerging in *The Edge of Heaven, Soul Kitchen* and *Goodbye Berlin*. Akin makes no pretence that such co-existence is easy, as the violence in his films underscores, most notably in *Short, Sharp, Shock, Head On* and *The Edge of Heaven*, as well as the recent *In the Fade*. Nevertheless, his films

166   O. EVANS

chime with Gerard Bouchard's understanding of interculturalism as a 'search for balance and mediation between often-competing principles, values and expectations':

> In this sense, [interculturalism] is a sustained effort aimed at connecting majorities and minorities, continuity and diversity, identity and rights, reminders of the past and visions of the future. It calls for new ways of co-existing within and beyond differences at all levels of collective life. (Bouchard in Cantle 2012: 153)

After the recent violence in three of Germany's most ethnically diverse cities, *Der Spiegel* suggested that the state must 'search for and foster discourse between and within social groups' (Baumgärtner et al. 2017: 14), in a striking echo of Ted Cantle's proposals for interculturalism after the riots in northern England in 2001. Fatih Akin's cinema of intercultural dialogue furnishes Germany with welcome pictures of a successful multicultural society to offset the disturbing media images from Cologne, Berlin and Hamburg. His films provide stories to counterbalance reports of the electoral success of the AfD, the chauvinistic utterances of certain segments of society and the more overt displays of racism that have returned to haunt everyday life in parts of Germany. His nuanced, objective views of home do much to celebrate the richness of Germany's ethnic diversity, by shifting the emphasis away from national and transnational concepts, and the anti-immigration rhetoric of the AfD and Pegida, onto individuals and communities, and ways to break down parallel lives by building bridges and finding communal spaces for those interactions and connections to take place. In so doing, his films militate against the rise of nationalist sentiment and any suggestions that Germany has failed as a multicultural nation, and propose instead a more positive view of home.

BIBLIOGRAPHY

Akin, Fatih. 2011. *Im Clinch: Die Geschichte meiner Filme* Reinbek: Rowohlt.
Appiah, Kwame A. 2007. *Cosmopolitanism: Ethics in a World of Strangers.* London: Penguin.
Baumgärtner, M. et al. 2017. Abgebrannt *Der Spiegel* 29: 12–20.
Bhabha, Homi. 1994. *The Location of Culture* London and New York: Routledge.
Briggs, Laura, Gladys McCormick and J.T. Wray. 2008. Transnationalism: A Category of Analysis. *American Quarterly*, 60 (3): 625–648.

Brockmann, S. 2010. *A Critical History of German Film*, Rochester: Camden House.

Cantle, Ted. 2012. *Interculturalism: The New Era of Cohesion and Diversity.* Basingstoke: Macmillan.

Connolly, Kate. 2010. Angela Merkel declares death of German multiculturalism. *The Guardian.* 17 October 2010. https://www.theguardian.com/world/2010/oct/17/angela-merkel-germany-multiculturalism-failures. Accessed 17 July 2017. Accessed 16th November 2017.

Deleuze, Gilles and Felix Guattari. 1986. *Kafka: Toward a Minor Literature* Minneapolis and London: University of Minnesota Press.

Eren, Mine. 2012. Cosmopolitan Filmmaking: Fatih Akin's *In July* and *Head-On.* In *Turkish German Cinema in the New Millennium: Sites, Sounds, and Screens.* Ed. Hake, Sabine and B. Mennel. New York and Oxford: Berghahn, 175–185.

Ezra, Elizabeth and Terry Rowden. 2006. General Introduction: What is Transnational Cinema? In *Transnational Cinema: The Film Reader.* Ed. Ezra, Elizabeth and Terry Rowden. London and New York: Routledge, 1–12.

Fenner, Angelica. 2012. Roots and Routes of the Diasporic Documentarian: A Psychogeography of Fatih Akin's *We Forgot to Go Back.* In *Turkish German Cinema in the New Millennium: Sites, Sounds, and Screens.* Ed. Hake, Sabine and B. Mennel. New York and Oxford: Berghahn, 59–71.

Hake, Sabine and B. Mennel. 2012. *Turkish German Cinema in the New Millennium: Sites, Sounds, and Screens.*New York and Oxford: Berghahn.

Halle, Randall. 2008. *German Film after Germany: Towards a Transnational Aesthetic* Urbana and Chicago: University of Illinois Press.

Hillman, Roger and Vivien Silvey, 2012. Remixing Hamburg: Transnationalism in Fatih Akin's *Soul Kitchen.* In *Turkish German Cinema in the New Millennium: Sites, Sounds, and Screens.* Ed. Hake, Sabine and B. Mennel. New York and Oxford: Berghahn, 186–197.

Johnson, Peter. 2006. Unravelling Foucault's "different spaces". *History of the Human Sciences.*19 (4): 75–90.

Johnson, Peter. 2013. The Geographies of Heterotopia. *Geography Compass,* 7 (11): 790–803.

Littler, Margaret. 2007. Cultural Memory and Identity Formation in the Berlin Republic. In *Contemporary German Fiction.* Ed. Taberner, Stuart. Cambridge: Cambridge University Press, 177–195.

Neufeld, Dialika. 2017. Unter der Haut. *Der Spiegel* 37: 58–64.

Rutherford, Jonathan. 1990. The Third Space: Interview with Homi Bhabha. *Identity, Community, Culture, Difference.* Ed. Rutherford, Jonathan. London: Lawrence and Wishart, 207–221.

Smoltczyk, Alexander. 2017. Einschlag ins Kontor. *Der Spiegel,* 25: 11–17.

Vertovec, Steven. 2003. Migration and Other Modes of Transnationalism: Towards a Conceptual Cross-Fertilization. *The International Migration Review.* 37 (3): 641–665.

CHAPTER 9

"Kapitalismus tötet": Liquid National Identities in the Cinema of the Berlin School

Anna Batori

Nearly thirty years have passed since the unprecedented unification of the German Democratic Republic (GDR) with the Federal Republic of Germany (FRG) under a single democratic political aegis of the new German state. The fall of the Berlin Wall not only opened a new chapter in the history of Europe but also raised questions as to what now constituted the nature of German national consciousness: the 'New German Question'. In the twenty-seven years since 1990, Germany has not only become one of the economic founding stones of the European Union (EU) but also a prosperous, modern and liberal multicultural state. The infamous wartime stigmatisation of Germany as a nationalist, right-wing nation has given way to a new reputation for *Willkommenskultur* (welcoming culture) so prevalent that Germany is now the number one destination for the asylum-seekers arriving from the Middle East and Africa (see Trauner and Turton 2017), even if it has come at the cost of increasing international and domestic criticism of its handling of the current refugee crisis (see Holmes and Castañeda 2016). While the 'New German Question' prompted radical shifts in German foreign policy to project a multinational image on the world stage, domestically, the socio-historical

A. Batori (✉)
Babeş-Bolyai University, Cluj-Napoca, Romania
e-mail: anna.batori@gmx.net

© The Author(s) 2018
J. Harvey (ed.), *Nationalism in Contemporary Western European Cinema*, Palgrave European Film and Media Studies,
https://doi.org/10.1007/978-3-319-73667-9_9

169

issues that continue to divide the society along imaginary East–West borderlines receive far less attention in German cultural discourse. Nostalgia for pre-unification West Germany and the GDR may be occasionally topical in the media, but the question as to what constitutes a united, twenty-first-century German identity in the midst of the current European refugee crises remains unanswered. Does the East–West divide continue to split the national psyche? Or has Germany achieved Helmut Kohl's dream of a united, wealthy society with a renewed, rehabilitated sense of nationhood?

To answer these questions, this chapter focuses on the films of Christian Petzold to examine how post-wall national self-image is represented in the productions of the Berlin School— a contemporary politico-aesthetic movement that includes German filmmakers such as Angela Schanelec, Christoph Hochhäusler, Benjamin Heisenberg, Maren Ade and Ulrich Köhler. While the New Berlin School has no explicit manifesto, common characteristics bind them together into an auteur-centred, coherent movement that rejects mainstream clichés to find new notions of national self-image framed by present-day struggles with post-wall capitalist structure and ideology.

To help model filmic manifestations of post-wall German identity, this chapter offers a liminal identity-structure that situates German national consciousness as caught between the socialist past and the capitalist present. Given this central trope concerning the loss of *Heimat* and the focus on self-reflective narratives, this chapter also argues that there is a politico-aesthetic continuity between the observational narratives of the German New Wave and the Berlin School filmmakers' preoccupation with the act of seeing. This continuity, as argued below, presents a critical framework to refute not only the allure of *Ostalgie* and *Westalgie* but also the current German socio-political establishment.

THE QUESTION OF GERMAN IDENTITY

In his book on New German Cinema, Thomas Elsaesser debunks the notion of a shared national and cultural identity for a profoundly divided Germany. He argues that,

> No other European country…is as unsure of the meaning of its culture as Germany, or as obsessed with its national identity. […] the post-war division of Germany into two political entities, each with its own version of national

history fixated on the phenomenon of Fascism, has ruptured and set up barriers to any notion of cultural and historical continuity. Germany never
became a nation state. (Elsaesser 1989: 49)

Although Elsaesser's argument dates back to pre-unification, it
remains valid when considering the national self-awareness still exhibited
by post-GDR and West German citizens to this day. As Elsaesser predicted, research into current socio-cultural and political understanding
of the past concludes that it is still formed along an Eastern and Western
German identity-border, rendering the construction of an integrated
national self-understanding and memory deeply problematic (Robertson
and Williams 2003). Firstly, a united Germany has to face the historical
baggage of two dictatorial establishments—the National Socialists and
the Soviet-backed German Democratic Republic—which, as argued by
Jarusch (2002), 'leaves a double burden of traumatic recollections'
(Jarausch 2002: 108) on German consciousness, resulting in a never-
ending cycle of negative self-questioning and doubt that renders the
construction of a positive, affirmative identity impossible. Secondly, the
division of Germany into East and West led to two very distinct kinds of
identity. The Federal Republic constructed a constitutional, post-nation-
alist West German society that tried to reckon with the ethnically homogeneous concept of nationhood that served the previous Fascist state
(Scharf 2008). Jürgen Habermas's concept of *Verfassungspatriotismus*
(constitutional patriotism) offered the idea of a post-nationalistic collective identity that unites its citizens under a democratic—rather than
emotional—bond. Although the concept contributed to developing a
positive self-image in the Federal Republic, it only widened the ideological gap between East and West Germany (Scharf 2008). The GDR too
distanced itself from the Third Reich and its crimes, but it did so by
founding a state on a fundamentally socialist consciousness, rather than
Western democratic values (McKay 2002). This perpetuated a cycle of
negatively defined counter-identities where the national consciousness of
the West rested on anti-Communist, democratic ideals (Cook 2005),
while the East relied on anti-Western, socialist ideals. Not only does this
ideological opposition appear to have been imprinted into the united
German subconscious (the unavoidable 'barriers' Elsaesser refers to),
but, it may have been exacerbated by the difficult and often disappointing post-wall transitional process that strengthened ambivalent feelings
on both sides.

Although the unification of Germany was a surprising and highly celebrated turning point in European history, the economic, social and political consequences that came with the 'Kohl-onization' (Saunders 2006) process left a bittersweet legacy for people from the Eastern region. When discussing the post-GDR unification process, Hefeker and Wunner (2002) argue that it was 'more like the accession of the GDR into the Federal Republic' (168) where the post-socialist state faced privatisation, harsh competition from companies from the West, and severe unemployment. Several scholars attest to the severe economic impact of unification with research revealing individual living conditions in the East, particularly a sharp rise in female unemployment (Young 1999; Münter and Sturm 2003). Worsening economic conditions aside, 'state unification', as Gellner and Robertson (2003) defines the post-1989 socio-historical process, focused primarily on the unification of state institutions and fundamentally neglected to answer the question of a common German citizenry in a fully operational constitutional agreement (Gellner and Robertson 2003). Thus, unification prioritised economy and governance in its approach to state cohesion and failed to acknowledge the importance of setting up a new, national identity structure.

The lack of a united national discourse on constitutional citizenship could only further polarise a nation whose unconventional identity seems to be based more on memory, than history (Vogt and Chong 2014). On the one hand, the remembrance of the Nazi past (Brockmann 2006) established a common ground of identity based on guilt and shame (Jarausch 2002). On the other hand, based on the East–West border, unification constitutionally and economically demarcated the population and, while shifting 'the ethnological burden of the past to an Eastern and Western other' (Boyer 2015: 371), created constant tension between the post-GDR and West German citizens. The current differential, marked as it is by economic deprivation, disappointment in the market economy and their treatment as second-class citizens in the new Germany (Ross 2002; Hodgin 2011), has motivated many to look back on their socialist past with greater fondness. 'Ostalgie', the post-2000 wave of nostalgia for East Germany, is 'an expression of defiance...against the western takeover' (Dale 2007: 171) and can also function as a 'secret handshake' between those who have 'a legitimate claim to east German memory' (Hodgin 2011: 154).

While Ostalgie helps East Germans form an alternative critical framework to judge the present situation and the capitalist establishment that has caused them such difficulties (Enns 2007), West Germans constantly provoke their Eastern compatriots for complaining about their situation in the united Germany (Grix 2002). There is no doubt that unification costs a lot, and especially for West German taxpayers who occupy an economically more privileged position. On the other hand, 'Westalgie', 'a copycat version of East German nostalgia' (Cook 2005: 40), is proof that post-FRG citizens also seek cultural glue that can keep West Germans together. That is, while East Germans have a stronger cultural and national identity (Cook 2005) that is mainly built on their everyday dominant experience in the GDR (McKay 2002), Westerners have less defined grounds for cohesion, and their longing for the pre-1989 universe is more an endeavour to change the Nazi past than to go back to the divided era (Boyer 2015). Whatever the case, the East–West opposition and the 'stubborn antimodernist tendency toward isolation remains a key constituent of German identity after unification' (Cook 2005: 53). The outcome of this very divisive East–West discourse is a fragmented, vulnerable and rather fragile liminal German identity whose definition becomes even more brittle when re-shaped to accommodate the question of long-standing Turkish migration and the current refugee-crisis in a more multicultural social portrayal of contemporary Germany.

In-between Identities, In-between Narratives

Trapped in a precarious in-between, East–West divided position, the future task of Germany, therefore, is to re-define its national identity along a new structural ideology that has the power to unite the nation. However, the persistence of an East–West psychological and mental wall (Vogt and Chong 2014) suggests that the Berlin Republic—as many name the united Germany—could be stuck in a socially historically transformative epoch for some time.

In his post-colonial reading, Bhabha (1994: 184) defines this discontinued historical position as 'time-lag' that, as a temporal caesura, forms an in-between state between the authorised, controlling narrative of the nation (sign) and its counter-part (signification) that constantly re-writes it. It thus 'describes the linguistic possibility of reordering or reinterpreting cultural symbols through a negotiation of difference', while drawing attention to the process of identification and the agency within the process (Runions 2001: 99). This hybrid in-flux position of the national narrative exposes the pedagogical and performative function of the German state.

174   A. BATORI

Germany's history is still in the 'process of being made', which is why, according to Bhabha, the nation as cultural authority can be 'caught...in the act of composing its powerful image' (Bhabha 1990: 4).

Drawing on the theories of Bhabha (1994) and Deleuze and Guattari (1987), David Martin-Jones (2008) identifies this time-lag as a gap in the constant shift between de- and re-territorialisation 'where one can see national identity as a repetition of difference' (Martin-Jones 2008: 35). In cinematic texts, re-territorialisation can happen via mirroring the memory-experience of the protagonists, which, as Martin-Jones argues, illustrates the 'process of national identity reterritorialisation' (Ibid.: 50).

In the constant struggle between the performative and pedagogical—the de-territorialised and re-territorialised state of national consciousness—filmic manifestations of Germanness can become stranded in the quagmire of just such a time-lag. As we will see, this insecure spatio-temporal position is accompanied by a constant feeling of homelessness and ghostliness that makes the characters absolute outsiders in the national context.

The lack of *Heimat* was one of the key characteristic of the films of the German New Wave (Elsaesser 1989). On the one hand, the feeling of homelessness in West German *Autorenkino* can be traced to the constitution of the Federal Republic that defined West Germany as a temporary construction, loosening the sense of belonging to a national identity (Scharf 2008). On the other hand, the American presence and the new consumer structure and cultural colonisation they brought with them left West Germany 'engulfed in foreign images' (Wenders, quoted in Cook and Gemünden 1997: 59), resulting in an asymmetrical relationship of Germans to their own Germanness, one overwritten by American dominance. In this way, West German identity became lodged between a German guilty past and Americanised present in a world of conflicting images. This imprisoned time-position is evident in the cyclical narratives of the New German Cinema that, as Scharf (2008) highlights, condemns protagonists to remain stuck in the past. In the German *Autorenkino* of the 1960s and 1970s, this cyclical sense of time (Scharf 2008: 122) created a self-reflexive, observative cinema that emphasised self-examination of the visual self. The polaroid images of Wenders in *Alice in the Cities / Alice in den Städten* (1974) or *Kings of the Road / Im Lauf der Zeit*, (1976) and the mirror and double-framing in the films of Rainer Werner Fassbinder (*Beware of a Whole Hore/Warnung von einder heiligen Nutte* (1971); *Effi Briest/Fontane Effi Briest* (1974); *Chinese Roulette/Chinesisches Roulette* (1976) all established spectatorial national narratives based on inescapable in-between spatial and temporal positions. The compulsively observational, self-reflexive approach of the protagonists to their physical space served as a reflection of their own and the nation's identity crisis and, as pinpointed by Scharf (2008), established the anti-*Heimat* cinema of 'existential homelessness' (Scharf 2008).

The Berlin School

In many respects, the current filmic stream of the Berlin School demonstrates a striking resemblance to the *Autorenkino* of the 1960s and 1970s. According to Marco Abel (2013), such an analogy would be deceptive, given that the disciplinary structure that was the critical target of the New German Cinema has changed its face to a biopolitically controlled society. According to this view, the current ideological structure of Germany has little continuity with the pre-1989 establishment. Despite the great many changes that unification, Europeanisation and the social market economy brought to Germany, it would be rather reductive to state that the German establishment-critique is designed along an entirely different aesthetic agenda. If the New German Cinema criticised an alienated, Americanised West Germany ruled by feelings of homelessness, anger and fear (Elsaesser 1989), the Berlin School is a comparable intensified thematic and aesthetic answer to the current historio-political situation and German identity-crisis.

The label 'Berlin School' covers a loosely affiliated group of filmmakers who forge a certain kind of counter-cinema in contemporary Germany by paying 'renewed attention to film form and aesthetics, [and the] life in Germany and Europe during the era of late capitalism and globalization' (Baer 2013: 72). The first generation of the school—marked by Thomas Arslan (*A Fine Day/Der schöne Tag* [2001]; *In the Shadows/Im Schatten*, [2010]), Angela Schanelec (*Passing Summer/Mein langsames Leben* [2001]; *Marseille* [2004]) and Christian Petzold (*The State I am In/ Innere Sicherheit* [2001]; *Wolfsburg* [2003]) who were educated at the Berlin film and Television Academy (*dffb*)—went against the comedic, superficial tone of the cinema of consensus (Rentschler 2000) to dig deep into quotidian post-wall life and the German identity-crisis. The filmmakers of the second generation—Christoph Hochhäusler (*The City Below/ Unter dir die Stadt* [2010]; *I am Guilty/Falscher Bekenner* [2005]), Benjamin Heisenberg (*This Very Moment/Milchwald* [2003]; *The Sleeper/ Schläfer* [2005]), Ulrich Köhler (*Bungalow* [2002]; *Windows on Monday/*

176   A. BATORI

Montag kommen die Fenster [2006]), Maren Ade (*Everyone Else/Alle Anderen* [2009]) and Valeska Grisebach (*Longing/Sehnsucht* [2006])—follow an 'aesthetics of refusal' (Cook et al. 2013) that refutes marketable tendencies and forces 'audiences to come to terms with the demand to *resee* that with which they assumed sufficient familiarity: *Deutschland* itself' (Abel 2013: 15). The Germany these filmmakers depict struggles with the alienating impact of free-market capitalism and globalisation on personal relationships, family relations and the individual herself/himself (Baer 2013). Alienation is thus a key feature of the films of the Berlin School, one that specifically derives from the breakdown in communication and unemployment that ensues when characters fail to embed themselves in the ruthless social market economy of the national text (Miller 2012). Characters respond to the crisis of their outsider, superfluous position in the national socio-political structure with constant movement, be that a travel within the country or aimless walking in the cities—as seen in Petzold's *Yella* or *Wolfsburg*, Köhler's *Bungalow* or Hochhäusler's *I am Guilty*. Despite the flux of in-between, non-places (Augé 1995) such as hotels, airports and highways, the plot of the films gravitates towards stillness. This stasis derives not only from absence of dialogue and emphasis on observation instead of action but also from a contemplative aesthetics that mediates the film to viewers in long takes and precise framing without extradiegetic music or overt narrative information to problematise the spectator's identification with the characters (Kopp 2010; Abel 2013).

In common with the *Autorenkino* of the 1960s and 1970s, the films of the Berlin School work within a self-reflexive, observational aesthetic that enacts the wariness of a spy's point-of-view in characters who keep their environment under constant surveillance, while they are also being watched by the gaze of the camera. Whereas some films— such as Heisenberg's *Sleeper*, Petzold's *Barbara* (2012) or Hochhäusler's *The Lies of the Victors/Die Lügen der Sieger* (2014)—clearly thematise surveillance, other Berlin School productions are more implicit in their attempts to focus on the grid of observation in the films. The narrative of *Bungalow*, for example, is based on the observational position of the deserted soldier Paul (Lennie Burmeister) who, as a ghost, wanders around his lost home, while constantly monitoring the house of his parents. In Hochhäusler's *The City Below*, the personal time of successful bank manager Roland Cordes (Robert Hunger-Bühler) is divided between watching his heroin-addicted son and spying on his young lover, Svenja (Nicolette Krebitz). In both films, the subjective shots of the protagonists, and the double-framed structure of the images construct a *mise-en-abyme* form that holds the characters in an in-between, watching–watched position.

In other productions, such as Grisebach's *Longing* and Hochhäusler's *I am Guilty*, the self-reflexive storytelling formula is framed by double-narration, consisting of dreams, computerised images and the very act of narration itself. In *Longing*, the tragic love-triangle depicted on screen gets summarised by a group of children who re-tell the fabula of the film, without revealing what happens after the suicide attempt of the main protagonist. In *I am Guilty*, Armin (Constantin von Jacheroff) escapes from reality in a homosexual dream-world; in Heisenberg's *Sleeper*, the staff of the research institute find shelter in videogames, while in Schanelec's *Orly* and *Marseille*, the travellers observe their environment through photographs. In all cases, the act of seeing mediates the world to escape into an alternative and in-between position where the protagonists are pure seers with a heavily mediated existence. They are identified as being stuck in time-lags—image-gaps—where their personal history is constantly being re-written by their position as observers.

Akin to the films of the New German cinema, this gap signifies an identity-crisis in which the characters only exist via memory-images or crystal-sequences, where actual and virtual, past and present, and subjective and objective are strongly interwoven in formation but rarely resolve. These time-images (Deleuze 1989) dramatize the alienated nature of consumer capitalism where characters are unable to respond to the massive flow of mediated reality. The protagonists of the Berlin School cannot cope with the hardship of economic reality and its inhuman face (*I am Guilty*), the alienated world that arises from the lack of communication (*Everyone Else; Marseille*) and the highly individualistic society that forces characters to watch, instead of taking any action (*The City Below; Windows on Monday*). As passive (object) as well as the active (subject) agents of the watching apparatus, the characters not only suffer psychic rifts but also drift from one place to the other. Their in-between identity thus manifests itself in a geographic dimension and/or is perpetuated in a homeless position. Be that the airport (*Orly; Windows on Monday; Yella*), the highway (*I am Guilty; Wolfsburg*) or another country (*Everyone else; Marseille*), there is no home for these characters in the postmodern world (Cook 2013; Baer 2013), only a possible wandering around as ghosts.

Like the *Autorenkino* of the 1960s and 1970s, to be embodied in the homeless position is an implicit and explicit critique of the highly capitalised structure of modern Germany. Homelessness as well as ghostliness is

178 A. BATORI

not only apparent in the explicit deprivation of these characters but also in their inability to discover the real image of themselves amid the flow of visuals. Alienated in this sense, they too are lost and untethered from the structural order. Thus, these films hold no stock with Westalgie and Ostalgie and refute both forms of remembrance and placement. The accelerated phenomenon of measuring family and social relations through progress, mobility and efficiency, that drove globalised Germany into an even deeper identity-crisis (Biendarra 2011), turns back on itself in a compulsive self-reflexivity in the Berlin School films. On the one hand, this intermedial gesture relies on the homeless, drifting tropes established by the New German Cinema. On the other hand, the Berlin School directors emphasise the accelerated alienated structure of the nation by turning the photographs and television of the New German Cinema into dreams, video-games and constant reflection on the storytelling process itself. Instead of looking back to the GDR or pre-1989 West German times, this aesthetic continuity reveals the bitter post-wall reality of society and draws attention to the suffocating reality of the excessive present.

LIQUID IDENTITIES: THE CINEMA OF CHRISTIAN PETZOLD

The aesthetic continuity between the New German Cinema and the Berlin School depicted above can be best illustrated by the films of Christian Petzold, whose narratives offer a comprehensive understanding of the in-between identity position of the German nation. Petzold, the most celebrated director of the Berlin School (Fisher 2013), draws on feelings of fear, alienation and homelessness and constructs his narratives from mediated images. What makes his works outstanding and different from the cinema of the 1960s and 1970s is that he actualises the topicality and relevance of homelessness to the East–West division and spotlights Germany's growing capitalist-globalist framework through his use of CCTV footage.

The films of Petzold are marked by surveillance: constant movement, empty, forgotten landscapes or 'anywhere-places' (Cook 2013) such as hotels, bridges or parks. Abel defines these geographic territories as places of 'no-where as a now-here' (Abel 2013: 71), which highlights the desire of the protagonists to find and own a home, while 'being affected in the now-here' (Ibid.), that is, the capitalist present, which keeps this desire unfulfilled. The characters are thus stuck in 'bubble spaces' (Fisher 2013), which gives them an outsider, isolated position in the narratives

(Biendarra 2011; Baer 2013). Whether they are in constant flux travelling from East to West, or *vice versa*, or stuck in various kinds of non-places in cities or countryside, they have a ghost-like phantom-identity (Webber 2011) that accentuates their imprisoned position in the time-lag of the East–West discourse.

Ghostliness, as Biendarra argues (2011), can become a political category and an aesthetic paradigm that illustrates the spatial-temporal globalising factors and precarity that force the characters to move. It also underlines their inability to identify themselves within the globalised framework, rendering them wandering ghosts, 'spectres and zombies' (Biendarra 2011: 476). This ghostliness, however, accrues a further political dimension for Petzold who portrays his protagonists against the symbolic, post-industrial landscapes of East Germany. In his films, the locations obtain a metaphoric, anti-*Heimat* quality that emphasises the effects of the division.

One of the key terms for understanding German identity, *Heimat* has 'more power of evocation than Fatherland or even nation' (Applegate 1990: 246). It denotes a very emotional belonging to a harmonious community of life (Dale 2007) and recalls the peaceful, romanticised landscape of German regions (von Moltke 2002) represented by the images of rural idyll contained in the *Heimatfilms* of the 1950s (Scharf 2008). These films—such as Harald Reinl's *The Fisher Girl of Lake Constance/Die Fischerin von Bodensee*, 1956; Hans Deppe's *Black Forest Girl/Schwarzwaldmädel*, 1950 or Rudolf Jugert's *The Farmer's Perjury/Der Meineidbauer*, 1956—linked the ideas of national traditions (*Volkstum*) with landscape (*Naturlandschaft*) and portrayed the archetypical German countryside—the Black Forest, the Lüneburg Heath, or the Alps—as home to happiness and peace. This romantic-idyllic natural landscape and rural tranquillity was identical to *Heimat* and became a metaphoric realm to Germanness.

The New German Cinema has radically changed this image of the 'rural, ultra-conservative never-never-land' (Boa and Palfreyman 2000: 98). As Clark points out, in the films of the German *Autorenkino*, 'the provincial setting is no longer portrayed as a space of continuity, community and reassuring tradition, but rather as oppressive and intolerant, maintaining its sense of identity and cohesion only through the exclusion of those who cannot conform to its rigid norms' (Clark 2011: 156). The anti-*Heimat* elements of the New German cinema—the constant travel, the lack of community and the emphasis on German division—all contributed to the feeling of homelessness (Scharf 2008). The lack of *Heimat* and sense of belonging have been inherited in the cinema of the Berlin School and function as central tropes in the films of Petzold. These post-*Heimat* (Hermann 2012) narratives of the German director feature provincial, forgotten landscapes, atomised communities and ghost-like characters who constantly wander in impoverished, impersonalised environments. The counter-images of *Heimat* thus reckon with the romantic notion of Germanness by featuring a strong anti-*Heimat* aesthetics that is further underlined by the protagonists' ghost-like status and the link between nature and death.

In *The State I am In/Die innere Sicherheit* (2000), the left-wing terrorist family on the run enters Germany via the Rhine, the western border of the country. Later, before crossing the Elbe—the virtual border of East and West—the trio realise they have no more money to travel around the country and hit a crisis point. The parents are forced to acknowledge their precarious homeless, ghost-like status in their home country: their friends in the West cannot help them, while a future travelling in the post-East Germany—a foreign, unknown territory—calls forth new fears. Disappointed and angry, the mother jumps out of the car and goes to sit at the riverbank with the Elbe in the background where her husband and later their daughter Jeanne (Julia Hummer) join her. Jeanne offers a solution to her parents' in-between status by pointing out that she knows a place where they can stay. Ironically, the shelter she comes up with is near Hamburg, on the shore of the Elbe, which further echoes their own psycho-geographical in-fluxus position. Trapped between two worlds that are both unknown to them, the parents are doomed to die, while their daughter—the only person who has entrance to the capitalist places in the city and can identify herself with the capitalist-consumerist culture—survives the fatal car accident.

The Elbe river as a liminal space of memories, dreams, and past and present holds a special place in Petzold's cinematic oeuvre. Wittenberge, the key location of *Something to Remind Me/Toter Mann* (2001) and *Yella* also lies at the emblematic river. The city was the most prominent industrial town of the region in the German Democratic Republic and was home to many sewing and cellulose factories (Biendarra 2011). After unification, however, it faced a period of serious economic downturn and severe unemployment that led to mass migration from the region (Willisch 2012). For Petzold, 'the failure of East Germany was the failure of all of Germany, the utter failure' (Petzold in Fisher 2013:153) that he

"*KAPITALISMUS TÖTET*": LIQUID NATIONAL IDENTITIES... 181

wanted to address in his productions following *The State I am In* (Ibid.). Although he never touches upon the topic explicitly, Petzold's decision to use Wittenberge as a location signifies his aim to provide a realistic portrait of the post-wall German economic and psychological struggle. By highlighting the role of the river and the forgotten East German landscape against the modern, alienated capitalist structure, he places his characters in an in-between situation that corresponds to their historio-geographical, as well as mental, state. In *Something to Remind Me* for instance, Leyla (Nina Hoss) escapes from Stuttgart to Wittenberge where Blum (Sven Pinnig), who murdered her sister, is on a post-prison re-integration programme. With the intention of ultimately torturing and killing Blum, Leyla invites him on romantic dates along the riverside of the Elbe. Moreover, she gifts Blum a book about bridges, which bestows the river and its emblematic link between East and West, with more sinister meaning.

The bridge connects Leyla's Western past and Eastern present and, while signifying her homeless status, also underlines her own dual identity. On the Eastern shore, she is a smiling, friendly kitchen maid, while on the Western side of the river, she turns into a wise, cautious woman preparing the perfect crime. Similarly, the East–West location and bridge represents the dual-identity of Blum—ruthless killer and shy, obese factory worker— who is trying to re-integrate into the now united German society.

Inevitably, the protagonists cannot escape their personal and national time-lags. Leyla finds herself incapable of murdering Blum, but he is eventually shot by the police. In this way, both characters remain in a dual identity-position between past and present, capitalism and socialism, and memories and dreams. Leyla continues to live with the burden of the memory of her murdered sister and the secret of her planned crime and is not released from her outsider, antisocial position. Blum, on the other hand, did not finish the re-integration process, and his in-between position eventually lead to his death.

The identification of the Elbe with death is a recurrent motif in other films too. In *Yella*, the eponymous protagonist wishes to re-locate from Wittenberge to Hanover but gets killed by her ex-husband when he drives his car into the river. Like *Something to Remind Me*, the emblematic jump into the water signifies the failed attempt of re-integration, trapping the protagonists in a liquid time-lag gap. Yella wanted to move to Hanover in the hope of a new job as an accountant but soon finds out that the company she was supposed to work for went bankrupt. She then gets an offer

182   A. BATORI

from Philip (David Striesow) who asks her to accompany him to various business meetings to help Yella learn the capitalist mode of thinking. From a startled, demure East German person, she soon turns into a cold-blooded business woman whose pressure on one of their possible clients lead to his suicide. Eventually, Yella must face her homeless position in the capitalist-consumerist structure, a point where the story returns to the East.

The narrative fantasy-frame of the film thus signals a failed de-territorialisation attempt by Yella who embraces her destiny to die in the Elbe. Having experienced the Western, capitalist flow of life and the liquid non-places that accompany this structure, the young woman realises that she cannot cope with the pressure the other Germany has to offer. At the same time, she also knows that she has no future in Wittenberge, a small, dilapidating Eastern town that guarantees no financial stability for her. For this reason, in contrast to the first accident, at the second attempt she does not try to impede the action of her ex-husband to drive the car off the bridge. Accepting her in-between position, Yella falls into death from the very architecture that symbolises her fractured identity.

Like *Something to Remind Me* and *Yella*, Petzold's other productions build their pro-filmic aesthetics around empty, barren Eastern landscapes that include rivers, the Baltic Sea and large, ghostly forests (Gerhardt 2013; Fisher 2013; Cook et al. 2013). These romantic motifs assemble an anti-*Heimat* collage that illustrates the insecure psychological state of the characters who are captured in a deteriorating, post-wall environment that keeps them imprisoned.

The main protagonists of *Something to remind me*, *Yella*, *Wolfsburg*, *Jerichow* and *Ghost* (*Gespenster*, 2005) are all incapable of identification with the capitalist world, which leaves them adrift as ghosts in memory-spaces, from West to East and *vice versa*. The only— albeit temporary— shelter for these characters is nature, but the emblematic symbols of *Heimat* narratives—the forest, the sea and the Elbe—only have lethal con-notations in these stories and only offer death as a possible solution to homeless identity-crisis.

BETWEEN IMAGES

The 'existential abeyance' (*Schwebezustand*), as Fisher (2013) defines the individual and collective gap prevalent in the cinema of Petzold, has not only a spatial (Staat 2016) but a temporal dimension that forces protago-

"KAPITALISMUS TÖTET": LIQUID NATIONAL IDENTITIES... 183

nists to have a ghost-like existence, in-between states. This flux in the territorialisation process is expressed through time-images that consist of dreams, fantasies and CCTV footage. On the one hand, this heightened intermediality may be motivated by Petzold's sense of the GDR as a utopian *dream* (Berghahn 2016) informed by his childhood memory of summers in the GDR. East Germany thus represents an imagined territory for him, a memory-space that reappears in the form of uncanny images.

On the other hand, Petzold often accentuates that, according to him, capitalism is in a state of severe crisis (Berghahn 2016). In common with other directors of the New German Cinema, capitalism is particularly represented by a mediated flow of images. In this way, Petzold depicts a surveillance society (Lyon 2001) whose main symbol is the immense proliferation of closed circuit television cameras (Norris and Armstrong 1999). This panoptic structure is built on the symbiosis of passive and active agency—a scheme that Baudrillard (2007) calls 'system of deterrence'—which is mirrored by a multifocalised narrative schema in his films.

In *Ghost* for instance, the observed outsider position of the orphan Nina (Julia Hummer) is emphasised via surveillance images. The young girl drifts in the grid of the haunted, transitional places of Berlin (Abel 2013), while also traversing the city's and her own past and present. As a child, Nina was kidnapped from a supermarket and grew up in an orphanage in Berlin. When her alleged mother from France finds her in Berlin, her childhood and adulthood re-unite, and images of the past start to re-appear. Petzold illustrates the kidnapping via CCTV footage in the film, while Nina's first meeting with her claimed mother happens after another CCTV-scene that depicts the girl and her friend after shoplifting (Fig. 9.1). The chain of observation emphasises Nina's subjected position—she is constantly spied upon in the capitalist framework (Webber 2011)—while the mediated images also identify her as an objectified commodity. In the first instance of her abduction, the CCTV footage shows how she, as a product, can be abstracted from the supermarket. In the second clip, Petzold again de-personalises Nina by concentrating on her shoplifter, criminal body leaving the mall. The computerised, bluish and almost mute images of the CCTV give the footage a cold, eerie atmosphere, while emphasising Nina's objectified-outsider position in the capitalist space. Thanks to the high-angle shot and the robotic-mechanical zoom of the camera that de-personalises the narrative space, her physical presence

Fig. 9.1 Nina's objectified position in *Ghost*

becomes a criminal-object that must be watched closely in the capitalist 'society of machinery' (Teurlings 2013). In both cases, the CCTV footage has a distancing affect, for it not only lies outside the narrative diegesis but also represents Nina as a lonely, depersonalised, ghost-like figure.

In the capitalist spaces of the city, Nina is the passive agent being watched; in nature, it is she who takes on the role of the observer. In the long opening sequence of the film, she witnesses the harassment of her future friend Toni (Sabine Timoteo) and follows her to a bridge in the park where she hides from Nina's workmates. Instead of subjective shots, Petzold emphasises Tony's physiognomy to register Nina's reactions. By accentuating the very physical presence of the girl, Petzold presents Nina's very active position as observer. Eventually, the shifts between the focalisational levels of the narrative and Nina's wandering in the city-text construct a memory-space through which Nina's very identity is constituted.

In the last sequence of *Ghost*, the girl returns to the park to check her mother's stolen wallet that Toni threw into a bin. In the pocket, she finds her own, digitalised phantom-images that were created to identify how she might look now. While she slowly unfolds the multi-layered paper, she faces the various stages of her life—first as a child, and then as a teenager (Fig. 9.2). Her position as observer and observed unite as her actual

Fig. 9.2 Nina's mirror image in *Ghost*

present and virtual past become indistinguishable in the act of watching herself in a digitalised mirror, a process that renders any distancing depersonalisation impossible. She thus becomes what Bogue, after Deleuze, defines as crystalline state: that which reveals 'different ways in which the whole of that great ocean of virtual past may be related to the ongoing actualization of time in a present moving toward a future' (Bogue 2003: 120). Nina's in-between spatio-temporal position thus crystallizes in the final sequence to unite past and present, objective and subjective to deposit her in a fractured time-lag.

The central conflict of the time-lag position, that which is caught between the virtual (past, observed) and actual (present, observer), is a recurring motif in the cinema of Petzold and plays a prominent role in the dream-images of *Yella*, the CCTV footages of Laura in *Wolfsburg* and those of Ana (Luna Zimic Mijovic) in *Beats Being Dead/Dreileben-Etwas besseres als den Tod* (2011). It also plays a part in Jeanne's movie-experience of Alain Resnais's *Night and Fog* (*Nuit et brouillard* [1956]) in *The State I am In*. Together with the observational aesthetic of these films, the crystalline rendering of time as time-lag forms a critical and aesthetical self-reflexive position that highlights the unstable liquidity of German national identity in the tense rift between East and West and their blurry sense of a national past and present.

CONCLUSION

In contrast to the protagonists of the *Autorenkino* who could not cross the Elbe because of the political-physical border, the characters in the films of the Berlin School move freely in the (post-)socialist and capitalist area. However, their constant ghost-like movement—or rather, flight—through a united national space signals an in-between identity resistant to simplistic notions of *Heimat*—one that re-formulates idyllic romantic landscape to signify death. The spatial time-lag of these contemporary characters also gains a temporal dimension. Stuck between memories and fantasies, and caught in the very grid of the act of seeing, the protagonists' short-lived existence is only possible in crystal images where the master, signifier past (passive, objectified) and present (active, interpolated) fuse. In this time-lag, contemporary Germanness is identified as an in-between, ghost-like state—not de-territorialised of its socialist past but not yet re-territorialised in the new narrative of Germany's future. This allows these films to depict the very essence of post-wall German nationalism and identity. As we have seen above, the films of Petzold resist any kind of explicit connection to the GDR and refuse Ostalgie or Westalgie, yet they still structure their narratives along the very divided East–West discourse and are clear in presenting their disappointment at the present capitalist-consumerist reality. In this way, they suggest that the German national identity built on a homeless, ghost-like state and the rejection of *Heimat* and romantic natural landscapes, is still fractured along its East–West intersection and can be only be driven further apart by the current, capitalist ideology.

BIBLIOGRAPHY

Abel, Marco. 2010. Imaging Germany: The (Political) Cinema of Christian Petzold. In *The Collapse of the Conventional German Film and Its Politics at the Turn of the Twenty-First Century*. Ed. Fisher, Jaimey and Brad Prager. Detroit: Wayne University Press: 258–285.

Abel, Marco. 2013. *The Counter-Cinema of the Berlin School*. Rochester: Camden House.

Anderson, Benedict. 1983. *Imagined Communities. Reflections on the Origin and Spread of Nationalism*, London and New York: Verso.

Applegate, Celia. 1990. *A Nation of Provincials. The German Idea of Heimat*. Berkeley and Los Angeles: University of California Press.

Augé, Marc. 1995. *Non-Places. Introduction to an Anthropology of Supermodernity*. New York: Verso.

"*KAPITALISMUS TÖTET*": LIQUID NATIONAL IDENTITIES... 187

Baer, Hester. 2013. Affectless Economies: The Berlin School and Neoliberalism. *Discourse*, 35(1): 72–100.

Baudrillard, Jean. 2007. *Forget Foucault*. Cambridge: MIT Press.

Berghahn, Daniela. 2016. DEFA's Afterimages: Looking Back at the East from the West in Das Leben der Anderen (2006) and Barbara (2012). In *Re-imagining DEFA. East German Cinema and its National and Transnational Contexts*. Ed. Allan, Sean and Sebastian Heiduschke. New York and Oxford: Berghahn.

Bhabha, K. H. 1990. Introduction: Narrating the Nation. In *Nation and Narration*. Ed. Homi K. Bhabha. London and New York: Routledge, 1–8.

Bhabha, Homi K. 1994. *The Location of Culture*. London: Routledge.

Biendarra, Anke S. 2011. Ghostly Business: Place, Space and Gender in Christian Petzold's Yella. *A Journal of Germanic Studies*, 47(4): 465–478.

Boa, Elizabeth and R. Rachel Palfreyman. 2000. *Heimat – A German Dream. Regional Loyalties and National Identity in German Culture 1890–1990*. New York: Oxford University Press.

Bogue, R. 2003. *Deleuze on Cinema*. London and New York: Routledge.

Boyer, Dominic. 2015. Ostalgie and the Politics of the Future in Eastern Germany. *Public Culture* 18(2): 61–382.

Brockmann, S. 2006. Normalization: Has Kohl's Vision Been Realized? In *German Culture, Politics and Literature into the Twenty-First Century*. Ed. Taberner, Stuart and Paul Cooke. Suffolk and Rochester: Camden House, 1–29.

Cook, Roger F. 2005. Recharting the Skies above Berlin. Nostalgia East and West. *German Politics and Society*, 74/23(1): 39–57.

Cook, Roger F. and Gerd Gemünden. 1997. *The Cinema of Wim Wenders. Image, Narrative, and the Postmodern Condition*. Michigan: Wayne State University Press.

Cook, R. F. 2013. Familiar Places. In *Berlin school Glossary. The ABC of the New Wave in German Cinema*. Ed. Cook, Roger F., Luty Koepnick and Brad Prager. Chicago: University of Chicago Press, 117–126.

Cook, R. F., Koepnick, L. and Prager, B. ed. 2013. *Berlin school Glossary. The ABC of the New Wave in German Cinema*. Chicago: University of Chicago Press.

Cooke, Paul. 2011. Watching the Stasi: Authenticity, *Ostalgie* and History in Florian Henckel von Donnersmarck's *The Lives of Others* (2006). In *New Directions in German Cinema*. Ed. P. Cooke and C. Homewood. New York: I.B.Tauris & Co. Ltd: 113–130.

Dale, G. 2007. Heimat, Ostalgie and the Stasi: The DGR in German Cinema, 1999–2006. *Debatte*, 15(2): 155–175.

Deleuze, Gilles. 1989. *Cinema II. The Time-Image*. Trans. Tomlinson, H. and R. Galeta. London and New York: Bloomsbury Academic.

Deleuze, Gilles. 1992. Postscript on the Societies of Control. *October* 59: 3–7.

Deleuze, Gilles and Felix Guattari. 1987. *A Thousand Plateaus. Capitalism and Schizophrenia*. Minneapolis: University of Minnesota Press.

Eigler, F. and Kugele, J. Eds. 2012. *Heimat. At the Intersection of Memory and Space*. Berlin: De Gruyter.

188   A. BATORI

Elsaesser, Thomas. 1989. *New German Cinema*. Basingstoke and London: Macmillan.

Enns, Anthony. 2007. The Politics of Ostalgie: Post-socialist Nostalgia in Recent German Film. *Screen* 48(4): 475–491.

Fisher, Jaimey. 2011. German *Autoren* Dialogue with Hollywood? Refunctioning the Horror Genre in Christian Petzold's *Yella* (2007), In *New Directions in German Cinema*. Eds. Cooke, Paul and Chris Homewood. New York: I.B.Tauris & Co. Ltd: 186–204.

Fisher, Jaimey. 2013. *Christian Petzold* Urbana, Chicago, Springfield: University of Illinois Press.

Foucault, Michel. 1977. *Discipline and Punish*. London: Allen Lane.

Gellner, W. and Robertson J. D. 2003. The Berlin Republic: German Unification and A Decade of Changes. In *The Berlin Republic: German Unification and A Decade of Changes*. Ed. Gellner, Winand and John D. Robertson. London: Franc Cass, 1–3.

Gerhardt, C. 2013. Winning a (Hi)story Out of Places: Christian Petzold's Germany in *Etwas Besseres als den Tod* (2011). *German Studies Review* 36: 617–625.

Gerhardt, Christina. 2016. Looking East: Christian Petzold's *Barbara* (2012). *Quarterly Review of Film and Video*, 33(6): 550–566.

Grix, Jonathan. 2002. Introduction to East German Political and Cultural Distinctiveness. In *East German Distinctiveness in a Unified Germany*. Ed. Grix, Jonathan and Paul Cooke. Birmingham: The University of Birmingham Press: 1–15.

Hefeker, Carsten and Norbert Wunner. 2002. Great Expectations, Hard Times: A Political Economic History of German Unification. In *Ten Years of German Unification: Transfer, Transformation, Incorporation?* Ed. Leonhard, Jörn and Lothar Funk. Birmingham: University of Birmingham Press: 168–183.

Herrmann, M. 2012. Geisterlandschaften. The Memory of Heimat on Recent Berlin School Films. In *Heimat. At the Intersection of Memory and Space*. Ed. Eigler, Friedrike and Jens Kugele. Berlin: De Gruyter: 158–175.

Hodgin, Nick. 2011. *Screening the East. Heimat, Memory and Nostalgia in German Film since 1989*. Berghahn.

Hodgin, Nick. 2011b. Aiming to Please? Consensus and Consciousness-raising in Wolfgang Becker's *Goodbye Lenin!* (2003). Eds. Cooke, Paul and Chris Homewood. New York: I.B.Tauris & Co. Ltd: 94–113.

Holmes, Seth M. and Heide Castañeda, 2016. Representing the "European refugee crisis" in Germany and Beyond: Deservingness and Difference, Life and Death. *American Ethnologist*, 43: 12–24.

James, Jason. 2010. Coming to Terms Through Cinema: The Lives of Others in Germany's Cultural Landscape of Memory. *Journal of the Society for the Anthropology of Europe*, 10(2): 29–40.

Jarausch, Konrad H. 2002. A Double Burden: The Politics of the Past and German Identity. In *Ten Years of German Unification: Transfer, Transformation,*

Incorporation? Ed. Leonhard, Jörn and Lothar Funk. Birmingham: University of Birmingham Press: 98–115.

Jordan, Jennifer A. 2006. *Structures of Memory.* Stanford: Stanford University Press

Kaussen, V. 2013. Ghosts. In *Berlin school Glossary.* Ed. Cook, Roger F., Lutz Koepnick, Kristin Kopp and Brad Prager. University of Chicago Press: 147–156.

Koepnick, L. (2013). Cars. In *Berlin School Glossary.* Ed. Cook, Roger F., Lutz Koepnick, Kristin Kopp and Brad Prager. University of Chicago Press: 75–82.

Kopp, Kristin. 2010. Christoph Hochhäusler's This Very Moment: The Berlin School and the Politics of Spatial Aesthetics in the German-Polish Borderlands. In *The Collapse of the Conventional German Film and Its Politics at the Turn of the Twenty-First Century.* Ed. Fisher, Jaimey and Brad Prager. Detroit: Wayne University Press: 285–309.

Lyon, David. 2001. *Surveillance Society: Monitoring Everyday Life.* Buckingham and Philadelphia: Open University Press.

Martin-Jones, David. 2008. *Deleuze, Cinema and National Identity. Narrative Time in National Contexts.* Edinburgh: Edinburgh University Press.

McKay, Joanna. 2002. East German Identity in the GDR. In *East German Distinctiveness in a Unified Germany.* Ed. Grix, Jonathan and Paul Cooke. Birmingham: The University of Birmingham Press: 15–31.

Miller, Matthew D. 2012. Facts of Migration, Demands on Identity: Christian Petzold's *Yella* and *Jerichow* in Comparison. *The German Quarterly* 85(1): 55–76

Moeller, Martina. 2013. *Rubble, Ruins and Romanticism. Visual Style, Narration and Identity in German Post-War Cinema.* Bielefeld: Verlag.

Münter, M. and R. Sturm. 2003. Economic Consequences of German Unification. In *The Berlin Republic. German Unification and a Decade of Changes.* Ed. Gellner, Winand and John D. Robertson. London: Frank Cass and Company Ltd: 179–195.

Mushaben, Joyce M. 2008. *The Changing Faces of Citizenship. Integration and Mobilization among Ethnic Minorities in Germany.* New York and Oxford: Berghahn

Norris, Clive and Gary Armstrong. 1999. *The Maximum Surveillance Society. The Rise of CCTV.* Oxford, New York: Berg.

Orr, John. 1993. *Cinema and Modernity.* Cambridge: Blackwell Publishers.

Prager, Brad. 2010. Passing Time since the Wende. *German Politics and Society,* 94(28): 95–110.

Rentschler, Eric. 2000. From New German Cinema to the Post-Wall Cinema of Consensus. In *Cinema and Nation.* Ed. Hjort, Mette and Mackenzie, Scott. London and New York: Routledge: 260–278.

Rentschler, Eric. 2013. Predecessors: The German Prehistory of the Berlin School. In *Berlin School Glossary.* Ed. Cook, Roger F., Lutz Koepnick, Kristin Kopp and Brad Prager. Chicago: University of Chicago Press: 213–221.

Robertson, John D. and Kim M. Williams. 2003. Analysing German Unification: State, Nation and the Quest for Political Community. In *The Berlin Republic.*

190 A. BATORI

German Unification and a Decade of Changes. Ed. W. Gellner and J.D Robertson. London: Frank Cass and Company Ltd: 3–19.

Ross, Gordon C. 2002. Second-class Germans? National Identity in East Germany. In *East German Distinctiveness in a Unified Germany.* Ed. Grix, Jonathan and Paul Cooke. Birmingham: The University of Birmingham Press: 61–75.

Runions, Eric. 2001. *Changing Subjects. Gender, Nation and Future in Micah.* London and New York: Sheffield Academic Press.

Saunders, A. 2006. "Normalizing" the Past: East German Culture and Ostalgie. In *German Culture, Politics and Literature into the Twenty-First Century.* Ed. Taberner, Stuart and Paul Cooke. Suffolk and Rochester: Camden House, 89–103.

Scharf, Inga. 2008. *Nation and Identity in New German Cinema: Homeless at Home.* New York and London: Routledge.

Staat, Wim. 2016. Christian Petzold's Melodramas: From Unknown Woman to Reciprocal Unknownness in *Phoenix, Wolfsburg* and *Barbara. Studies in European Cinema,* 13(3): 185–199.

Teurlings, Jan. 2013. From the Society of the Spectacle to the Society of the Machinery: Mutations in Popular Culture 1960s–2000s. *European Journal of Communication* 28(5): 514–526.

Trauner, Florian and Jocelyn Turton. 2017 "Welcome culture": The Emergence and Transformation of a Public Debate on Migration. *Austrian Journal of Political Science,* 46(1): 33–42.

Uecker, Matthias. 2013. *Performing the Modern German. Performance and Identity in Contemporary German Cinema.* Bern: Peter Lang.

Vogt, Roland and Li Chong. 2014. German National Identity: Moving Beyond Guilt. In: *European National Identities. Elements, Transitions, Conflicts.* Ed. Vogt, Roland, Wayne Cristaudo and Andreas Leutzsch New Brunswick and London: Transaction Publishers: 71–95.

Von Moltke, Johannes. 2002. Evergreens: The Heimat Genre. In *The German Cinema Book.* Ed. Bergfelder, Tim, Erika Carter and Deniz Göktürk. Suffolk: St Edmundsbury Press: 15–18.

Webber, Andrew J. 2011. Topographic Turns: Recasting Berlin in Christian Petzold's Gespenster. In *Debating German Cultural Identity since 1989.* Ed. Fuchs, Anne Kathleen James-Chakraborty and Linda Shortt. Rochester: Camden House: 67–82.

Willish, Andreas. Ed. 2012. *Wittenberge ist überall. Überleben in schrumpfenden Regionen.* Berlin: Christoph Link Verlag.

Young, Birgitte. 1999. *Triumph of the Fatherland. German Unification and the Marginalization of Women.* Michigan: The University of Michigan Press.

CHAPTER 10

Resistance Against Itself: Austrian Cinema's Responses to the Far-Right

Nikhil Sathe

The Austrian far-right Freedom Party (FPÖ), initially under the leadership of Jörg Haider, was the first populist, far-right party in post-1989 Europe to enter a national government and, after some setbacks, retain its domestic electoral success and its international influence. The party's ascent and reliance on nationalist and xenophobic rhetoric since the early 1990s are paralleled, with a gap of less than a decade, by a renaissance of a critical Austrian film that has earned international acclaim. Both directly and indirectly, the far-right has figured prominently in Austrian cinema. The following chapter will examine Austrian cinema's treatment of the far-right since the late 1990s. After an overview of the post-1945 development of the Austrian far-right Freedom Party, this chapter will briefly discuss how the more prominent examples of critical Austrian cinema since the 1990s have primarily taken an indirect response to the far-right's ascent. The chapter will then offer detailed readings of three films that adopt a more direct approach: the omnibus film, *Zur Lage: Österreich in sechs Kapiteln*, (Michael Glawogger, Michael Sturminger, Barbara Albert and Ulrich Seidl 2002); *Franz Fuchs: ein Patriot* (Elisabeth Scharang 2007) and finally,

---

N. Sathe (✉)
Ohio University, Athens, OH, USA
e-mail: sathe@ohio.edu

© The Author(s) 2018
J. Harvey (ed.), *Nationalism in Contemporary Western European Cinema*, Palgrave European Film and Media Studies,
https://doi.org/10.1007/978-3-319-73667-9_10

191

Todespolka (Michael Pfeifenberger 2010). Examining the considerable stylistic differences and the different contexts that these three films address will reveal their attempts to raise political consciousness, shape historical awareness, and enact critique of the populist far-right, illustrating as well their sensitivities to the dynamics of representing the far-right and their shared concern for engagement with the political sphere.

The nativist, right-wing populism that fuelled the rise of the FPÖ marks a shift from the nationalist focus of the party's origins. In 1949, recently re-enfranchised former National Socialists and pan-German ideologues formed a political union called the Federation of Independents [Verein der Unabhängigen]. In 1955, a rift in that union led to the founding of the FPÖ. Austria's political elites in the early post-1945 era began promoting an Austrian national identity to establish an independent sense of nationhood in a populace that largely perceived itself as belonging to a German nation. This strategy also sought to create distance between present-day Austria and its past complicity with National Socialism and to hasten a release from Allied occupation. For the FPÖ, however, German cultural nationalism would remain integral to the party platform for decades, even as most Austrians gradually came to accept its separate national identity. Until the early 1990s the FPÖ rarely earned more than 10% in national elections and had only a brief stint as a junior partner in coalition government from 1983–86. Jörg Haider's assumption of party leadership in 1986 shifted its electoral fortunes and initially maintained its cultural focus, with Haider continually shocking with positive assessments of National Socialism and dismissing Austrian nationhood as an "ideological miscarriage." Haider's media-savvy charisma and controversial statements contributed to his stardom across the European far-right and the rapid growth of his party to 26.9% of the electorate by 1999, but, as Heinisch notes, he and his party profited from specific Austrian circumstances as well as their opportunistic ideological flexibility (2008: 44). The FPÖ's electoral gains took advantage of voter dissatisfaction with declining economic growth and with the Grand Coalition between the Social Democrats (SPÖ) and the conservative People's Party (ÖVP) that had prevailed for most of the post-1945 era. This coalition was anchored by the so-called Social Partnership, a centralised corporatist system uniting political, business and labour interests, which by the 1980s was widely criticised for its unchecked power and corruption scandals. Haider's FPÖ also capitalised both on the uncertainties arising with Austria's entry into an expanding European Union, and especially on the radical transformations of 1989, which unsettled the country's image as a bridge between East and West and initiated a period of increased immigration. Since Haider's rise, the FPÖ's ideological positions have been fluid and adaptable: their original primary support from libertarians and business owners is now from working-class voters, their early opposition to EU membership has been replaced by strong EU-scepticism, yet a leading role the EU Parliament's far-right ENF group (Europe of Nations and Freedom), and finally the party's earlier allegiance to German nationalism has been transformed by the party platform's commitment to "Austria first."

The party's focus on Austria first, to be sure, has little to do with asserting a separate Austrian nationhood and instead serves the FPÖ's most successful tactic, namely constructing itself as a defender of a national community against external threats—in particular, foreign migrants, asylum seekers and refugees. After 1989, migration to Austria increased through refugees from the Balkan wars, economic migrants from within and beyond the EU, and more recently, refugees from conflicts in the Middle East. Haider's FPÖ exploited Austrian anxieties about this influx, perhaps most notoriously with its "Austria First" referendum of 1993, also known as the "Anti-Foreigner" referendum.[1] Although this plebiscite failed, its xenophobic rhetoric and its aggressive stance regarding migrants expanded the party's appeal by drawing working-class voters away from the SPÖ. With its 1999 federal campaign, which ran on a platform against "Überfremdung" [over-foreignisation], the FPÖ had its best electoral result and became the junior partner in a coalition government with the ÖVP, which sparked widespread international criticism.[2] As a largely symbolic response to the first entry of a far-right party among its member governments, the EU imposed a series of bilateral measures against Austria. These actions had some adverse effects: the right portrayed them as sanctions, which allowed the coalition to cast itself as a victim of foreign attacks, eliciting a defensively nationalistic response.[3] The EU's measures also had positive impacts, forcing resolution to long-stalled deliberations on reparations to victims of National Socialism and to the official status of ethnic minorities in Austria. The measures also

---

[1] For more on this referendum see Kryzanowski and Wodak (2009: 103–5), and Gärtner (2002: 23–6).

[2] All translations in this chapter are by the author.

[3] For more on the positive and negative impacts of these measures see Wodak et al. (2009: 223–7).

194 N. SATHE

prompted a domestic rejuvenation of civic society and substantial protest against the coalition government, most significantly the weekly "Thursday demonstrations" in Vienna.[4] The FPÖ's tenure in a governing role proved unsuccessful, but as Zaslove demonstrates, one of its accomplishments was making the country's immigration laws more restrictive (2004: 109–11). Party infighting played a role in the FPÖ's failure in the federal government. Haider, who at the start of the coalition shifted his role as party leader to serve as a provincial governor, eventually resigned to form his own party, the Alliance for the Future of Austria (BZÖ). After Haider's untimely death in 2008, however, the BZÖ could only retain provincial representation. Haider's earlier rival, Heinz Christian Strache, assumed leadership of the FPÖ and after initial setbacks, has gradually steered the FPÖ to electoral success. If lacking Haider's natural charisma, Strache maintains his aggressively provocative campaigning, employing social media and youth-oriented platforms.[5] Amid voter dissatisfaction with neoliberalism, Strache's FPÖ adopts an anti-elitist, "common-man" populism. His party's trademark xenophobia has shifted focus to Islamophobia, which has become mainstream across Europe and has even been legitimised by the centrist Austrian parties (Opratko 2015). In the 2016 presidential election, for the first time in the post-war era, the candidates of the SPÖ and ÖVP were eliminated, and in the runoff between the FPÖ candidate and a former Green Party independent, the FPÖ narrowly lost, revealing the continued appeal of its populist nationalism for the country's volatile electorate.

The rise of the FPÖ since the 1990s is a significant backdrop for the rejuvenation of a critical Austrian cinema, highlighting the primarily younger generation of Austrian filmmakers and the prominence of women directors among them. Dassanowsky and Speck have dubbed this a "New Austrian Cinema" that has earned international acclaim and success on the arthouse and festival circuits (2014: 9–10). The formal precision, even rigidity of this cinema and especially its intense yet stylised realism and its unflinching predilection for abject and taboo societal elements have led a *New York Times* critic to call Austria the home of a "feel bad

---

[4] See Krylova (2017: 10–15) for a comprehensive overview of the civic response to the election.

[5] For a full analysis of Strache's electoral strategies, see Wodak (2015: 134–48).

cinema" (Lim 2006). Aligning with predominant trends in recent European cinema, a key focus of Austrian cinema's social realism has been on the broad complex of migration. This focus by feature and documentary filmmakers in Austria, however, must also be understood as a response to the rise of the far-right. The FPÖ or other instances of the far-right, however, are not explicitly depicted in these films. Instead, their narratives are driven by migrants, refugees, and the undocumented—precisely those targeted by the FPÖ's exclusionary, racist rhetoric.[6] In stories revolving around journeys to Austria or westward, daily struggles of migrants of all stripes, or dilemmas of integration, the protagonists must navigate a context profoundly shaped by the far-right. Barbara Albert's celebrated *Nordrand* (1999) offers a paradigmatic example of this indirect response to the far-right. In this film, an election poster featuring Haider appears on screen for barely a second, but the viewpoints his party espouses provide the film with its contours, such as the threat of random raids and checkpoints plaguing the undocumented characters, or the hostility and unspoken racism directed at the Serbian-born protagonist. The film also counters the viewpoints proffered by the far-right through its critical portrayal of a border guard's personal anxieties, through its emphasis on a Bosnian refugee's struggles, and through the budding, multiethnic friendships of the film's resolution. With its critical depiction not of far-right politicians or supporters but of a society influenced by them, Albert's film illustrates the more common and widely received treatment of the far-right in Austrian films.[7] This chapter will examine three under-examined films with a more direct approach to depicting the far-right, and will provide information on related films. The three films addressed below do not turn their cameras on foreigners or minority figures, but examine domestic responses to FPÖ victories, xenophobic violence, and, in a satirical manner, the policy goals of the far-right.

[6] Examples of this range of films include documentaries, such as Ulrich Seidl's *Good News* (1990) or Ed Moschitz's *Mama Illegal* (2011), as well as feature films, such as Houchang Allahyari's *Geboren in Absurdistan (Born in Absurdistan)* (1999), Erwin Wagenhofer's *Black Brown White* (2011) or Sudabeh Mortezai's *Macondo* (2015).

[7] Another indirect response to the far-right can be found in films that are set in different historical periods, but whose depictions of authoritarianism and exclusionary violence are clearly reflections on contemporary society. Such examples include Michael Haneke's *Das weiße Band (The White Ribbon)* (2009) and Andreas Prochaska's *Das finstere Tal (Dark Valley)* (2014).

ZUR LAGE: ÖSTERREICH IN 6 KAPITELN [STATE OF THE NATION: AUSTRIA IN 6 CHAPTERS]

Zur Lage by Barbara Albert, Michael Glawogger, Michael Sturminger and Ulrich Seidl, was conceived as a reaction to the entry of the FPÖ into the federal government in 2000 and the protest movement that it prompted.[8] More broadly, this omnibus documentary participates in a European trend of collective films, in which prominent directors address the contemporary context of a nation or place (Diffrient 2014: 182–3). As Seidl describes it, *Zur Lage* was conceived as a film that would "look more closely at Austria. One that attempts to resist complacency and the everyday and to hold a critical mirror to our society. Thus, a resistance film, but one against ourselves" (N.N. 2002b).[9] The filmmakers conduct this critical assessment through a collection of documentary episodes, in which ordinary citizens discuss political issues, sometimes directly addressing the election. Although there is considerable stylistic variation, the predominance of subject interviews in most episodes approaches what Bill Nichols refers to as the participatory mode of documentary cinema (2010: 31). In his review, Dominik Kalmazadeh faults *Zur Lage* for its greater emphasis on chronicling the extremes of this "state of the nation" rather than exploring the factors that led to it (2002). Such a reading, to be sure, rests on the filmmakers' choice to have the subjects speak for themselves. Attention to their subjective involvement with and arrangement of the footage, however, lays bare their focus on the relationship between the private and the political. While parts of the film's critical mirror to Austrian society agitate resistance to deplorable viewpoints of the far-right, much of the film targets indifference and apolitical ignorance.

Michael Glawogger's episode, entitled "A Journey," was filmed during the director's hitchhiking trek along Austria's borders and consists of statements by those offering him a ride. Glawogger's comments and ques-

---

[8] The FPÖ is the subject of a previous critical documentary, Helmut Grasser's *Die Wahlkämpfer (The Campaigners)* (1993), but its electoral victory in 1999 prompted numerous filmic responses, such as Ruth Beckermann's *homemad(e)* (2001) or British filmmaker Frederick Baker's retrospective on the resistance, *Widerstand in Haiderland (Resistance in Haider-land)* (2010). Belgian filmmaker Nathalie Borgers examined the phenomenon of the party's former leader in her *Fang den Haider (Catch Haider)* (2015).

[9] "*Zur Lage* sollte ein Film sein, der genauer auf Österreich schaut. Einer, der sich Selbstgefälligkeit und Alltag widersetzen und Menschen in unserer Gesellschaft kritisch widerspiegeln will. Ein Widerstandsfilm also, aber einer gegen uns selbst" (N.N. 2002b).

tions are omitted, leaving solely the drivers' monologues. An early interviewee is explicitly critical of the ÖVP for inviting the FPÖ into a coalition. The sole female driver is dismayed by Haider's success, locating it in his ability to bedazzle with his charm and novelty, especially given voter malaise with the establishment. Glawogger devotes the longest time to a driver, who rails abstractly against the decline of the traditional nuclear family and of the subservient position of the female, both of which he sees as responsible for societal ills and an increase in homosexuality. Only later does he express his frustrations about his ex-wife, who presumably left him for another. While this driver, as Christoph Huber notes, illustrates the episode's emphasis on the import of the personal situation on political views, another segment foregrounds a divergence in this regard. It features a young, long-haired driver who scorns the bourgeois mentality and conformity of his peers. Given his unconventional attitude and gothic appearance, it is jarring when this subject not only expresses his agreement with Haider's views of foreigners as outsiders whose numbers should be reduced, but even casually suggests that Hitler would have had more success with non-violent means rather than attempting to eradicate Jews. The contradictions between this young man's stylisation of his own alterity and his rejection of ethnic others as outsiders lay bare his incongruence with the other interviewees' greater historical consciousness or at least awareness of the bearing of their personal history.

Continuing the illumination of parallels between the private and the political, Michael Sturminger's episode, "Three home visits," is focused on family structures. Sturminger foregrounds the artificiality of his intervention by replicating the format of television infotainment. Employing as interviewer Dieter Chmelar, a well-known host of a daytime lifestyle programme, the episode unsettles viewer expectations by having Chmelar employ leading questions and a fluff journalistic style to inquire about political dynamics that engage anxieties upon which the FPÖ has capitalised. Targeting the transmission of political awareness within the family, Sturminger's interviewer visits three homes across Austria. In the first, the patriarch expresses his vehement objection to mosques as incompatible with Tyrolean values. In a separate interview, his son then states that he gets along with his Turkish schoolmate, yet when posed an uneasy question, he looks at his parents and answers that he rejects the other's faith as false. A later visit is to an innkeeper near the Hungarian border and begins with the proprietor's vehement dismissal of Eastern Europeans as freeloaders. The remainder of the interview focuses on his personal life and attempts implicitly to link his intense rejection of the eastern EU expansion to the strict order and discipline that he wishes to impose in his business and within his family. For the longest visit, the interviewer starts by asking two suburban teenagers about their opinions of politicians, only to get their tortured response that they have never thought about those kinds of things. In the subsequent interview with the grandmother, she describes her imprisonment in a concentration camp because of her relationship with a Polish forced labourer and her arduous return on foot after liberation. Intercut with shots of the teenagers listening, the grandmother's retelling foregrounds a gap between the profound impact of historical events and institutional racism and the youngest generation's apathy. Whereas the first two visits highlight the overbearing influence of the older generations, this final visit offers an implicit warning of the younger generations to recognise potential parallels between the family history and the contemporary political climate.

Albert's episode, titled simply with the names of the eight women interviewed, attempts most directly to link the personal with the political. Crosscutting among the different interviewees places their divergent perspectives in a critical dialogue. One woman's allegation that foreigners exert an undue strain on the welfare state is juxtaposed both with segments featuring women of foreign descent working at an assembly line and with another in which an Austrian woman is waiting at the benefits office. Similarly, claims of foreigners' unwillingness to learn German are opposed to a scene showing an interviewee of Turkish descent correcting the German of her young daughter, who proudly describes how she refused to speak Turkish with a schoolmate. The girl's comments both refute the earlier stereotype and tellingly expose the pressures toward self-censorship and hyper-assimilation she perceives at a young age. In a different interview, the single mother of a bi-racial child details the racism she has encountered through her daughter. Her experiences are juxtaposed with a factory worker's considerations about adopting an African child. When asked whether the child would face discrimination, this woman disagrees, citing contemporary Austrians' greater tolerance toward foreigners. This same woman, however, is the subject most critical of foreigners and, when asked about her political viewpoint, states her preference for "Jörgl." Her use of the affectionate diminutive stresses her emotional attraction to Haider's charismatic appeal rather than the ideological aspects that colour her other statements. Albert's interviewees articulate diverse political viewpoints, but when asked about their political participation,

RESISTANCE AGAINST ITSELF: AUSTRIAN CINEMA'S RESPONSES... **199**

nearly all, even the FPÖ supporter, answer that they do not vote, with only two affirming. The first, the mother of the bi-racial child, not only describes her thoughts on participation, but is also shown marching with her daughter in an anti-coalition demonstration. The second is a handicapped artist, who states her fear that this new government will be a threat to her well-being. Underscoring the implicit focus of Albert's diverse perspectives, these two women explicitly foreground their keen awareness of how the political context can impact their lives.

Ulrich Seidl contributes several pieces to *Zur Lage*, all of which are characterised by the director's unique visual style and penchant for showing human extremes. As Florian Mundhenke argues, Seidl's filming of awkward, unpleasant moments and the exaggerated artificiality of his settings conspicuously break with the expectations of the documentary format and constitute a recurring aesthetic strategy employed to unsettle viewers and provoke critical reflection on societal realities and how they are represented (2011: 125). In the film's second episode, entitled "Johann Leeb, Bad Vöslau" Seidl has the eponymous older man address the camera directly, as he is placed in front of tightly composed backgrounds that emphasise the rigid orderliness of his home. Seidl cuts between scenes of Leeb running around his yard, detailing the meticulous order of his wardrobe, and painstakingly sweeping his already clean foundation. These stylised framings offer a visual correspondence to Leeb's paranoia and extremism, such as his Islamophobic fears of a de-Christianised Europe or his ranting against anglicisms in German.

Seidl contrasts his segment on Leeb by following it with a short episode entitled "A Song," in which three men, composed in a static image, look directly at the camera as they sing "No greater country" ["Kein schöner Land"]. The openness of this nineteenth-century folk song expressing harmony with nature and with one's immediate community has enabled its multiple adaptations by diverse ideological impulses (Linder-Beroud and Widmaier 2007). By placing it alongside the xenophobic paranoia of the Leeb episode, Seidl is ironically invoking the song's nationalistic appropriation and implicating the defensive reaction to the international condemnation of Austria's recent election.[10] The myopic perspective of that kneejerk reaction is underscored through the placement of the singers in front of a world map drawn in a naïve, distorted style, resembling a child's drawing.

---

[10] Seidl further undermines the song's traditional folk context by clothing the men not in Lederhosen, but modern business attire.

200   N. SATHE

Seidl's other episode, "At the wine tavern," presents the viewer with a more intense unease. Constructed with Seidl's characteristic "tableaux vivant" style (Mundhenke 2011: 119), the episode's static camera is frontally centered on a seated couple, interrupted only by edits shot from a slightly closer length. With no visual escape or break, the viewer's focus is forced onto the couple's increasingly heated, cascading diatribe. Their anti-Semitism and xenophobia conjure the far-right's perceptions of a world threatened by an allegedly radical Islam and of an Austria under siege—both by an influx of foreigners, who are perceived as criminal, parasitic others, as well as by liberal critics who are imagined as betrayers of Austrian cultural identity. The couple denounces, without specifically mentioning the FPÖ, the international reproach over the election and recent scandals. They are particularly dismissive of the criticism regarding the case of Marcus Omofuma, a Nigerian who died from mistreatment during his deportation in 1999.[11] The couple end their tirade by suggesting that the state should encourage its citizenry to return to the Nazi-era tactic of denunciations to eliminate all potential threats. In their animated and surely drunken display, the couple exaggeratedly professes knowledge, for example, of police procedures or American weaponry, that they cannot have, and their words offer a distillation of the far-right's most abhorrent views. Against the earlier episodes' more speculative tone and looser, open focus that invite the viewer's reflective engagement, Seidl's segment, in its unavoidable fixing on the couple's radical views, most directly confronts and implicitly challenges the viewer. If Seidl, as noted earlier, describes the film as enacting resistance "against ourselves," his episode presents its imagined Austrian audience with the film's most reprehensible, shameful self-image (Fig. 10.1).

This call to resistance is perhaps invoked by the film's ambiguous final image. It features a shot of an older man playing an accordion and singing a melancholic Viennese folk song. The lyrics question the point of any action or resistance, bemoaning the inevitability that things will transpire as they must: "It will happen as it has to."[12] The static frame and the singer's frontal pose immediately betray Seidl's handiwork, as does the

---

[11] Andreas Gruber's 2004 film, *Welcome Home*, reflects indirectly on the example of Omofuma through its depiction of a Ghanaian who is deported from Austria. When the film's racist police officer who deports him is deprived of his passport in Ghana, however, the Ghanaian man must help the Austrian navigate the analogous situation he faced in Austria.

[12] "Es kommt, wie es kommen muss."

Fig. 10.1 *Zur Lage*: Jörg Haider appearing in an icon-like image

deliberately staged background: on the wall behind the singer is a small picture of Haider—his sole appearance in the film. Religious motifs and imagery recur throughout Seidl's oeuvre, and this image is indeed framed and hung much like a religious icon. Conspicuous on the bare wall and elevated to command attention or perhaps ironic reverence, Haider's image invites the viewer's reflection on the figure, who, though never appearing onscreen, drives the film through his words and actions. Placed in the context of the singer's lament at the present state of things, the image of Haider can be read as a final challenge for the viewer to resist the resignation of the lyrics and strive toward other potential outcomes.

Franz Fuchs: Ein Patriot (Franz Fuchs: A Patriot)

While *Zur Lage* ends with one couple's fantasy of intimidation and violence, Elisabeth Scharang's *Franz Fuchs: ein Patriot* revisits a period of actual violence carried out in the name of the far-right. From 1993 until 1997, Austria was terrorised by a series of letter and pipe bombs directed at minorities and at people and institutions aiding minorities and asylum seekers. Numerous people were severely injured by the letter bomb attacks and in the eastern town of Oberwart, four Roma men were murdered by a pipe bomb affixed with a xenophobic message. The letter bombs, addressed as coming from Count Ernst Rüdiger von Starhemberg, a historical figure who fought against the Ottoman Empire during the 1683 Siege of Vienna, were claimed to be the work of the "Bajuwarische Befreiungsarmee" (BBA Bajuvarian Liberation Army), a term referencing the Germanic tribes inhabiting what would become Bavaria and Austria. These references steered investigators into the milieu of neo-Nazis and the extreme right and failed to produce credible suspects, proving an embarrassment for the police and the Interior Ministry. This changed in 1997 when, during an unrelated traffic stop, a man attempted to blow himself up, severing both hands. In custody this man, Franz Fuchs, confessed to the bombings, claiming that he, as a BBA member, was defending Austria against its alleged infiltration by foreigners. Fuchs received a life sentence in 1997 and committed suicide in prison in 2000. Fuchs' refusal to speak on certain topics has allowed some speculation to persist whether he acted alone.

A project conducted to mark the tenth anniversary of Fuchs' arrest, Scharang's television film adopts the form of the docudrama. For Bill Nichols, docudramas derive their plot structure and meaning from the larger historical context yet employ filmmaking modes that are both non-fictional and fictional (2010: 145). Scharang, whose fictional and nonfictional works centre on topical and historical political issues, notes that the docudrama format appealed to her because, with Fuchs' suicide, there is no way to gain insights into his thoughts and actions other than through creative interpretation of his confessions (Scharang 2007). The interplay between the factual and fictional is evident in the opening sequence. It starts with a re-enactment of Fuchs, played by Karl Markovics, pacing in his cell and then being taken down a corridor.[13] In an implicit cut, the film then shifts to news footage of the real Fuchs entering a courtroom spewing political slogans. The sequence then shifts to a re-enactment of an interrogation, before closing with conventional, talking-head interviews with Fuchs' real-life interrogators.

The film's non-fictional segments not only offer factual support for the fictionalised elements, but also introduce speculation. Detailing events from nearly a decade earlier, the newsreel footage supplies viewers some context to the events, devoting particular attention to the media coverage

---

[13] For *Franz Fuchs*, Markovics is cast against his previous role in Houchang Allahyari's *Geboren in Absurdistan (Born in Absurdistan)* (1999), where he plays a hard-line bureaucrat who undergoes a change of heart through his interactions with the foreigners he is supposed to deport, a storyline his role repeated in Allahyari's *Die verrückte Welt der Ute Bock (The Crazy World of Ute Bock)* (2010).

of the bomb victims and to the investigation of Fuchs' residence. The interviews with Fuchs' acquaintances and real interrogators provide further background, yet also proffer psychological readings of Fuchs' personal life. Cautiously foregrounding their limited perspective, the interviewees venture their speculations on Fuchs' failures in education and the workplace, an early attempted suicide, or his romantic relationships.

The film's fictionalised passages continue the psychological profiling of Franz Fuchs, but also attempt to add dramatic counterpoint. The fictionalised re-enactments, which according to the film's prefacing intertitle, are based solely on Fuchs' interrogation proceedings, both depict the interrogations themselves, but also dramatize details from Fuchs' confessions and his interrogators. These scenes, which often feature subdued, yet intense musical accompaniment, include depictions of Fuchs' clandestine delivery of the letter bombs and the increasingly paranoid measures he undertook to avoid his presumed surveillance. The fictionalised re-enactments establish and propel the film's dramatic arc: namely, the question whether Fuchs acted alone.

A possible answer is suggested by the film's treatment of Fuchs' most fatal attack, the Oberwart bombing. Here, the re-enactments clearly break with the stated adherence to Fuchs' statements. The film portrays re-enacted interrogations and shows the normally reserved Fuchs having an emotional breakdown when describing Oberwart. The film then ventures into the fictional by constructing a scene in which Fuchs, after setting up the bomb, witnesses the explosion from afar. As his real interrogators detail, Fuchs never admitted to being present. His interrogators, however, suspect that he was indeed at the attack because of his uncharacteristically emotional account. Perhaps to counter the speculative nature of this re-enactment, Scharang juxtaposes it with interviews she conducted at the bomb site with the victims' families, who detail its lingering impact. This footage stands out not only because of its length, but also because they are Scharang's only interviews with any of Fuchs' victims or in which she appears. The speculative re-enactments and the extensive interviews of the Oberwart sequence underscore the director's thesis of Fuchs as the sole perpetrator. Dismissing the suspicions of Fuchs' ties to neo-Nazi groups as a narrative that sought to give meaning to the tragedy, Scharang instead cites the lack of evidence of collusion and the investigators' conclusions about Fuchs' capabilities and loner inclinations (Scharang 2007). To that end, her film privileges the psychological motivations behind Fuchs' actions.

The film's psychological portrait of Fuchs as a single perpetrator, however, leaves any emphasis on the historical context under-explored. With the first bombings in December 1993, Fuchs' actions began after racially motivated attacks against foreigners were occurring in Germany and other parts of Europe. Furthermore, they occurred after years of the FPÖ's xenophobia, most recently its "Austria First" referendum that ended in February 1993. After the attacks began, the FPÖ was criticised for its inflammatory rhetoric and Haider even pledged to adopt a milder tone, while at the same time insinuating that the attacks may have been planned by leftists. This background is largely absent in Scharang's film.[14] Even the longer sequence devoted to the Oberwart bombing excludes the historical and political backdrop, which illustrates historian Oliver Rathkolb's point that many have forgotten how entwined Oberwart was in contemporary debates on immigration (2011: 35). Fuchs' motivations are presented only through re-enactments, some of which attest to the real Fuchs' reaction to contemporary events, such as his mention of former chancellor Franz Vranitzky's pledges to accept more refugees. The film also paraphrases Fuchs' anger at the opening of a Slovenian language school in Carinthia, an issue that occupied a central position for FPÖ politics, especially for Haider's early rise in that province.[15] Other re-enactments stress vague motivations, such as Fuchs describing his self-image as a patriot defending his antiquated moniker, "German-Austrians" [Deutschösterreicher], or his disavowal of his Austrian identity for a "German cultural heritage" [Deutschstämmigkeit]. Other references to political contexts are presented to encourage psychological readings. For example, in one re-enactment Fuchs explains his targeting of Helmut Zilk because of the Vienna mayor's joke that the city has benefitted from all immigrants, including those from Styria, Fuchs' home province. In a subsequent interview, Fuchs' psychologist describes Fuchs' sense of persecution and his dismay at childhood episodes of discrimination for his rural roots and Styrian dialect. Through this juxtaposition, the film invites the viewer to consider Fuchs' focus on Zilk from a psychological perspective, implying his perception of Zilk's comments as an attack on his threatened sense of identity.

[14] Scharang's film indirectly addresses this historical context during interviews with two police officers, who explain how their search for the bomber led them to numerous suspects with similar viewpoints as Fuchs, none of whom translated them into actual violence.

[15] The struggles for minority recognition, and right-wing backlash, for Carinthian Slovenians is the subject of the 2005 documentary, *Artikel 7 – Unser Recht!* by Thomas Korschil and Eva Simmler.

A decade after Fuchs' arrest, Scharang's film provided viewers with a useful revisiting of the facts of the case, but its docudrama format has limits for the film's engagement with the most significant act of right-wing inspired violence in Austria. Noting that "individual actors draw upon the prevailing threats and views of history," historian Gerhard Botz argues that the actions of Franz Fuchs "reflected the political climate in a certain way" (N.N. 2013).[16] In the film, *Franz Fuch: ein Patriot*, however, such a reflection is limited by the docudrama focus on Fuchs' personal history and psychological temperament. This serves Scharang well in supporting her conviction that Fuchs acted alone, yet creates an artificial vacuum around Fuchs, implicitly divorcing him from the political zeitgeist. The incendiary words and, in some cases, violent deeds that emanated from the far-right in Austria and across Europe surely were an influence on Fuchs. An emphasis on them in the film would deepen its exploration of Fuchs' earlier actions and, for the film's viewers in 2007, would open up contemporary parallels with continuing significance of the far-right.

TODESPOLKA [DEATH POLKA]

Inflammatory rhetoric is central to Michael Pfeifenberger's *Todespolka*: a fictional take on the far-right. A work of independent cinema, *Todespolka* employs a low-budget style and attitude to imagine an Austria where the far-right has taken control.[17] With its satirical portrayal, *Todespolka* aligns itself with Walter Wippersberg's 2001 mock-documentary presenting a right-wing corrective to history, *Die Wahrheit über Österreich: oder wie man uns belogen hat* [*The Truth about Austria: or how we have been lied to*], and with Peter Kern's 2002 film *Haider lebt - 1. April 2021* [*Haider lives – 1 April 2021*], which depicts an Austria after twenty years of the ÖVP/FPÖ coalition. The far-right party in *Todespolka* is the Citizens Party and it exhibits clear parallels with election strategies of the FPÖ and the BZÖ. Like the real Austrian parties, the Citizens Party is helmed by a charismatic leader who is shown donning a traditional dirndl at an all-night summer solstice festival, where she animates the crowd and even dances to polka music. This character is given the blatantly loaded name, Sieglinde Führer,

---

[16] "Einzeltäter greifen in der Gesellschaft vorhandene Bedrohungsszenarien und Geschichtsbilder auf. Die Tat von Franz Fuchs hat in gewisser Weise das Klima widergespiegelt" (N.N. 2013).

[17] See Fiddler (2011a) for detailed readings of these films.

206   N. SATHE

which channels National Socialism not only through the surname, but also the affection nickname, "Siegi," which her followers sometimes use with the interjection "heil." As her name signals, Führer's policies draw on the Nazi era: she has instituted penal labour camps to punish her undesirables: criminals, drug dealers, foreigners, "sexual perverts," child molesters, and anyone critical of the party. In addition to its xenophobia, the Citizen Party's opposition to the EU links it to the real far-right, and in *Todespolka*, the party has successfully exited Austria from the supranational organisation and reinstated the Schilling as its currency. The film's protagonist is Rafael, a medical student, who has recently moved into a suburban neighbourhood, where his neighbours suspect that, as a student, he must be seditious and drug-addicted. Rafael hopes to have a relaxing evening with fellow student Michael, an Austrian citizen of African descent. Accusing Michael of criminal behaviour, however, Rafael's neighbours murder Michael, and by the film's bloody finale, they, with the eager help of the corrupt police, kill Rafael and even fellow neighbours who refuse to support their cover-up of the murders.

The amateurish style and exaggerated elements in *Todespolka* signal its trash cinema aesthetics. This is clearly announced by the film's deliberately grotesque first image, which would not out of place in a work by iconic trash director John Waters. It opens on the naked backside of a far-right politician, from which a dominatrix loudly removes a dildo just before he expires from a heart attack after hearing a broadcast proclaiming Sieglinde Führer's election victory. If the remainder of *Todespolka* does not aspire to the same level of shock and provocation, it does conform to expectations of trash cinema. In addition to what Sarkhosh and Menninghaus describe as the "deformation of the standard mainstream formulae and anti-illusionist excess" (2016: 41), trash films exhibit exaggerated performances, unsophisticated costumes and settings, clumsy dialogue and editing, and deliberately unpolished production values.[18] Discussing what he calls trash or "paracinema," Jeffrey Sconce writes that this cinema's excessive qualities offer "a freedom from constraint, an opportunity to approach a film with a fresh and slightly defamiliarised perspective" (1995: 391). The extremes to which trash cinema is willing to go, for Sconce, allow it to offer 'a cinema so histrionic, anachronistic and excessive that it compels even the most casual viewer to engage it ironically' (1995: 393),

---

[18] A similar aesthetic is employed in Peter Kern's aforementioned satire *Haider lebt – 1. April 2021* (2002).

which opens the possibility for heightened critical awareness. This excess is evident in the portrayal of the grotesque, overly stereotypical neighbours, who are easily captivated by Führer's speeches. Similarly, with the party leader's name, the police force's brown uniforms resembling Nazi storm-troopers, and the party's penal camps, the film exploits opportunities to colour the Citizens Party in the most extreme position, as updated National Socialists. Most successfully over the top is the campy portrayal of Führer. Having her played by a non-native speaker, Israeli actress Tamara Stern, allows her exaggerated, histrionic speeches to become all the more de-familiarised. Despite the film's attempts at trash subversion, however, numerous reviewers are correct that these endeavours remain too tame to be effective, lacking the "sufficient extremity [...] analytical sharpness, or dramatic verve" (Kriest 2010), and thus wind up "a toothless banging away at the mere edges of acceptable taste" (Petraitis 2010). [19]

The real extremes of far-right discourse in Austria prove daunting for *Todespolka* to achieve the excess expected of trash cinema. Writing about post-VHS era filmmakers' difficulties in truly shocking an audience given the diversity of cinematic content and broader opportunities for film dis-tribution and production, Sconce ponders: "is it even possible to signify 'excess' or provoke controversy anymore? Some cultural center would have to remain to be attacked and defended" (2008: 48). Applied to the political context addressed by *Todespolka*, Sconce's question is particularly relevant because the "centre" of acceptable political discourse has already been breached by the extremes to which the Austrian far-right has gone in its campaign rhetoric. As a number of reviewers note, the campaign slo-gans and speeches of the far-right party in *Todespolka* are not particularly shocking because they seem very much like those of the FPÖ and BZÖ (Zlabinger 2010; Kurz 2010).[20] For example, the fictional Sieglinde Führer's rhetorical question to her audience whether they want "Burkas or

---

[19] Even as a grotesque depiction of suburbia, *Todespolka* does not distinguish itself as espe-cially shocking or disturbing when compared with such films as Harald Sicheritz' comedies *Muttertag* (1993) and *Hinterholz 8* (1998) or Ulrich Seidl's drama *Hundstage* (2001). Similarly, the scene in *Todespolka* in which Rafael's neighbours are astounded by the sado-maso basement studio can only pale in comparison with the real basement horrors of then recent cases sensationalized in the media: namely of Natascha Kampusch, who was held cap-tive for eight years until her escape in 2006, and of Josef Fritzl, who held his daughter captive for twenty-four years until her release in 2008.

[20] See Liebhart (2016: 73–5) and Wodak (2015: 143–8) for further discussion of far-right campaigns in Austria.

208   N. SATHE

our traditional folk clothing" finds ready parallels in the FPÖ 2008 campaign posters that promised "Daham statt Islam" [Home instead of Islam) or "Pummerin statt Muezzin" (The bell of St. Stephen's cathedral instead of the call of the muezzin).[21] Führer's posters in the film declaring "Wir räumen auf" [we are cleaning up] are synonymous with the BZÖ's 2008 slogan "Wir säubern Graz" [we are cleansing Graz]. Another reviewer even finds striking similarities between the film's Sieglinde Führer and FPÖ politician and former presidential candidate Barbara Rosenkranz (Kriest 2010). As extreme as Sieglinde Führer's call to have child molesters chemically castrated may sound, this was a campaign talking point for FPÖ leader H. C. Strache (N.N. 2006).

The depiction of a far-right party, however, was secondary, as the filmmakers note, to representing its potential influence on individuals. This is reinforced in that Sieglinde Führer only appears as a media presence. Her image is ubiquitous, plastered on posters and broadcast on radio and television, and Rafael's neighbours and the police are consistently shown listening or watching Führer's performance at the festival, which recalls the image-conscious media focus characterising both Haider's and Strache's political presence.[22] Despite this specific similarity, producer and screenwriter Stephan Demmelbauer notes that *Todespolka* could have taken place in any country, reminding instead:

> It has more to do with the long-distance effects of political actions on the lives of the individuals, of whom the populists cannot or do not want to take notice. [...] What politicians at campaign events spew into the crowds to charge up the atmosphere can, in the right place and time, lead to brute violence. With *Todespolka*, our concern was making this, in its most radical form, clear even to a mass audience. (Winsemann 2010)[23]

---

[21] Another poster in the film declares "Wir sind die Retter des Abendlands" (We are the saviours of the Occident), which recalls FPÖ campaign posters calling for "Abendland in Christenhand" (The Occident in Christian hands).

[22] For a discussion of Haider's image construction, see Gingrich (2002: 70–81) and on Strache, see Wodak (2015: 136–41).

[23] "Es geht vielmehr um die Fernwirkung politischen Handelns auf das leben einzelner Menschen, die Populisten gar nicht zur Kenntnis nehmen können oder wollen.[...]Was Politiker bei Wahlveranstaltungen in die Menge werfen, um Stimmung zu machen, kann im rechten Moment zu roher Gewalt führen. Dies in aller Radikalität verständlich zu machen, auch einem massenpublikum, war das Anliegen des Projektes Todespolka." (Winsemann 2010).

With its characteristically blunt manner, *Todespolka* stages numerous instances in which political discourse triggers threatening reactions. After presenting a snippet in which Führer rails against criminal foreigners, the film shows two listeners debating the merits of immediately executing foreign criminals or first interrogating them about accomplices. After that scene, Rafael is shown witnessing a dark-skinned man being brutally taken into custody for no apparent reason. In a scene at a convenience store, the clerk watches Führer on television denouncing the so-called "Gutmenschen" [goody two-shoes], a term the real FPÖ uses pejoratively to describe humanitarian or liberal-minded supporters of immigrants and asylum seekers (Parigger 2007). When Rafael approaches, the suspicious attendant calls him a "Gutmensch," who, she claims, belongs in a penal camp.

The film's most violent example of political influence is Michael's murder. The neighbourhood residents, all staunch supporters of Führer, eagerly watch her speeches conjuring up criminal foreigners and promising law and order. Seemingly conditioned by Führer's words, the neighbours, when confronted with Michael's mere presence, can only see him as dangerous and assume he is Rafael's drug supplier. When one neighbour covers up his own misdeeds by falsely accusing Michael of attacking his wife, the mob feels justified in executing Michael. They rely on similar logic with Rafael, whom they murder as a witness to their actions, but whose death they sanction because of his presumed criminality and hostility to the state.

To communicate with a mass audience, scriptwriter Demmelbauer and director Pfeifenberger adopt a trash cinema approach for their dystopian satire of an Austria under the grip of the far-right. Of the few non-documentary films directly addressing the Austrian far-right, such as *Todespolka* and the aforementioned films by Kern and Wippersberg, most employ paracinematic and satirical modes. This constitutes a striking index of the severity of the far-right's political rhetoric and the challenge it poses for artists reflecting on it. As Alysson Fiddler argues, this challenge demands that artists "cut across contemporary political discourse" in order to counter the "so-called 'truths' continually performed and perpetuated by populist far-right politics" (Fiddler 2011a: 127). If *Todespolka*, undermined by its tameness, may not achieve the expected grotesque irreverence of trash cinema, it does, as a reflection on the far-right, undermine their discourse and campaigns. The film's Citizen's Party deconstructs the agendas of the FPÖ by mocking their style and fictionally

210   N. SATHE

taking their proposals to their logical extreme outcomes, for which, in some aspects, only a slight degree of de-familiarisation was needed. The strong correspondences between the film and reality prompted one reviewer's remark that *Todespolka* presents "a horribly familiar Austria that appears much too less exaggerated as one might wish" (Brenner 2010).[24] The most shocking aspect about the far-right party in this trash film, then, might be, unintentionally, not its distance from the real far-right but its similarities with it.

CONCLUSION

The three films discussed above distinguish themselves from many other Austrian works in that they are less focused on those affected by the far-right's rhetoric or policies and instead focus more directly on the far-right's supporters. Their depictions of the ideologies and instances of the far-right, however, are carefully managed. In *Zur Lage*, the different extreme right-wing viewpoints shown are presented either through almost caricatured extremes or alongside contradictions—thus in contextualisation that allows their ready debunking. In *Franz Fuchs*, the intense focus on the titular figure's individual psychology misses opportunities to explore connections to the far-right to their fullest. Even in *Todespolka*, the far-right ideologies and politicians are omnipresent, but are always enveloped in the satirical packaging of trash cinema. This tendency is surely an indication of the filmmakers' sensitivity to the potential of allowing representations of far-right discourse to become its legitimation or distribution. The challenge of more penetrating, in-depth representations of what motivates and sustains far-right supporters and figures thus remains unanswered by these films. They do, however, clearly exhibit a unifying concern with an engagement in the political sphere against the populist far-right in Austria. The filmmakers of *Zur Lage* take stock of their fellow citizens in the hopes of awakening a critical consciousness about the significance of the political for their lives. With *Franz Fuchs*, Scharang seeks to heighten and shape historical awareness about a deadly act of political violence connected to the far-right's discourse. *Todespolka* attempts to illustrate the dangerous potential of inflammatory political ideas and, through exaggerated satire, to dismantle the electoral strategies of the

---

[24] "... ein entsetzlich vertrautes Österreich, das viel weniger überzeichnet wirkt als wünschenswert wäre ..." (Brenner 2010).

FPÖ. As the electoral success of the populist and nationalist far-right in Austria and across the continent, indeed the globe, continues, there will surely be cause for future filmmakers to mobilise the cinematic engagement and even resistance that is evident in these three films.

Bibliography

Ajanovic, Edma, Stefanie Mayer and Birgit Sauer. 2015. Umkämpfte Räume Antipluralismus in rechtsextremen Diskursen in Österreich', *OZP – Austrian Journal of Political Science* 44 (2): 75–85.

Ajanovic, Edma, Stefanie Mayer and Birgit Sauer. 2016. Spaces of Right-Wing Populism and Anti-Muslim Racism in Austria: Identitarian Movement, Civil Initiatives and the Fight against "Islamisation." *Politologický Časopis/Czech Journal of Political Science*, 2: 131–148.

Albert, Barbara. 2002. Der Regierungswechsel erforderte unbedingt eine Reaktion. Interview. *Der Standard*, June 9. http://derstandard.at/971586/Der-Regierungswechsel-erforderte-unbedingt-eine-Reaktion. Accessed 3 June 2017.

Brenner, Gini. 2010. Review of *Todespolka*. *SKIP.at*. https://www.skip.at/film/13853/. Accessed 20 May 2017.

Dassanowsky, Robert von. 2006. Austria Hungry. *Bright Lights Film Journal*. http://brightlightsfilm.com/austria-hungry-return-film-nation/#.WXyRnRiZPVo. Accessed 1 November 2008.

Dassanowsky, Robert von and Oliver Speck. 2014. Introduction. In *New Austrian Film*, eds. von Dassanowsky, Robert and Oliver Speck. New York: Berghahn.

Diffrient, David Scott. 2014. *Omnibus Films: Theorizing Transauthorial Cinema*. Edinburgh: Edinburgh UP: 1–20.

Fiddler, Alysson. 2006. Shifting Boundaries: Responses to Multiculturalism at the Turn of the Twenty-First Century. In *A History of Austrian Literature*, ed. Kohl, Katrin and Ritchie Robinson. Rochester, NY: Camden House. 265–289.

Fiddler, Alysson. 2011a. Fooling around with Film: Political Visions of Austria—Past, Present and Future. *Austrian Studies* 19: 126–141.

Fiddler, Alysson. 2011b. Lights, Camera, … Protest! Austrian Film-makers and the Extreme Right. *Journal of European Popular Culture* 2 (1): 5–18.

Gärtner, Reinhold. 2002. The FPÖ, Foreigners, and Racism in the Haider Era. In *The Haider Phenomenon in Austria*, ed. Wodak, Ruth and Anton Pelinka. New Brunswick, New Jersey: Transaction: 17–32.

Gingrich, Andre. 2002. A Man for All Seasons: An Anthropological Perspective on Public Representation and Cultural Politics of the Austrian Freedom Party. In *The Haider Phenomenon in Austria*, ed. Wodak, Ruth and Anton Pelinka. New Brunswick, New Jersey: Transaction: 67–94.

212 N. SATHE

Heinisch, Reinhard. 2008. Right-Wing Populism in Austria: A Case for Comparison. *Problems of Post-Communism* 55 (3): 40–56.

Heinisch, Reinhard and Kristina Hauser. 2016. The Mainstreaming of the Austrian Freedom Party: the more things change… In *Radical Right-Wing Populist Parties in Western Europe*, ed. Akkerman, Tjitske, Sarah L. de Lange, and Matthijs Rooduijn. New York: Routledge: 73–93.

Hipfl, Brigitte and Daniela Gronold. 2011. Asylum Seekers as Austria's Other: The Re-Emergence of Austria's Colonial Past in a State-of-exception. *Social Identities* 17 (1): 27–40.

Huber, Christoph. 2014. Austria Plays Itself and Sees *Da Him*: Notes on the Image of Austria in the Films of Michael Glawogger. In *New Austrian Film*, ed. von Dassanowsky, Robert and Oliver Speck. New York: Berghahn: 335–342.

Kalmazadeh, Dominik. 2002. Hausbesuche und Stammtischreden. Review of *Zur Lage*. https://derstandard.at/973107/Hausbesuche-und-Stammtischreden. Accessed 3 June 2017.

Kriest, Ulrich. 2010. Review of *Todespolka*. *Filmzentrale.de*. http://www.filmzentrale.com/rezis2/todespolkauk.htm. Accessed 20 May 2017.

Krylova, Katya. 2017. *The Long Shadow of the Past: Contemporary Austrian Literature, Film, and Culture*. Rochester, NY: Camden House.

Krzyzanowski, Michal and Ruth Wodak. 2009. *The Politics of Exclusion: Debating Migration in Austria*. New Brunswick, New Jersey: Transaction.

Kurz, Joachim. 2010. Die totale Sieglinde. Review of *Todespolka*. *Kino-zeit.de*. http://www.kino-zeit.de/dvd/todespolka-dvd. Accessed 20 May 2017.

Liebhart, Karin. 2016. A Multi-Method Approach to the Comparative Analysis of Anti-Pluralistic Politics. In *German Perspectives on Right-Wing Extremism: Challenges for Comparative Analysis*, ed. Kiess, Johannes, Oliver Decker, and Elmar Brähler. New York: Routledge: 61–80.

Linder-Beroud, Waltraud and Tobias Widmaier. 2007. Kein schöner Land in dieser Zeit, *Historisch-kritisches Liederlexikon*. http://www.liederlexikon.de/lieder/kein_schoener_land_in_dieser_zeit/. Accessed 20 September 2017.

Lim, Dennis. 2006. Greetings from the Land of Feel-bad Cinema. *New York Times*, 26 November. http://www.nytimes.com/2006/11/26/movies/26lim.html. Accessed 1 November 2008.

Lorenz, Dagmar. 2004. The Struggle for a Civil Society and beyond: Austrian Writers and Intellectuals Confronting the Political Right. *New German Critique* 93 (Autumn): 19–41.

Marchart, Oliver. 2002. Austrifying Europe: Ultra-Right Populism and the New Culture of Resistance. *Cultural Studies* 16 (6): 809–819.

Mathijs, Ernest and Jamie Sexton. 2011. *Cult Cinema: An Introduction*. Malden, Massachusetts: Wiley-Blackwell.

Mundhenke, Florian. 2011. Authenticity vs. Artifice: The Hybrid Cinematic Approach of Ulrich Seidl. *Austrian Studies* 19: 113–125.

RESISTANCE AGAINST ITSELF: AUSTRIAN CINEMA'S RESPONSES... 213

N., N. 2002a. Zur Lage: Befund für Österreich. Review of *Zur Lage: Österreich in sechs Kapitel.* *Der Standard*, 22 March. http://derstandard.at/899372/Zur-Lage-Befund-fuer-Oesterreich. Accessed 3 June 2017.

N., N. 2002b. Review of *Zur Lage: Österreich in sechs Kapiteln.* *SKIP.at.* https://www.skip.at/film/3625/. Accessed 20 May 2017.

N., N. 2006. "Kommen Sie näher, ich beiße nicht": H.C. Strache auf Stimmenfang am Rochungsmarkt. *News.at*, 12 September. https://www.news.at/a/kommen-sie-h-c-strache-stimmenfang-rochungsmarkt-150873. Accessed 1 July 2017.

N., N. 2010. *Todespolka*: Im Würgegriff des Mob. Review of *Todespolka. Der Standard*, 5 May. http://derstandard.at/1271376008494/Im-Wuergegriff-des-Mob. Accessed 20 May 2017.

N., N. 2013. Franz Fuchs: Ein Spiegel des Klimas in Österreich. *Kleine Zeitung*, 3 December. http://www.kleinezeitung.at/steiermark/graz/4106279/20-Jahre-Briefbomben_Franz-Fuchs_Ein-Spiegel-des-Klimas. Accessed 3 June 2017.

Nichols, Bill. 2010. *Introduction to Documentary.* 2nd ed. Bloomington, Indiana: Indiana UP.

Öner, Selcen. 2014. Different Manifestations of the Rise of Far-Right in European Politics: The Cases of Germany and Austria. *Marmara Journal of European Studies* 22 (2): 85–106.

Opratko, Benjamin. 2015. Austria's New Right. *Jacobin*, December 1. https://www.jacobinmag.com/2015/12/austria-freedom-party-strache-fpo-nazi-right-wing/. Accessed 7 July 2017.

Parigger, Robert. 2007. Strache beklagt "Meinungsdiktate von Gutmenschen. *Die Presse*, 2 June. http://diepresse.com/home/innenpolitik/308005/Strache-beklagt-Meinungsdiktate-von-Gutmenschen#. Accessed 1 July 2017.

Petraitis, Marian. 2010. Review of *Todespolka. Filmstarts.de.* http://www.filmstarts.de/kritiken/139607/kritik.html. Accessed 20 May 2017.

Pichler, Barbara. 2012. The Construction of Reality: Aspects of Austrian Cinema between Fiction and Documentary. In *Cinema and Social Change in Germany and Austria*, eds. Gabrielle Mueller and James Skidmore. Waterloo, Ontario: Wilfrid Laurier UP: 267–281.

Rathkolb, Oliver. 2011. *Die paradoxe Republik: Österreich 1945 bis 2010.* Innsbruck: Haymon.

Reyes, Damaso. 2011. Living in the Shadows: Navigating Austria's Evolving Asylum Policy. *World Policy Journal*, Winter: 87–95.

Richardson, John E. and Ruth Wodak. 2009. Recontextualising Fascist Ideologies of the Past: Right-wing Discourses on Employment and Nativism in Austria and the United Kingdom. *Critical Discourse Studies* 6 (4): 251–267.

Sarkhosh, Keyvan and Winfried Menninghaus. 2016. Enjoying Trash Films: Underlying Features, Viewing Stances, and Experiential Response Dimensions, *Poetics*, 57: 40–54.

Scharang, Elisabeth. 2007. Regisseurin Scharang über den Franz Fuchs-Film: "Wo sind die Beweise?" Interview. *Der Standard*, 3 August. http://derstandard.at/2921072/Regisseurin-Scharang-ueber-den-Franz-Fuchs-Film-Wo-sind-die-Beweise. Accessed 3 June 2017.

Sconce, Jeffrey, Joe Bob Briggs, John Hoberman, Damien Love, Tim Lucas, Danny Peary, and Peter Stanfield. 2008. Cult Cinema: A Critical Symposium. *Cineaste* Winter: 43–50.

Sconce, Jeffrey. 1995. "Trashing" the Academy: Taste, Excess and an Emerging Politics of Cinematic Style. *Screen* 36 (4): 371–393.

Winsemann, Bettina. 2010. Ein Ort des Friedens und der Sicherheit. Review of *Todespolka*. *Telepolis*, 26 May. https://www.heise.de/tp/news/Ein-Ort-des-Friedens-und-der-Sicherheit-2016412.html. Accessed 20 May 2017.

Wodak, Ruth., Rudolf de Cillia, Martin Reisigl, and Karin Liebhart. 2009. *The Discursive Construction of National Identity*. 2nd ed. Edinburgh: Edinburgh UP.

Wodak, Ruth. 2015. *The Politics of Fear: What Right-Wing Populist Discourses Mean*.Washington, DC: Sage.

Zaslove, Andrej. 2004. Closing the Door: The Ideology and Impact of Radical Right Populism on Immigration Policy in Austria and Italy. *Journal of Political Ideologies* 9 (1): 99–118.

Zlabinger, Ralf. 2010. Review of *Todespolka*. *Filmtipps.at*. https://www.filmtipps.at/kritiken/Todespolka/. Accessed 20 May 2017.

CHAPTER 11

Frivolity and Place Branding in Martínez Lázaro's 'Nationalist Comedies'

Alfredo Martínez-Expósito

This chapter puts forward the hypothesis that Martínez Lázaro's nationalist comedies *Ocho apellidos vascos/Spanish Affair* (2014) and *Ocho apellidos catalanes/Spanish Affair 2* (2015) draw together several of the most salient aspects of nation branding (Anholt 2010). These include commodification of place, authentication of local stereotypes, promotion of communication strategies that privilege a tourist's gaze, selective recycling of history, and the emergence of commercial nationalism. *Ocho apellidos vascos*, the biggest Spanish box office 'hit' of all time, was released in the wake of ETA's historic ceasefire declaration. A year later, *Ocho apellidos catalanes* was released against the backdrop of an unprecedented pro-independence mobilisation in Catalonia. Concurrently, the Spain's central government demoted the Brand Spain strategy (Marca España) from an overarching government policy to a mere tactic in its 2014 Law of Exterior Action.

In a national context marked by a deep realignment of political agents in Catalonia on both sides of the independence debate, and by domestic

---

A. Martínez-Expósito (✉)
School of Languages and Linguistics, University of Melbourne,
Melbourne, VIC, Australia
e-mail: alfredo.m@unimelb.edu.au

© The Author(s) 2018　　　　　　　　　　　　　　　　　　215
J. Harvey (ed.), *Nationalism in Contemporary Western European Cinema*, Palgrave European Film and Media Studies,
https://doi.org/10.1007/978-3-319-73667-9_11

decline in the popularity of Brand Spain, *Ocho apellidos catalanes* mobilises branding and ideological discourses. These sober discourses are present in the film in impactful ways that belie its seemingly innocuous reliance on clichés and stereotypes. This chapter explores the influence of these discourses on the films' treatment of key 'places'—specifically, Spain, Catalonia, the Basque Country, and Andalucia. Through an analysis of Martínez Lázaro's two nationalist comedies the aim is to engage with the notion of political frivolity, which gained critical clout as a comprehensive critique of the historical revisionism associated with former prime minister Rodríguez Zapatero. As a cultural category, the notion of frivolity has often been used in the Catalan independence debate as a rough equivalent to populism. In *Ocho apellidos catalanes*, strategies of place branding and nation branding seem to coincide extremely well with those ideas of political frivolity that are expected to illuminate the debate on nationhood in both the Spanish and European context—a debate that is increasingly urgent and complex.

Peripheral Nationalisms as Real Context for the *Ocho apellidos* Diptych

Of course, nationalism is a distinctive feature of contemporary Spain, yet its main frame of reference is no longer the centralising agenda of Franco-era far-right ideology. Rather it is most manifestly associated with the centrifugal movements in Catalonia, Valencia, the Balearic Islands, the Basque Country, Navarre, Galicia, and the Canary Islands, where a number of local political parties define themselves as nationalist. While the sentiment of Spanish nationalism has largely failed to find explicit political expression in recent decades, the so-called 'peripheral' nationalisms that were repressed by Franco's dictatorship have enjoyed a vigorous revival, especially in Catalonia and the Basque Country. The right-wing coalition Convergència i Unió ruled Catalonia from 1980 until 2003 and returned to power in 2010. Euzko Alderdi Jeltzalea (the Basque Nationalist Party) formed governments in the Basque Country in the years 1980–2009, and has done so again since 2012. Both parties have used their parliamentary majorities to foster their respective 'national' cultures, which includes promoting the Catalan and Basque languages.

The two comedies of nationalist themes directed by Emilio Martínez Lázaro and released in 2014 and 2015 became blockbusters, their social

FRIVOLITY AND PLACE BRANDING IN MARTÍNEZ LÁZARO'S 'NATIONALIST... 217

and cultural impact transcending the strict limits of film consumption.[1] Both films display many constitutive elements of the idea of 'nation branding' originally proposed by Simon Anholt (2010; Aronczyk 2013). Specifically, both films evidence the commodification of the physical space, the authentication of regional stereotypes, the use of communication strategies based on the tourist gaze, the selective recycling of history, and the emergence of an embryonic commercial nationalism. Both films implicitly compare the local brands involved (Basque Country, Catalonia) with the Brand Spain strategy, which was launched by the central government in 2002 based on previous experiences dating back to1998. This chapter contends that to interpret these comedies as texts of local and national promotion is to broach the idea of political frivolity, a concept that recurs in Spanish public debate as part of a critical response to the historical revisionism promoted by all tiers of government since 2002. The concept of political frivolity encompasses a set of strategies of resistance that can work on a wide variety of levels, ranging from the use of language (Derrida 1980) to tactical use of the masses as element of resistance (Chesters and Welsh 2006)—including populist resignification of culture and of public spaces.

Martínez Lázaro's nationalist comedies have been described as frivolous by film critics who perceive an historical imbalance between the sternness of the themes presented and the comical tone used to 'dress them up' for popular consumption. It may be argued that any cinematic use of the rhetoric of 'nation branding' is likely to generate trivial political interventions; nonetheless, in the case of the two *Ocho apellidos* films the conflict between seriousness and humour can be observed to have ethical repercussions.

In *Ocho apellidos vascos*, Amaia (Clara Lago), a young Basque girl on holidays in Seville, meets Rafa (Dani Robira). Straightaway they have a

---

[1] *Ocho apellidos vascos* (2014) was produced by Snow Films, LaZona Films, Kowalski Films, and Telecinco Cinema. Set in Seville (Andalucia), Leitza (Navarra), Getaria, San Sebastián, Zarautz, and Zumaia (Basque Country), its published budget was €3 million and its first-year box office domestic results exceeded €55 million. By way of comparison, for 2014 the top four Spanish market hits were *El Niño* (Spain, €15.9 million), *Maleficent* (UK, €12.5 million), and *Dawn of the Planet of the Apes* (USA, €12.4 million; all figures are sourced from IMDb). *Ocho apellidos catalanes* (2015) was produced by LaZona Films for Telecinco Cinema, in collaboration with Mediaset España and Movistar+. The film was shot on location in Sevilla, Madrid, Girona, and Baix Ampurdá (Catalonia). With a budget of €4.5 million, it grossed more than €32 million (Boletín informativo 2015).

sexual intercourse; because both are highly intoxicated, it concludes unsatisfactorily. Amaia returns to her village, the fictitious Argoitia in the Basque Country, where her boyfriend Antxon has just put an end to their engagement. Meanwhile, in Seville, Rafa decides to travel to Argoitia to meet Amaia once more, and attempt to resume their love affair, ignoring his friends' advice to the contrary. Ominously, they remind him of the poor reputation of Basque people, and the reciprocal acrimony between Basques and Andalusians.

Seeking to anticipate difficult situations, Rafa tries to familiarise himself with the Basque language—amusingly, he begins pronouncing Castilian with a heavy Basque accent. Upon arrival at Argoitia, Amaia rejects Rafa, and their affair seems to have ended. However, at the same time, Amaia's father, a tuna fisherman known as Koldo (Karra Elejalde), returns to Argoitia to spend a few days with his daughter after a long absence. Proud and obstinate, Amaia does not want her father to find out about her breakup with Antxon, whom he has not had the chance to meet. So Amaia begs Rafa to impersonate her fiancé during her father's short visit. With the help of Merche (Carmen Machi), a widow who has resided for many years in the Barque Country, Rafa/Antxon and Amaia prepare their masquerade. They hope that Koldo will leave before the date set for the wedding; however, at the last minute Koldo changes his mind and decides to stay for the ceremony. On the wedding day, standing at the altar, Amaia surprisingly accepts the vows, but Rafa/Antxon refuses to take the plunge into formal matrimony. Believing he has lost Amaia forever, Rafa then returns to Seville. Yet, as a surprise ending, in Seville he finds that Amaia has left Argoitia to follow him to Andalusia and resume their relationship.

Ocho apellidos catalanes (2015) is conceived as a plot continuous with that of *Ocho apellidos vascos*. Amaia has broken up with Rafa: she has left for Catalonia where she plans to marry a Catalan hipster named Pau (Berto Romero). Alarmed by this news, Koldo travels to Seville and persuades Rafa of the need to prevent the wedding. Once in Catalonia, Koldo and Rafa meet Pau, whose aesthetic sensibility seems to embody a satirised cosmopolitanism that contrasts vividly with Koldo's rusticity. The location for the prospective wedding is the farmhouse of Pau's grandmother, a pro-independence activist called Roser (Rosa María Sardá). Roser believes that Catalonia has become an independent country; her family and all her neighbours have led her to believe that the fake referendum of 9 November of 2014 was actually legal and successful. Given

Roser's dominant and controlling nature, and to avoid disappointing her, all the family and town maintain the pantomime of Catalonia's independence. The romantic tangle is resolved with the break-up of Amaia and Pau—not at the altar, but in front of the local mayor who is charged with performing their marriage ceremony. The film also ends with the improvised marriage of Koldo and Merche.

Ocho apellidos vascos and *Ocho apellidos catalanes* were released against a backdrop of intense political changes in the Basque Country and Catalonia. A basic chronology for these changes should include the following key dates: 16 May 2010, last political assassination by ETA; 10 July 2010, demonstration in Barcelona against the ruling of the Constitutional Court suspending parts of the 2006 Catalan Statute of Autonomy; 20 October 2011, ETA's definitive ceasefire; June to November 2013, production and filming of *Ocho apellidos vascos*, released in 14 May 2014; 8 April 2014, public release of *Estrategia Basque Country*, a Basque government's internationalisation policy (Eusko Jaurlaritza and Gobierno Vasco 2014); 20 November 2015, *Ocho apellidos catalanes* opens on the day of the fortieth anniversary of Franco's death.

Martínez Lázaro's Constructions of Foreignness and Place

The huge box office success and public appeal of Martínez Lázaro's two comedies of nationalist humour are inseparable from a comic plot based on effective narrative tools such as ambiguity, misunderstanding, the made-up story, and double meanings. Both films combine elements from comedic sub-genres such as the romantic comedy and the sitcom. Yet these are subordinated to the overarching structure delineated by the main characters' travels. Critical commentaries frequently centred on the presumed cathartic effects in Spanish society of the films' parodies of Basque and Catalan nationalisms. Following decades of unrest, the Spanish public had become habituated to a perspective that privileged dramatic and tragic representations of all matters related to the Basque Country. And once ETA's decades-long terror campaign seemed to be coming to an end, Spanish society found itself immersed in a process of escalating separatist tension in Catalonia.

The thematisation of national difference is one of the most interesting aspects of these films. Obviously, as comedies, their treatment of the cultural diversity is not free from stereotypes. Cultural stereotypes and clichés help to simplify potentially complex discourses, while providing the necessary dose of humour required by the comical context. In both films the construction of foreignness is particularly interesting since it literally negates any existing conception of Spanish culture as a homogeneous entity. Without a doubt, such cultural homogeneity belongs neither to the collective imaginary of Spanish cultural diversity, nor to the official policies issued from Madrid since the reinstatement of democracy in 1977. However, the myth of Spanish homogeneity occupies a prominent place within Basque and Catalan nationalist discourses as an assigned attribute of Spanishness—as a monolithic repressor of all differences. Martínez Lázaro's films, therefore, juggle with a fundamental double perspective, which can be summarised as follows. One of these is the Basque perspective described by some of the characters as *arbertzale* (Basque nationalist left): for instance, the youngsters that Rafa meets in jail talk about *kale borroka* (Basque for 'urban guerrilla'), and their contacts with an organisation that cannot be other than ETA.[2] The second perspective is associated with fisherman Koldo, Amaia's father, who stands for possibilist nationalism and, at times, represents a vehement supporter of old school politics identifiable with the conservative Basque National Party. Other secondary characters can be easily ascribed either to the *arbetzale* realm (the tavern and its members seem like a nod to the aesthetics of the *herriko tabernas*) or to the world of the Basque National Party (the traditionalism represented by the town's church and priest).

For the stereotyped representatives of Basque nationalism, the Spanish stereotype consists in cultural and linguistic arrogance that naturally leads to an oppressive political centralism, and to a symbolic order that seeks to impose homogeneity. In *Ocho apellidos catalanes* the Basque point of view is also complemented by a stereotype of the Spanish people attributed to the Catalonian rural bourgeoisie, according to which Spaniards are inferior, incapable, and aggressive. In addition to these, there is a third point of view—an Andalusian or Sevillian perspective, nourished by several cultural clichés associated with music, *joie de vivre*, and the like. Yet this

---

[2] Recent Spanish films about ETA have never used comedy as a genre. Some of the more well-known titles include dramas and political thrillers such as *La voz de su amo* (Martínez Lázaro 2001), *Todos estamos invitados* (Gutiérrez Aragón 2008), *Celda 211* (Monzón 2009), *Asier ETA biok* (Merino and Merino 2012), *Lasa y Zabala* (Malo 2014), and *Fuego* (Marías 2014).

FRIVOLITY AND PLACE BRANDING IN MARTÍNEZ LÁZARO'S 'NATIONALIST... 221

perspective does not have a steady and unequivocal denomination: Rafa's friends refer to themselves as Andalusians, while Rafa often uses Seville as a marker of identity; Basques and Catalonians categorise all of these characters as Spanish. As such, the third, unsteady perspective correlates Seville, Andalucia, and Spain, and in this sphere there is no political qualification that allows for identifying characters and spaces in terms of Spanish nationalism.

Between both groups linked with the essential double perspective, two particular characters act as hinges: these are Merche, who takes a leading role in both films, and Judit (Belén Cuesta), who first appears in *Ocho apellidos catalanes*. Merche is a woman from Extremadura, widow of a *guardia civil* police officer. She is been living for years in the Basque Country, where she feels totally integrated.

As a hinge character, she is presented in relation to the notions of foreignness in both films. The scene in which Merche and Rafa first meet is particularly significant: in a rural bus packed with serious and impenetrable Basque men, the friendly, cheerful Merche becomes the first welcoming sign to a land that, so far, Rafa has experienced as hostile. Whether from Rafa's body language, or from the tourist guide he is reading, Merche unequivocally infers that Rafa hails from Spain's south. Their shared geographical origin is enough for them to engage in friendly conversation. Merche's character is defined, both structurally and thematically, as that of a mediator, the quintessential translator between two worlds that pretend not to understand each other. In the Catalan case, the foreign but perfectly integrated character is Judit, a Galician wedding planner who wishes to pass as Catalan at all costs.

In *Ocho apellidos vascos* the dynamics of place branding and nation branding, as well as the concurrent social and political discourses, are constantly emphasised. The cinematic construction of three such 'places' is particularly relevant: Spain, Seville, and the Basque Country. These 'places' prove interdependent in their functions. Importantly, the signifier 'Spain' seems to vanish from the ideological world of the film; it is subject to a subtle process of erasure, whereby some of the traditional attributes associated with 'Spain' are transferred to the signifier 'Seville'. The latter and the signifier the 'Basque Country' are shown through the perspective of an outsider who simultaneously eroticises and exoticises the region for Spanish film audiences. These perspectives are not symmetrical: Amaia's visit to Seville is not presented as a shocking or unpleasant experience, whereas Rafa's trip to the Basque Country is full of the traumatic elements a comedy can possibly exploit to humorous effect. Rafa's othering gaze places the film in the orbit of the Spanish imaginary, and thus renders it barely consistent with the official Brand Basque Country as this was adopted by the Autonomous Government just weeks before the film's release in 2014.[3]

A key signifier in both films, 'Spain' was the object of a major nation branding strategy coordinated by Spain's central government from 2002, which gained strong media visibility between 2002 and 2010. *Ocho apellidos vascos* and *Ocho apellidos catalanes* invoke rhetorics of Spain's self-image and hetero-image. The Spanish self-image is constantly challenged by Spaniards who find themselves in situations that seem to question their own Spanishness. The Basque characters, meanwhile, are presented as 'different': they are the object of Rafa's othering gaze, which is also the perspective of the films' implicit viewer. Much of the plot development depends on the dramatic tension between the Spanish questioned self-image and the Basque hetero-image. Yet the signifier 'Spain', including its name and national symbols, is almost nowhere to be seen. Such careful avoidance of references to Spain produces a fascinating semiotic effect through the whole saga: namely, the idea of Spain is at once both present and absent. In a manner somewhat reminiscent of Martin Heidegger's negative writing, Spain in these films is a phantasmatic entity, a crossed-out idea that is simultaneously necessary and rejected (Heidegger 1956).

As a precondition for 'Seville', Andalusia is the second key place. Andalusia frames each film's story as both the starting and returning point of the protagonist-traveller. Whereas it can be observed that other autonomous communities such as the Basque Country and Catalonia have been very agile in adopting holistic city branding and nation branding strategies, Andalusia has focused its branding in the tourism sector.[4] Therefore, Brand Andalusia can be defined by the hypertrophy of its well-rehearsed sun-and-sand tourism model (Martínez Pastor and Nicolás Ojeda 2014). Another important element of Brand Andalusia is the perpetuation of the synecdoche Andalusia-as-Spain, a trope that dates back

---

[3] John Urry's original notion of the tourist gaze as a set of expectations placed upon local communities by tourists who are in search of authentic cultural experiences implies the notions of differentiation and reification that are present in all *othering* practices (Urry 1990: 120–128).

[4] Anholt's classic hexagon includes tourism/exports, governance, foreign investment, immigration, cultural patrimony, and social articulation (Anholt 2010).

to the early nineteenth century, and one that was strongly reinforced in tourism campaigns throughout the twentieth century (Liáñez Andrades and Puche Ruiz 2016). Since the Brand Spain's tourism promise has never fully abandoned the sun-and-sand message, it is obvious that Brand Spain and Brand Andalusia play on very similar themes. Overall, with regard to tourism their value proposition is virtually indistinguishable. Both *Ocho apellidos vascos* and *Ocho apellidos catalanes* support and reinforce the identification of Andalusia with Spain. Therefore the signifier 'Andalusia' fills the semantic void left by the erased signifier 'Spain'.

One strategy in the cinematic construction of the synecdoche Andalusia-as-Spain is the use of yet another place brand—that of the city of Cáceres in Extremadura. Although pertinent as Merche's birthplace, this city is never seen in the *Ocho apellidos* films, whether diegetically or as a location. Even so, Merche refers to Cáceres in two relevant ways. First, as her place of origin and, therefore as a mark of her identity that she considers perfectly compatible with her adoptive Basque identity. In declaring herself as a Cáceres-born Basque, Merche ironically echoes the popular saying that Bilbao dwellers have the right to be born wherever they please. The second way in which Cáceres reinforces the synecdoche Andalusia-as-Spain is through an elaboration of the first: Merche and Rafa recognise one another as fellow Spaniards and *also* as Spaniards who, for different reasons, are forced to hide their true identity and national sentiments. Rafa's faked identity when he impersonates the Basque Antxon is obvious throughout *Ocho apellidos vascos*. Close to the film's end, Merche reveals her true identity and her treasured photos and memories of Cáceres/Spain, all of which she keeps hidden from her Basque neighbours. The theme of the hiding Spaniards resurfaces in *Ocho apellidos catalanes* as one of the most politically intense moments of the saga.

The construction of the Basque Country as a brand in both films contains a number of well-known stereotypes, as well as some unexpected turns. Among the popular Basque stereotypes shared by the rest of Spain, weather and landscape clichés are prominent: scenery that is rainy, cloudy, cold, and dark; coastal locations, small towns; traditional and rural architectures. Allusions to well-built men and sexually conservative women abound. *Abertzales* are characterised by their clothes, hairstyle, and young age. Among the unexpected turns, it is surprising to find the synecdochical reduction of the Basque Country to a small emblematic village. The fictional village of Argoitia is composed from the Basque locations of Getaria and Zumaia, and the town of Leitza in Navarre. The use of cities as synecdoches or allegories of a larger territory has a long tradition in Spanish cinema; *Ocho apellidos vascos* seems to use this trope to create a characteristic, archetypical place-idea that signifies the Basque Country as a whole. As a result, the Basque Country is framed by the perspective of an outsider, as a hetero-image that is both different and alien (Buse and Triana-Toribio 2015). This said, the narrative of *Ocho apellidos vascos* also seems to point to a reversal or revocation of the outsider's gaze: towards the film's end, it is suggested that—northern and southern, respectively—Basques and Andalusians have more in common than they credit themselves for.

The Emergence of Brand Spain as an Iconic Brand

Spain's centuries-long concern with its national image went through a period of intense scrutiny in the first decade of the twenty-first century. In part this was due to the theoretical and policy-making impact of nation branding: as a relatively new concept with origins in the business and marketing arena, nation branding came to inspire the central government's strategy known as Marca España, or Brand Spain (Chislett 2008; Guillén 2005). Coined in 1996 by British brand consultant Simon Anholt, the idea that nations and cities could be reinvented as consumer-oriented brands rapidly caught the imagination of public administrators and tourism boards in Europe and elsewhere. Anholt proceeded to develop the seeds of a theoretical apparatus (Anholt 2007, 2010), as well as a double ranking instrument, the *Anholt Nation Brands Index*^{TM} and the *Anholt City Brand Index*^{TM}.[5] Despite the countless versions and applications of the concept, at its heart nation branding can be defined as 'a compendium of discourses and practices aimed to reconstituting nationhood through marketing and branding paradigms' (Kaneva 2011: 118). Earlier formulations of this neoliberal concept—that is, that the market can and should shape the national State—can be traced back to the origins of economic liberalism.

In Spain, the first attempt to employ the nation branding paradigm took place in 1999 with the creation of the Leading Brands of Spain Forum (Foro de Marcas Renombradas Españolas), a partnership between the central government (the Ministry of Industry, Tourism and Commerce; the Ministry of Foreign Affairs and Cooperation; the Spanish Institute of

---

[5] In 2004 Anholt founded the academic journal *Place Branding and Public Diplomacy.*

Foreign Trade, and the Spanish Patents and Trademark Office) and a group of companies listed on Spain's principal stock exchange, the IBEX 35.[6] The Forum's main goal was to drive a future Brand Spain strategy that should add value to Spanish companies and institutions abroad.[7] The Forum itself took charge of advertising and disclosing the activities of those companies and institutions to the public. As part of its communications strategy, the Forum implemented a programme of Honorary Ambassadors for Brand Spain, which achieved significant media coverage. Honorary Ambassadors were chosen from amongst those individuals and institutions that had made a significant contribution to the image of Spain abroad. The array of such names came to include, over the years, tennis player Rafael Nadal; tenors Plácido Domingo and José Carreras; basketball player Pau Gasol; film director Pedro Almodóvar; former Olympic Games executive Juan Antonio Samaranch; Inditex CEO Amancio Ortega; chef Ferrán Adrià, and institutions such as Instituto Cervantes, the Spanish National Soccer Team, Real Madrid and many others. This unusual combination of popular celebrities from sports and culture with financial and corporate names would allegedly contribute to normalising the idea that culture and market 'go hand in hand' in the task of redefining the country as a competitive brand in a globalised world.

In 2001, the Leading Brands of Spain Forum, the Spanish Institute of Foreign Trade, the Ministry of Foreign Affairs, the Association of Communication Executives, and the Elcano Royal Institute formalised the Brand Spain Project (Proyecto Marca España). This working group was created with the purpose of further constructing an image of Spain that was coherent with the country's strong financial and cultural indicators.[8] In sharp contrast with the optimism of the Brand Spain Project, from 2007 Spain's economy suffered a drastic transformation: the beginning of the Global Financial Crisis (GFC) and the stock market crisis in Spain would in turn bring about an unprecedented loss of public confidence in the State. In their timely analysis of the weakening of Spain's image in the

---

[6] The first recorded use of the word *brand* in relation to the nation appeared in a set of sociological papers penned by Amando de Miguel in the early 1970s, focusing mainly on notions related to national character (Miguel 1972).

[7] 'Ser el impulsor, junto con las administraciones públicas, de la Marca España a todos los niveles como una marca que aporte valor a las empresas e instituciones españolas en el extranjero' http://www.marcasrenombradas.com/info/foro/.

[8] 'Avanzar de forma coordinada en la construcción de una imagen de España que responda a la nueva realidad económica, social y cultural del país' (Noya 2003).

226   A. MARTÍNEZ-EXPÓSITO

aftermath of the 2007 GFC, Javier Noya and Fernando Prado proposed a refined definition of Brand Spain as a much broader paradigm that should not be limited to the economy.[9] Their differentiation between the overall image of the country and the specific reputation of the different sectors (such as the economy or culture) is relevant as demonstrated significant asymmetries exist between the market, politics, society, and culture. Such enlargement of the paradigm became one of the most visible features of a new branding institution, the Brand Spain High Commission (Alto Comisionado para la Marca España). Created in 2012, this High Commission focused on seeking overarching strategies encompassing all angles of Anholt's hexagon model of branding (Anholt 2010), in relation to Spain's image within the country and abroad.

Efforts to publicise the activities of the Forum, the Brand Spain Project, and the High Commission have been largely successful. Unlike Cool Britannia, Australia Unlimited, Pure New Zealand, Deutschland: Land der Ideen, and similar branding strategies around the world, the popularisation of Brand Spain was so successful that a media mythology about the image of Spain emerged, and this was soon crystallised into products of popular culture, especially in films and television. In fact, twenty-first century Spanish cinema has displayed a renewed interest in the themes popularly associated with Brand Spain, such as tourism, gastronomy, sports, and the new socio-sexual values (Martínez-Expósito 2015). Meanwhile, as a consequence of the 2007 GFC, the popular echo turned mainly negative and critical of Brand Spain; for many it came to signify a strategy that seemed to serve only the interests of the elites. Popular views of Brand Spain after 2007 focused mainly on its inappropriateness, since the booming country it sought to promote no longer existed.

In many respects, Brand Spain became an iconic brand for the Spanish people. Indeed, any brand, whether commercial or national, can become a fetishised social icon, because all brands are capable of conferring meaning and identity upon users and consumers (Arvidson 2006). Yet some brands work at more subtle levels: for Douglas Holt, some brands are particularly successful in addressing asymmetries and contradictions between reality and the consumer's expectations (Holt 2004). According

---

[9] 'La 'Marca España' no es la imagen de España, pues se refiere sólo a la imagen económica y financiera. Por mucho que contamine a otras dimensiones, sobre todo a la política, y al revés, siguen existiendo otros activos de España que pueden no estar intoxicados (cultura, sociedad, etc.)' (Noya and Prado 2011).

to Holt's theory of cultural branding, iconic brands do not stop at providing consumers with meaning and identity. They operate in a different way, by identifying consumers' anxieties and convincingly suggesting solutions for them. This can only be achieved, according to Holt, through the representation of certain identity myths in fictional scenarios, far from the everyday life of the consumers. These myths contribute to relieve the social—or national—anxiety that consumers experience:

> Identity myths are useful fabrications that stitch back together otherwise damaging tears in the cultural fabric of the nation. In their everyday lives, people experience these tears as personal anxieties. Myths smooth over these tensions, helping people create purpose in their lives and cement their desired identity in place when it is under stress. (Holt 2004: 8)

Holt's first axiom refers to an iconic brand's capacity to identify a social anxiety and relieve it at an individual level. Some city brands in Spain seem to follow this principle. For example, Brand Barcelona succeeds in combining in a single coherent narrative the myths of Catalanness and cosmopolitanism. Such a comforting narrative was an effective antidote against the anxieties linked with parochial nationalism. At a national level, the successful popularisation of corporate and political discourses concerning Brand Spain suggests that the brand was able to address some collective anxieties concerning Spanishness. Provisionally, it is not difficult to point out three well-known anxieties: firstly, Spaniards' inferiority complex in the European context; secondly, the idea that the Spanish nation was a product of Franco's dictatorship; thirdly, the fear of Balkanisation. Brand Spain's promise of selling a competitive, modern, and efficient image of the country was probably a perfect antidote against such anxieties. Perhaps surprisingly, for the same promoters of Brand Spain, a broad cross-section of the Spanish public came to accept the idea that a positive image is good for the national self-esteem—not only for improving sales. It is in this sense that Brand Spain can be understood as an iconic brand.

As stated earlier, commercial cinema is one of the pillars on which the popular version of Brand Spain has been built. Holt recalls that iconic brands stage identity myths in fictional scenarios, and this is precisely how the cultural industries, including cinema, serve Brand Spain. The film industry's competence in coining images of the country for international circulation has been asserted frequently by Brand Spain and by the film industry itself. As eminent examples, Pedro Almodóvar was appointed Honorary Ambassador for Brand Spain in 2007, and Antonio Banderas was appointed in 2013.

For all its glossy packaging of a nation in the most favourable and positive ways that marketing allows, nation branding cannot escape its fundamental aporia—that of considering the nation as market. As a sophisticated tool of neoliberal capitalism, nation branding has been the subject of fundamental criticism from a cultural studies perspective (Kaneva 2011; Volcic and Andrejevic 2011). Firstly, if nation branding belongs with the economical superstructure, then it is part of the hegemonic powers that sustain today's advanced capitalism, which is intrinsically undemocratic. Secondly, nation branding refracts the principles of plurality and diversity: far from fighting stereotypes, brands reinforce them (Widler 2007: 148). Thirdly, nation branding is only possible in a globalised economy (Jansen 2008: 122), which renders unclear how to effect a fair distribution of its economic and symbolic gains. Fourthly, branding can very easily become an instrument of propaganda at the service of hegemonic powers (Kaneva 2007).

Institutional and social experiences of Brand Spain visibly influenced local and regional administrative bodies that later decided to adopt branding techniques for cities and autonomous communities. Such experiences are clearly indicative of the fragility of the branding paradigm: advocates speak of long-term strategies based on deeply held social values, and of permanent dialogue with the public. However, the experience of Brand Spain has shown that the brand holds up only as long as the country's image holds up at home. Thus, when Spain's image collapsed in 2007 together with its economic pride, the popularity of Brand Spain sank. Strong criticism in the post-crisis years led the central government of Spain to demote Brand Spain from an organising strategic policy to a promotional tactic in its 2014 Law of External Action.

COMEDY, PLAUSIBLE FICTION, AND FRIVOLITY

Returning to the idea that Brand Spain can be construed as an iconic brand, it is possible to read the *Ocho apellidos* saga as a fictional scenario in which the Brand's identity myths are lived out. This kind of reading is consistent with the films' unprecedented box office success in Spain. The films' fictional scenarios entered popular speech, with the expression 'eight surnames' (which in Peninsular Spanish refers to the two surnames of one's four grandparents) now commonly used to denote local or regional ancestry. Needless to say, the films generated their own spin-offs and merchandising. Indeed, together they have become a social phenomenon with an influence felt well beyond the limits of film consumption. As part of this development, the films soon became an advertising phenomenon of the kind that seeks to turn a product into something desirable—and also into a social trend. This strategy does not seek to build consumer loyalty towards the product or the brand; rather it seeks to generate a social behaviour that individual consumers may find difficult to avoid. After all, cultural products that successfully generate social trends have the potential to foster anxieties about social conformity. Furthermore, *Ocho apellidos* worked intermedially and intertextually: some of the seminal ideas pertaining to both films had already appeared in Basque and Catalan satirical television programmes. The television-cinema feedback loop works in such a way that the popularity of the story in each medium benefits the other.

Politically, the films have been received and interpreted as calculated interventions in two unrelated processes, namely: in ETA's 2011 ceasefire, and the sudden rise of the pro-independence movement in Catalonia since 2012. Both processes have caused significant changes in the political landscape, and in the composition of the parliaments of the Basque Country and Catalonia. Ideologically, the films' intervention is closely related to the debate on nationalism: a long-lasting discussion in Spain that has hardened into a set of vitriolic polarisations between nationalists and non-nationalists, and between advocates of the various nationalist movements that co-exist in the country. Each of these movements received Martinez Lázaro's films according to their own ideological principles. For some Basque and Catalan nationalist commentators, the films were little more than a regressive use of traditional regionalist humour; for some Madrid-based commentators, the films interfered in the political debate and sought to 'whitewash' radical nationalism.

The one aspect of the films that such comments have glossed over is their comical tone, which contrasts sharply with the much more severe tone traditionally used in political fiction. A more recent social phenomenon centred on ETA's terror campaign is the much acclaimed, award-winning novel *Patria* (2016) by Fernando Aramburu. The differences between Aramburu's socio-political drama and Martínez Lázaro's *Ocho apellidos* comedies could not be more striking. The films are light and fun, employing well-known comic tropes such as accidental love stories, happy

230 A. MARTÍNEZ-EXPÓSITO

endings, social and gender stereotypes, one-line jokes, and the like. Aramburu's novel is a dark fictional recreation that delves into complex characters and situations, and deploys sophisticated narrative resources such as perspectivism, multiple temporalities, and polyphonic narrative. Unlike the novel, which urges the reader to solemnly assess the ethics of a dysfunctional and broken society, the films comfort the viewer with positive ideas, including the end of terrorism, the possibility of a peaceful coexistence, and the promise of civilised dialogue across cultures.

The key difference is, of course, genre. The use of comedic genres in films that thematise cultural differences is common in politically stable contexts. Recent European cases include *Bienvenue chez les Ch'tis* (Dany Boon, 2008), as well as *Benvenuti al Sud* (2010 dir. Luca Miniero), and its sequel *Benvenuti al Nord* (2012). In the Spanish case, however, the cultural differences between the Basque Country, Catalonia, and Andalusia have become amplified into political and ideological differences grave enough to have generated terror campaigns and political assassinations. Although ETA declared a unilateral and permanent ceasefire in 2011, none of the political conflicts seems to have been overcome.

As such, it remains somewhat puzzling that Martínez Lázaro's two popular *Ocho apellidos* films enlist comedy to address the issue of cultural differences in a post-violence and pre-independent context. Why risk what Aristotle described as lack of *decorum* by dealing with such serious matters in a light way? Most commentators have pointed to the films' genre as the apparent cause of their success. In an industry where it is customary to consume the themes of nationalist, terrorist, ideological debate and linguistic and cultural differences in severe, sometimes even dramatic or tragic tones, a mere change of genre is sufficient to shock or otherwise unsettle viewer's expectations. Television political satires *Vaya semanita* (Basque ETB) and *Polònia* (Catalonia's TV3) have used these techniques for years with remarkable success. Martínez Lázaro's films do the same at the Spanish national level. Comedy is highly popular because it fosters empathy with the viewer through the use of humour and other positive emotions. Branding strategies and election campaigns make abundant use of comedic tropes; it is widely appreciated that comedy is the preferred genre for persuasion. Furthermore, comedy appeals to the externalisation and communication of feelings, eschewing introspection; it is uncommon to find in comedies examples of psychological introspection or detailed analyses of character's motivations. Instead, comedies tend towards psychological oversimplification by using typical characters, stereotypes, and clichés that allow the viewer a fast and effective understanding. The complexity of comedy it is often found in the plot—in the twists and unexpected turns of the argument. In sum, popularity, persuasion, and simplification are three chief reasons why genre is key to understanding Martínez Lázaro's nationalist comedies.[10]

Structured as a diptych, *Ocho apellidos vascos* and *Ocho apellidos catalanes* work as two different parts of the same story. In the second or Catalan part, the plot revolves around a great masquerade in which each character has the sole objective of making Roser (Pau's grandmother) believe that the world is different from reality. As outlined above, Roser's family and the whole town acts as if Catalonia were already an independent country. This narrative turn obviously invokes the famous second part of Miguel de Cervantes' classic Spanish novel *Don Quixote de la Mancha*: every single character actively colludes to help Roser (*à la* Don Quixote) live out her dream, in this case the dream of Catalonia's independence. Her 'achieved utopia' allows the other characters, as well as the viewer, to experience the effects of bringing a dream to life. Whether in the novel or the film, so as to participate in the masquerade, most characters develop double identities (the real and the performed), which in turn make possible discussion of existential and ethical matters. The tremendous dramatic potential of mirror-like effects, however, is realised very differently in both texts: the anodyne superficiality of *Ocho apellidos catalanes* contrasts markedly with the literary and philosophical depth of Cervantes' achievement.

The theme of the wedding, an almost mandatory subplot in the romantic comedy genre, has a strong presence in both *Ocho apellidos* films. The heterosexual wedding ceremony, either religious (*Ocho apellidos vascos*) or civil (*Ocho apellidos catalanes*), creates a dramatic tension through the ceremonial exchange of questions and answers that functions as narrative climax. The frivolity of this approach raises several sociocultural questions—for example, the question of the degree to which the theme of the romantic wedding still bears any resemblance to current social practices in Spain, where religious wedding ceremonies now represent a shrinking minority. Along the same lines, there arises the question of why these films, while

---

[10] Unfortunately, most commentators who have addressed this subject have tended to reduce the debate about comedy to remarks on the role of humour. Certainly humour is a key resource in these films, but as a focus for analysis it does not cover some of the issues relative to comedy that this chapter is concerned with—and surely leaves out the question of decorum.

apparently questioning social stereotypes, seem to take seriously the literal wording of formal wedding vows, as if the bride's 'yes' or 'no' had any legal weight whatsoever. More broadly, the theme of the heterosexual wedding seems to add little to films that, arguably, seek to explore alternative models of masculinity (Martínez-Expósito 2017).

'What if … ?'. Testing possible scenarios is a main trait of utopian genres, science fiction, post-apocalyptic world narratives, and political and historical fictions. These genres share an ontological commonality: reality is modified in a plausible way, which does not break with the rules of verisimilitude. Once the viewer consents to participate in this hypothetical discourse, willingly suspending disbelief, such stories can introduce all kinds of modification regarding any state of reality from which distance is sought. Thus this kind of fiction is only limited by a need to respect the integrity of the baseline reality that serves as the reference point for the creation of the fictional world. Unlike *Don Quixote*, *Ocho apellidos catalanes* does not seek to explore such limitation. In other words, if Martínez Lázaro had decided in any way to question the baseline reality—the reality of the regionalised Spain that generates stereotypes and clichéd narratives—the viewer's interest would immediately wane: the film would become an implausible fiction; the element of social ghoulishness (a by-product of the friction between reality and alternative reality) would disappear. Above all, the atmosphere of frivolity would be lost. Implausible fiction cannot be frivolous, since it has no possible effects on reality. Only a fiction firmly anchored in the real can be frivolous, and frivolity becomes possible precisely when the intervention on the real is carried out from the ethics of fiction—and not from the ethics of reality.

The foregoing proposes, then, a definition of the frivolous in narrative terms: a frivolous story is one that reflects reality, pretending to act on it but without coming to accept that reality has its own norms. A frivolous story aspires to transform reality by imposing rules that are alien to it because they exist only in the fiction of history. In turn, this narrative definition makes possible the observation that self-absorbed, solipsistic, and frivolous stories which have managed to modify the world according to their own criteria tend to be described as sacred texts, or self-fulfilling prophecies.

Martinez Lázaro's nationalist comedies of 2014 and 2015 would have gone unnoticed in the history of Spanish cinema had it not been for their unexpected box office success. Is this social phenomenon emblematic of a frivolous popular culture, perhaps excessively influenced by overheated

FRIVOLITY AND PLACE BRANDING IN MARTÍNEZ LÁZARO'S 'NATIONALIST... 233

and tense media, but unable to give voice to rational and complex discourses? Jean-François Lyotard has warned of the risks of simplifying representations of an increasingly complex world. The indignation of the so-called 15M movement (the anti-austerity movement in Spain) was precisely a sign of resistance to the simplification of a culture that had been creating an impression of ease and clarity while reality became less and less transparent. Contemporary sycophantic populisms are, among other things, a frivolous response to a complex reality: a hastened response that seeks to modify reality without truly having attempted to grasp its nuanced, multifaceted, and often paradoxical nature.

Ironically, press reviews of Martínez Lázaro's films published in the Basque *arbertzale* and Catalan pro-independence newspapers underlined the Spanish director's frivolity when reducing Basque and Catalan culture into stereotypes. The frivolity of using stereotypes to examine complex problems is only comparable to the narcissism of the small differences (Buse and Triana-Toribio 2015) that Sigmund Freud observed between neighbouring cultures as an expression of an ego-affirming anxiety. Frivolity and narcissism can certainly become strategies of resistance as well as defence mechanisms in a globalised world. Ultimately, however, the success of the *Ocho apellidos* saga demonstrates that in the transition from the nation-as-brand to the nation-as-a-frivolous-story, audiences seem to have lost their capacity to understand what must be resisted. Perhaps inadvertently, it also demonstrates the need to understand better the cultural dynamics that nurture and support frivolous politics in times of indignation and political disengagement.

BIBLIOGRAPHY

Anholt, Simon. 2007. *Competitive Identity: The New Brand Management for Nations, Cities and Regions*. New York: Palgrave.

Anholt, Simon. 2010. *Places: Identity, Image and Reputation*. New York: Palgrave.

Aramburu, Fernando. 2016. *Patria*. Barcelona: Tusquets.

Aronczyk, Melissa. 2013. *Branding the Nation: The Global Business of National Identity*. New York: Oxford University Press.

Arvidson, Adam. 2006. *Brands: Meaning and Value in Media Culture*. London and New York: Routledge.

Boletín informativo. 2015. Películas, recaudaciones, espectadores. Ministerio de Educación, Cultura y Deporte, Instituto de la Cinematografía y de las Artes Audiovisuales (Madrid). http://www.mecd.gob.es/cultura-mecd/dms/mecd/cultura-mecd/areas-cultura/cine/mc/anuario-cine/ano-2015/Boletin-2015.pdf

Buse, Peter and Núria Triana-Toribio. 2015. *Ocho apellidos vascos* and the Comedy of Minor Differences. *Romance Quarterly* 62 (4): 229–241.

Chesters, Graeme and Ian Welsh. 2006. *Complexity and Social Movements: Multitudes at the Edge of Chaos*. London: Routledge.

Chislett, William. 2008. *Spain: Going Places. Economic, Political and Social Progress 1975–2008*. Madrid: Telefónica.

Derrida, Jacques. 1980. *The Archeology of the Frivolous: Reading Condillac*. Trans. John. P. Leavey. Pittsburg: Duquesne University Press.

Guillén, Mauro. 2005. *The Rise of Spanish Multinationals: European Business in the Global Economy*. New York: Cambridge University Press.

Heidegger, Martin. 1956. *Zur Seinsfrage*. Frankfurt-am-Main: Klostermann.

Holt, Douglas. 2004. *How Brands Become Icons: The Principles of Cultural Branding*. Boston: Harvard Business School Press.

Jansen, Sue C. 2008. Designer Nations: Neo-liberal Nation Branding. Brand Estonia. *Social Identities* 14 (1): 121–142.

Kaneva, Nadia. 2007. Meet the New Europeans: EU Accession and the Branding of Bulgaria. *Advertising & Society Review* 8 (4). https://doi.org/10.1353/asr.2007.0051.

Kaneva, Nadia. 2011. Nation Branding: Toward an Agenda for Critical Research. *International Journal of Communication* 5: 117–141.

Liáñez Andrades, R. and M.C. Puche Ruiz. 2016. Cinema, paesaggio e turismo 'andaluzadas': La Spagna andalusizzata, patrimonio retroproiettato. *Il capitale culturale*. Supplementi 4: 379–391.

Martínez-Expósito, Alfredo. 2015. *Cuestión de imagen: Cine y Marca España*. Vigo: Academia del Hispanismo.

Martínez-Expósito, Alfredo. 2017. Hegemonic Masculinities and Staged Authenticity in *Ocho apellidos vascos* (2014). In *The Dynamics of Masculinity in Contemporary Spain*, ed. L. Ryan and A. Corbalán. London and New York: Routledge, 229–243.

Martínez Pastor, Esther and Miguel Ángel Nicolás Ojeda. 2014. The Construction of Tourist Space by Public Administration and Institutional Communication: The Image of the Brand Andalucia as a Tourist Destination. *Journal of Promotion Management* 20 (2): 181–199.

Miguel, Amando de. 1972. *España, marca registrada*. Barcelona: Kairós.

Noya, Javier. 2003. *La nueva etapa de la marca España*. Madrid: Real Instituto Elcano de Estudios Internacionales y Estratégicos.

Noya, Javier and Fernando Prado. 2011. *¿Cuánto ha empeorado la imagen de España?* Madrid: Real Instituto Elcano de Estudios Internacionales y Estratégicos.

Urry, John. 1990. *The Tourist Gaze: Leisure and Travel in Contemporary Societies*. London: Sage.

Volcic, Zala and Mark Andrejevic. 2011. Nation Branding in the Era of Commercial Nationalism. *International Journal of Communication* 5: 598–618.

Widler, Janine. 2007. Nation Branding: With Pride Against Prejudice. *Place Branding and Public Diplomacy* 3(2): 144–150.

CHAPTER 12

After the Crisis: Europe and Nationhood in Twenty-First-Century Portuguese Cinema

Mariana Liz

Ten years after the start of the financial crisis that has shaped much of the first two decades of the twenty-first century, a general narrative on crisis and austerity, bailouts and recoveries, even if told from different perspectives and by a number of different actors, has started to be consolidated. According to this general narrative, a property-led financial crisis hits the USA in 2007 and is followed by a euro-zone debt crisis in 2008; austerity is imposed in a series of European countries from 2010; a 'rescue package' is 'offered' to Greece in 2010, followed by a 'bailout' to Portugal in 2011 and the 'rescue' of Spanish banks in 2012; and by 2014, there are some signs of improvement. In Portugal, such signs include the end of the three-year agreement between the Portuguese government and the *troika* (the European Commission, the European Central Bank and the International Monetary Fund) in 2014; the unexpected results of the 2015 general election and the innovative government solution found since 2016[1]; the reversal of a series of austerity measures, and, by 2017, the first

[1] The most voted for party in the Portuguese national elections in 2015 was the centre-right PSD (Partido Social Democrata), with 36% of the votes. However, PSD did not obtain

M. Liz (✉)
Instituto de Ciências Sociais, Universidade de Lisboa, Lisboa, Portugal
e-mail: mariana.liz@ics.ulisboa.pt

© The Author(s) 2018
J. Harvey (ed.), *Nationalism in Contemporary Western European Cinema*, Palgrave European Film and Media Studies,
https://doi.org/10.1007/978-3-319-73667-9_12

235

news pieces on the country's successful recovery, even if far from the economic and social health experienced prior to 2007 (OECD 2017).

As a story now apparently close to its end, and as a narrative spanning approximately ten years, 'the crisis' begins to emerge more clearly as an event with a longer history than first assumed. Understandings thereof are increasingly tied to the development of capitalism and neoliberalism (Harvey 2010), of Europeanisation and globalisation (Habermas 2012), and of modernity and postmodernity (Bauman and Bordoni 2014). Arguing for the importance of studying the crisis within specific contexts and adding to the analyses focused on the crisis and austerity in Portugal in this ten-year period as social, political and cultural facts (Santos 2012; Freire et al. 2015; Leone 2016), this chapter uses the contemporary crisis to explore visions of nationhood in twenty-first-century Portuguese cinema. On the one hand, it suggests twenty-first-century Portugal, as well as its national cinema, cannot be dissociated from the idea of, and indeed the reality, of the 2007–2017 crisis. On the other, it argues for the importance of placing the notion of crisis, and this particular decade of crisis, in time and in space, understanding it as a phenomenon with a history and a geography that go further back than 2007 and beyond Portugal's boundaries.

My analysis considers both the changing notions of Portugal, Portuguese culture and Portuguese cinema in the past two decades, and the extent to which, through economic, political and social indicators, the country, its culture and cinema have changed. As such, it discusses the link between visions of Portuguese nationhood in the twenty-first century, particularly since 2007, and conceptions of periphery, smallness and nostalgia developing within cinema. As the examination of an auteur and a popular film will show, a cinematic engagement with political and cultural ideas of Portugal and the crisis suggests new conceptions of Europe and globalisation are emerging. These carry significant implications for the definition of Portuguese nationhood in the twenty-first century.

a majority. As a result, the second most voted for party, PS (Partido Socialista), on the centre-left, with 32% of the votes, signed an agreement with the (other) two left parties with parliamentary representation in Portugal: the Communist Party, PCP (Partido Comunista Português), with 8% of the votes, and a party of Trotskyist affiliation, BE (Bloco de Esquerda), with 10% of the votes. This agreement meant PS was able to form a government, and to present to the Portuguese President a viable political programme. Neither PCP and BE are in government, but both parties have signed deals agreeing to vote in favour of some of the most important reforms proposed by PS, namely on social and fiscal policies aiming to reverse austerity. For more on this, see Freire and Santana Pereira (2016) and, in English, Finn (2017).

Portugal and Nationhood in the Twenty-First Century

For Boaventura de Sousa Santos, 'since the fifteenth century, Portugal has existed, as a bundle of social representations, in two zones or time-spaces simultaneously: the European zone and the colonial zone' (2011: 403). These two 'zones' carry significant cultural implications. It is in the face of Europe (more precisely, of the European Union [EU] in this particular historical period) and in the face of Portugal's former colonies, particularly in Africa, that ideas of Portuguese nationhood have been constructed since the last decades of the twentieth century. The relationship between Portugal and Europe, as well as between Portugal and its former colonies, was also transformed by the crisis. This chapter is focused on Portugal's relationship with Europe, not least because the link between Portugal and Europe, and particularly between Portugal and the EU, is the one most obviously challenged during the euro-zone crisis.

The period in which this analysis is centred tells a circular story about the country's support for European integration, from suspicion towards the EU to wide support for this political project, and once again back to mistrust. Portugal's accession to the EU (EC [European Communities] at the time) in 1986 was met with cautious enthusiasm by some, and even direct opposition by many, including the then prime minister Aníbal Cavaco Silva. Yet soon, and particularly once major structural funds were transferred from Brussels to Lisbon and the results of their impact were visible to the public eye (the most emblematic of these probably being the conclusion of the motorway linking the country's two main cities, Lisbon and Porto, in 1991), popular support for European integration grew considerably. Portugal's interest in Europe was essentially founded on the availability (and indeed the amount) of EU funds, which sustained a huge transformation of the country, in terms of infrastructures, political importance and culture. By 1991, according to Eurobarometer data, and only five years after Portugal's accession to the EU, over 80% of the Portuguese population thought Portugal had benefitted from joining the EC.[2]

The transition to the twenty-first century can be seen as the honeymoon phase in the relationship between Portugal and the EU. The 1990s

---

[2] All Eurobarometer survey reports are available online. The 1991 Spring wave (Standard Eurobarometer 35) can be accessed at http://ec.europa.eu/commfrontoffice/publicopinion/archives/eb/eb35/eb35_en.pdf (21 June 2017).

238 M. LIZ

were Portugal's most European years. By that time, national authorities were involved in a huge public relations campaign that aimed to show a new image of a modern and successful country that could overcome the perception of a retrograde Portugal. The hosting of high-profile international events such as the world exhibition Expo'98 and the football competition Euro 2004 are key examples of this turn of the century and turn of the millennium effort. This is despite the fact that, according to Soares, these events actually,

> fostered the idea of a country concerned mostly with its foreign image, which was able to spend millions on superfluous buildings, such as football stadiums or useless railway stations, instead of investing in crucial areas for economic growth, like education, research and development. (2007: 466)

Soares echoes here the voices of a number of critics opposing the realisation of these events in Portugal. While Portugal's membership of the EU was seen as undoubtedly positive not just by the politicians in charge, but also, as testified by the Eurobarometer survey cited above, by the majority of the Portuguese population, as the European integration process moved forward, criticism emerged from different corners of Portuguese society. Europe and the EU were seen as either promoters of a necessary and beneficial modernisation, or as imposers of an unstructured opening to capitalism and globalisation. Such visions have implications for the notion of nationhood in Portugal too: the country has either been perceived to be a new, developed nation, or one losing its sovereignty and unique character, as its economic development is undermined and its culture becomes diluted into the engulfing wave of globalisation.

Portugal enters the twenty-first century as one of the most pro-European nations within the EU: approval for EU membership stays very strong until 2001, never falling below 67% (Lobo 2003: 102). Yet, as perhaps predicted, and in a reversal of the shift to strong approval for the Portuguese membership of the EU in the mid-1980s, there is, since 2010, a sharp decline: from this year onwards, and at least until 2013, just over 40% of Portuguese people say being part of the EU is a good thing (Magalhães 2013: 50). The austerity measures imposed on the nation no doubt have an impact on perceptions of Europe and of European institutions. But the direction the European integration process was taking had already started to be questioned by a growing number of people.

AFTER THE CRISIS: EUROPE AND NATIONHOOD... 239

Two key films challenged the European modernisation of the country even before 'crisis' was a buzzword. *Slightly Smaller Than Indiana* (Daniel Blaufuks, 2006), for instance, is a personal documentary structured as a road movie, in which the director travels through Portugal to show what he identifies as several instances of abuse suffered by the landscape, which had been torn apart by construction projects, many of them unfinished. Shot just after the end of Euro 2004, the film depicts a country on the brink of collapse, as a place where speed and progress appear as illusions waiting to be shattered. In a similar vein, *Ruínas/Ruins* (Manuel Mozos, 2009) is a non-narrative essay-film that features a series of empty spaces, editing together shots of abandoned settings of domestic and industrial character, privately and publicly owned, in rural and urban areas across the country. These are brought together by fragments of direct but non-diegetic sound (because it is edited off-sync with the images), as well as dissonant electronic music. These add to the eerie depiction of contemporary Portugal as a timeworn and disconnected country embarking on a process of precarious development. As these two film examples show, the crisis should not be taken as a moment of exception, but rather be understood as the almost obvious consequence of a particular economic and financial history—and one which draws on and simultaneously helps to shape the cultural history of the nation.

The vision of Europe as the geopolitical entity guaranteeing the future and modernity of the nation—as well as the acceptance that this is necessarily positive—might be justified by what Sousa Santos (2012) identifies as a teleological narrative of progress that is dominant in Western nations, and that Portugal's elites hoped to replicate. According to this narrative, nations can only get better in time, which means the past is constantly retro-shaped as being 'backwards'—the exception being the re-telling and re-appropriation of history in a logic of consumption, as in the expansion of the so-called heritage industry (Samuel 1994). This (positive) association between European Portugal and an idea of future might also explain why, since the turn to Europe, Portuguese culture can be seen to operate an almost complete cut with the past. This meant, for instance, that the colonial issue was only seldom addressed since EU membership was attained (Sabine 2009), to the point that, at the time of writing in 2017, there are still calls for the country to be 'decolonised' (Câncio 2017).

Whereas the dictatorial New State regime had built its core ideology around the idea of a glorious past (this vision is for instance depicted in the documentary *Fantasia Lusitana/Lusitania Illusion* [João Canijo, 2010]),

240   M. LIZ

democratic European Portugal was almost entirely constructed as a nation with a promising present and an improving future. This political and cultural narrative repressed, as much as possible, historical facts and the association with any sense of (past) backwardness, and therefore left unattended pressing issues in contemporary Portuguese society, including immigration, racism and social inequality (Medeiros 2015; Vale de Almeida 2016). If Europe represented modernity and the future, the break with Europe, once the crisis hit, led to a renewed interest in the past. Problematically, though, as this history and past had been left untouched, the history-based conception of twenty-first-century Portugal has easily turned into an utterly faint, when not distorted, vision of what the nation had been. The politics of *Tabu* (Miguel Gomes, 2012), for instance—probably the most international of recent Portuguese films—were extensively debated, as the film has been received as a parody of colonial times, and one that, because it has been seen as humorous, fails to make a clear political point, being seen as indifferent at best, and uncritical at worst (Faulkner 2015; Medeiros 2016; Owen 2016; Nagib 2017).

The different stages and modes of the relationship Portugal establishes with Europe hint at two possible definitions of nationhood in this country—or, as argued below, at two seemingly contrasting but deeply interconnected visions of nationhood. One, related to modernity and progress, is particularly embraced at the start of the 1990s, but denied after 2008, and especially since austerity hits the country, meaning conceptions of the nation might no longer be safely based on positive, transnational visions of a European future. The other, structured on a discourse promoting the vision of a confident past, and emerging particularly after 2014, offers a distorted and problematically nostalgic vision of history. These two aspects of Portuguese nationhood in the twenty-first century have also been explored by contemporary Portuguese cinema. On the one hand, recent Portuguese films gaining recognition abroad focus on the present, explicitly alluding to Portugal's financial crisis, and re-thinking the nation's connection to the European space. These include Miguel Gomes's *As Mil e Uma Noites/Arabian Nights* (2015) trilogy, Marco Martins's *São Jorge/ Saint George* (2017), Teresa Villaverde's *Colo* (2017) and Pedro Pinho's *A Fábrica de Nada/The Nothing Factory* (2017). On the other, a significant number of Portuguese films released since the *troika* years, and particularly successful with national audiences, show an emotional attachment to the past. This is for instance the case of *Os Maias: Cenas da Vida Romântica/ The Maias: Scenes from Romantic Life* (João Botelho 2014), *O Pátio das*

Cantigas (Leonel Vieira 2015), *Cartas da Guerra/Letters from War* (Ivo Ferreira 2016) and *Jacinta* (Jorge Paixão da Costa 2017).

The extent to which visions of nationhood are articulated in twenty-first-century Portuguese cinema is not just a matter of representation and political engagement, but also of aesthetics. While Portugal might not be depicted in film as a European nation, what is problematised in cinematic terms is the expression of the distance and/or proximity to Europe, which stands for ideas of modernity, progress and potential standardisation. Similarly, the films examined here are not about the Portuguese colonies or the nation's (post)colonial status—even if studies on the empire, memory and post-colonialism are a rich field of enquiry in contemporary Portuguese cinema (see for instance Owen and Klobucka 2014; Vieira 2015; Faulkner and Liz 2016). Rather, they express a sense of longing for and an emotional attachment to the past that at the same time denounces a worrying ignorance about that same past. *Saint George* and *O Pátio das Cantigas* are examined in greater detail below as vivid illustrations of the complex relationship between Portugal and Europe in the transition to the twenty-first century: as utopian promise and present disappointment in the first case, and as growing nostalgia for a specific vision of the past of country and its cinema, as well as, potentially, a coherent national identity, in the second.

Portuguese Cinema, Crisis and Austerity: The Case of *Saint George*[3]

Despite a lack of data and the limited number of systematic studies on these issues, an article mapping cultural policy in Portugal suggests the impact of austerity has been particularly felt in the cultural sector (Garcia et al. 2016). As part of the measures imposed by the *troika*, the Portuguese government suspended all funds to the audiovisual sector in 2012. This was an acutely hard blow to a sector historically perceived to be in a permanent state of crisis. Labelled the 'year zero' of Portuguese cinema, 2012 was a year of protests by all those involved in the film business in Portugal (Kourelou et al. 2014). It was also the year that saw the creation of a new Cinema Law, which aimed to boost film production in Portugal, bringing

---

[3] I am thankful to the film's production company, Filmes do Tejo II, for giving me access to *Saint George*; the film was no longer in theatres and not yet commercially available at the time of writing.

242 M. LIZ

together funds from the public and private sectors (Pinazza 2017). However, the law was never fully implemented, which has led producers, filmmakers and others, to argue 'Portuguese cinema is in danger' (Gomes and Urbano 2013). The tension between professional associations and the government has been growing since 2012. More recently, in February 2017, Portuguese filmmakers staged another protest at the Berlin Film Festival against this Cinema Law.

The episodes described here highlight the extent to which cinema has become an important field to challenge notions of crisis and practices of austerity. Like the national cinemas of other European countries affected by austerity, Portuguese cinema has also been producing films *about* the crisis, and directly depicting its effects. Iván Villarmea Álvarez, for instance, has been mapping what he calls the 'cinema of austerity' in Portugal and Spain. He divides this cinema into two main phases: the first, between 2007 and 2010, is composed of a number of films that seem to preclude the crisis, and are almost premonitions of events to come (*Slightly Smaller than Indiana* and *Ruins* would be included in this category); the second, between 2011 and 2017, comprises films that instead address head-on the consequences of austerity. The films that are part of this second phase tell the stories of people who lost their jobs, their houses and/or their families, and often turn to violence as a result. Frequently allegorical, these films 'show an atomised mosaic of society, waiting for the wind to change' (Villarmea Álvarez 2017; my translation).

Marco Martins's *Saint George*, released in 2016, is one of the films listed by Villarmea Álvarez as an example of this second phase of the cinema of austerity. Seen by over 40,000 viewers, *Saint George* was one of the most watched national films in Portugal in 2017.[4] Undoubtedly the film's topic and extensive promotion campaign, which stressed its realistic depiction of Portugal in 2011, contributed to this success. Portuguese Prime Minister António Costa, for instance, alluding to the aim of his government to reverse austerity, tweeted his support for the film, describing it as 'a hard punch of reality that inspires us to continue with change'. Following art cinema conventions, the film constructs a realistic portrait of the nation. But *Saint George* also comes to occupy the terrain of what could be defined as a 'middlebrow cinema' (Faulkner 2016)—it is a quality film,

---

[4] Statistics as of July 2017, the time of writing. Box office numbers are made available by ICA—the Portuguese Institute of Cinema—on their webpage: http://www.ica-ip.pt/en/downloads/box-office/ (accessed 3 July 2017).

with high production values, and it is appealing to audiences. It not only adopts a plot-based narrative, telling an essentially straightforward story, it also casts a popular Portuguese star, Nuno Lopes, who has worked in numerous film, TV and theatre productions at national and international level. Nuno Lopes also significantly won a Best Actor award at the Venice Film Festival for his performance in *Saint George*—a prize he dedicated to the 'heroes' who had been fighting the 'dragon of austerity'.[5]

In *Saint George*, Jorge (played by Nuno Lopes) is an unemployed factory worker and an amateur boxer. The link between boxing and life under austerity is drawn clearly from the start: *Saint George* is a film about someone forced against the ropes. Similar to films such as Ken Loach's *I, Daniel Blake* (2016), *Saint George* is a vivid account of austerity, which leaves viewers with a feeling of impotence and anger. As the narrative progresses, it might look like there is a way out (of claustrophobic housing, isolated neighbourhoods, and a life of poverty)—but despite Jorge's endeavours, there never really is a solution to his problems. In an attempt to stop his wife Susana (Mariana Nunes), from whom he is separated, leaving for Brazil with their son Nelson (David Semedo), Jorge finds a job as a debt collector. He hopes to save some money and to be able to rent a flat for his family, away from his abusive father, with whom he currently lives. His experience in the boxing world and his athletic physique frame him as the perfect candidate for a job that essentially requires the ability to physically intimidate those owing money to his employers. However, Jorge is neither comfortable in his role nor able to actually turn to violence. His characterisation as a boxer who is unable to be violent is one of the many contradictions that the film explores, anchored in a story of richness and poverty, coldness and sensitivity, modernity and backwardness.

The film's beginning is very similar to the scenes in *Ruins*. *Saint George*'s very first sequence edits together a series of empty, abandoned or destroyed locations, including office buildings, advertising boards and restaurants (Fig. 12.1). Unlike *Ruins*, however, *Saint George* then goes on to explore not so much these spaces and the meaning they convey, but rather the lives that are caught in between such emptiness. The neighbourhoods where Jorge and Susana live, for instance, could also be first recognised as abandoned spaces or locations under construction. By placing the narrative in such spaces, the film highlights smallness, periphery and confinement, as

---

[5] Lopes's acceptance speech can be watched in full at https://www.youtube.com/watch?v=L9aZ7m7-UNo (accessed 2 August 2017).

Fig. 12.1 Empty, abandoned and destroyed locations mark the initial sequence of *Saint George*

well as a tension between a sense of belonging and exclusion, as its key themes—themes that effectively mirror Portugal's historical relationship to Europe.

Two main stylistic devices support the film's themes. Firstly, camerawork privileges close ups. Framing is often tight and claustrophobic, focusing on details and inserts. When shots are wider, people and objects block what viewers should actually be looking at. This sort of strategy, that at the same time highlights and delimits the different layers of each image, contributes to the notion that obstacles are omnipresent: in the shot, in the narrative and in Jorge's life. The constant tight framing highlights the sense of entrapment that defines Jorge's character—in the boxing ring, in his professional life and in his personal life. From the start, Jorge is reduced to insignificance by framing choices that see people and buildings constrain him. He sleeps in a small room with his son Nelson, in a two-bedroom flat that seems to house at least six people; he prepares for a fight in a packed dressing room, and is then cornered in a limited boxing ring; he talks to Susana between parked buses, his body and face out of focus, oppressed between the urgency of what he has to say and the weakness of the promises he can make (Fig. 12.2).

Fig. 12.2 Jorge being physically and visually oppressed in *Saint George*

Secondly, sound tends to hide what characters say—either by capturing and making particularly prominent background noises, which obscure dialogue, or by voicing things viewers do not actually see, as in the case of the scene where a group of men discuss unemployment benefits at Jorge's father's flat. Sound is crucial for the feelings of simultaneous entrapment and intimacy developed in *Saint George*. The film begins with a sigh by the main character. He is then heard praying to Saint George, while training. Whispered prayers to Saint George and repeated mantras can be heard throughout: for instance, Jorge's coach keeps telling him, 'You are great' [*Tu és grande*], in a bid to offer encouragement just before the start of another fight. Dialogue is constant, but not consequential. Questions are repeated but no answers are presented. Speaking to Susana, Jorge insists: 'Why don't you come back home?', but she shrugs and moves away rather than explaining her reasons. The closeness and disconnectedness of the sound matches the tightness of the image, in a claustrophobic narrative that moves slowly, but not far.

Portuguese critic Vasco Câmara (2017) argues the film draws from different cinematic genres, namely melodrama and film noir. The film's emotional density seems to derive from a melodramatic streak already present in Martins's previous work (see for instance his film *Alice* [2005], also starring Lopes as its protagonist), whereas from film noir, *Saint George* inherits a characteristic anxiety about identity and disorientation. Fragmentation emerges not just as a main topic of the film, but also as a key feature of contemporary society. This is an issue that is made worse by austerity policies and that is well expressed in the construction of Jorge as a character. He is a father, but cannot perform that role fully because he needs money. He is strong but sensitive, unable to hit people when working for the debt-collecting agency, and unable to win fights, supposedly for being too soft. A sense of disorientation is vividly mirrored in the expression of the film's protagonist. Despite being at the centre of the narrative, and having an overwhelming percentage of screen time in relation to other characters, Jorge spends most of the film on the side-lines, watching events as they unfold, learning and copying behaviours and attitudes, trying to understand what is happening and what his role might be. For instance, when he starts working for the debt collectors, he travels in the back seat of the car, and his facial expression seems to indicate his puzzlement and a sense of being lost, as if he is wondering why he is there and what he is meant to be doing. In fact, it is when he travels alone for the first time (now in the driver's seat), that the narrative takes a turn for the worst: Jorge is not in control of his life, and when he tries to take the initiative, he is seemingly punished by structural hierarchies.

This is a realist, almost documental film. Yet, *Saint George* appears as a realist film about illusion. Boxing is framed as an illusion (for instance, when, clearly bruised after losing another fight, Jorge tells his son he is not hurt), and wealth is framed as an illusion (as represented by the character of the chef at a Michelin-starred, modern and bright-lit restaurant who cannot pay his debts), in the same way that the work of the debt collectors is fictitious (they don't actually help anyone, and the actions they carry out are illegal). While *Saint George* is absolutely centred on the present, the film suggests there has been a better past. It hints at the glorious old times of boxing, for instance, by referencing Fernando Lopes's *Belarmino* (1964), a classic of Portuguese cinema on a similar topic. The very recent past is also framed as more positive than the present: the scenes at the restaurant and in the city centre hint at periods of development, even if these are only in the film to show the viewer what no longer exists. The sense of illusion is heightened by the fact that this is Martins's first digitally shot feature film. But mostly, this is the story of the illusion that were the *troika* years in Portugal (a topic also explored in Miguel Gomes's *Arabian Nights*)—the illusion of being helped while in reality people's lives were made worse,

AFTER THE CRISIS: EUROPE AND NATIONHOOD... 247

which mirrors the illusion of progress European integration projected into peripheral nations like Portugal from the mid-1980s onwards.

Despite the clear denouncing of such issues, the film is not entirely political. Race and gender, embodied by Nelson and Susana, for instance, are ignored. *Saint George* is centred on yet another white male protagonist, who is seen dealing with his frustration and impotence. The film can be read as a problem of postmodern complexity, as it pinpoints fragmentation and acceleration as crucial setbacks for a potentially European Portugal. Europe appears in *Saint George* as an imposer of inequality. In turn, Portugal is here seen at its least European, as it is no longer a nation characterised by progress and development. *Saint George* is a film about the illusion that is/was European Portugal–a nation for which unsustainable development meant significant gaps in progress and high levels of inequality became very quickly evident across its disintegrating society.

NOSTALGIA FOR NATION AND FILM IN *O PÁTIO DAS CANTIGAS*

Whereas *Saint George* denounces the unequal, uneven and inconstant relationship between Portugal and Europe, focusing its narrative and form on ideas of fragmentation, decadence and entrapment, *O Pátio das Cantigas* is constructed on a sense of nostalgia. *O Pátio das Cantigas* is also set in the present, but its production and promotion history, as well as its narrative, stress the vision of a Lisbon and a country that is continuously compared to those of a supposed 'golden age'. The present, officially emerging as post-austerity, is not entirely bleak. However, promises of a better future are constructed on very thin foundations. As such, *O Pátio das Cantigas* offers important insight into how Portugal's relationship to Europe shifted during and immediately after the *troika* years, as well as into Portugal's supposed new positioning in a globalised world.

O Pátio das Cantigas is a remake of the homonymous film directed by Francisco Ribeiro in 1942. The 1942 version of *O Pátio das Cantigas* is regarded as the quintessential example of the *comédia à portuguesa*, a popular genre in the 1940s (Shaw 2003). These comedies were known for drawing a simile between neighbourhood life and family life. Accordingly, *O Pátio das Cantigas* tells the story of a group of people living in a small area of Lisbon's historical centre. Focused particularly on the love triangle formed by Rosa (Dânia Neto), a modest, hard-working, and very attractive young woman; Evaristo (Miguel Guilherme), a widower in his fifties, owner of a gourmet grocer's; and Narciso (César Mourão), a bon vivant in his thirties working as a tourist guide and *tuk tuk* driver, the film tells the story of this particular community through episodes relating to these and other characters—their partners, children and other relatives, all somehow attached to this area of the city.

This remake of *O Pátio das Cantigas* was part of an initiative supported by public television channel RTP. In addition to this version of *O Pátio das Cantigas*, remakes were also made of *A Canção de Lisboa* (Pedro Varela, 2016) and *O Leão da Estrela* (Leonel Vieira, 2015), originally shot in 1933 and 1947, respectively, and considered some of the finest examples of the *comédia à portuguesa*. The films were also screened as a mini-series on RTP after their commercial premiere on the big screen. The fact that these remakes were produced and then watched by so many people in the years after austerity was implemented in Portugal shows an apparent shift in society to a desire to look back not with negativism (to a recent past) but with nostalgia (to a more ancient history), as well as a willingness to engage in escapism through entertainment.

O Pátio das Cantigas is particularly relevant for the discussion about cinema and nationhood in contemporary Portugal as it was an incomparable hit with national audiences. This is the most watched Portuguese film ever, with 607,976 viewers, also according to data published by ICA. In the same way that *Saint George* is a film about austerity and can simultaneously be seen as a product of the austerity imposed in the film industry, *O Pátio das Cantigas* aimed to launch a debate not just about Portugal's supposed greatness, but also about the vitality of Portuguese cinema. However, unlike the international success many art films, including, to an extent, *Saint George*, were achieving in film festivals around the globe, Portuguese popular films, often derided by critics, might achieve impressive box office figures, but they almost always fail to recover their production costs, as the Portuguese internal market is too small and there are limited opportunities for export.

The debate about the possibility of existence and development of a popular Portuguese cinema, which would be different from the 'international' Portuguese cinema praised abroad, but is rarely seen by national audiences (Liz 2017), has a long history. The 1940s films have been particularly important for those defending the existence of a commercial cinema in Portugal, as they are perceived to be role models for audience interest. By contrast, many filmmakers and critics have repeatedly dismissed not just the endeavour to produce 'films that please audiences', but also the notion that the films of the 1940s would be the appropriate standard to build on. João Mário Grilo, for instance, argues these films 'contribute, in a relevant way, to the resurrection of a nightmare of the ill-famed "national cinema", which defined the isolation of the Portuguese cinematic production in the 1930s and 1940s' (2006: 31; my translation). The national specificity of Portuguese popular cinema is one the most contentious issues being raised, particularly in the era of transnational, global and world cinema(s), as well as increasing globalisation.

As Lisa Shaw (2003) notes, the *comédia à portuguesa* films of the 1930s and 1940s were cheap to produce. By contrast, the new version of *O Pátio das Cantigas* had a budget of €1 million, a spectacular figure for a film 'industry' (if the term can even be applied) the size of the Portuguese film sector. With high production values, the film's ensemble cast included a long-list of mostly TV stars, in addition to a series of cameos by media and entertainment personalities. With the aim to modernise not just the plot (see below) but also the looks of the film, the remake was characterised by a series of over-lit images and fast-paced sequences, often accompanied by popular songs. With plenty of colour, light and catchy music, the film has a shiny and glossy look, not too dissimilar from the one adopted by the French directors of the *cinéma du look*. However, unlike the films of Luc Besson and others in the 1980s, *O Pátio das Cantigas* seems to lack the supposed postmodern irony generally attributed to their French counterparts (see for instance Vincendeau 1995). The lack of distancing (Oliveira 2015), as the feature that would allow *O Pátio das Cantigas* to think the present in relation to the past, is precisely what compromises the film's vision of nationhood imposed on the viewer.

O Pátio das Cantigas both pays homage to 1940s Portuguese cinema and departs from its canon. A number of sequences in the new version are direct retakes from the original film, such as the scene in which Evaristo, having drunk a bit too much, wanders through the neighbourhood, stumbling, and has a lengthy conversation with a street lamp. The opening sequence is also essentially a shot-by-shot retake of the original film, although there are a number of important differences in terms of aesthetics and narrative focus. In the 1942 film, we see the opening credits over images of traditional buildings and small neighbourhoods in the historic centre of Lisbon. The 2015 version of *O Pátio das Cantigas* opens with the film's credits appearing on bunting, hanging from similar houses and blocks of flats. The flags in evidence at the centre of the screen are the colour of the Portuguese flag (green, yellow, red) and the music, first

250   M. LIZ

cheerful, quickly turns melancholic, echoing fado tunes and guitar cords. The sequence immediately marks the 'Portugueseness' of the film and its narrative, alluding not just to the flag, but also to fado—the perceived Portuguese 'national song' (Holton 2006)—in a nationalist streak that seems inherited from the 1940s dictatorial censorship, but feels out of place (and out of time) well into the twenty-first century.

A key difference between the two films is the age of the protagonists. Almost every character from the original film is here replaced by a much younger avatar. The exception is Evaristo, who stays the same age. Hence, in the 2015 version of *O Pátio das Cantigas* Evaristo is even more clearly marked as different from the rest of the ensemble, in terms of his cultural references and taste. For instance, in a knowing reference to the film's status as a remake, Rosa tells Evaristo: 'I love the way you speak; it is as if you are a character in those old movies.' This is despite the fact that, as discussed in greater detail below, *O Pátio das Cantigas* modernises all characters, even Evaristo, in terms of their jobs and pastimes.

The film is at the same time contemporary and full of anachronisms— particularly with regards to gender representations. *O Pátio das Cantigas* actualises age, but not gender equality. As was the case in the original film, the opening sequence of the 2015 remake presents us with a narrator. Looking down at Rosa as she leaves her flat to go to work in the morning, the narrator presents the protagonists of the film—most of them, the same as in the 1942 version. His POV shot shows Rosa from above, as he claims that she is 'so hot' (Fig. 12.3). The camera then moves to street level to show mostly her legs, as she walks past in a tight dress and high heels—a shot that will be replicated when we have the introduction of another young, female character, Amália. It is not just the women that are reduced to being 'desirable' or 'undesirable' (as in the case of Amália's sister, Susana, apparently overweight). Men too are presented drinking beer around a table, discussing how hot women are, but not expressing any other interests or concerns.

O Pátio das Cantigas fails to address a series of political and historical issues, such as the link between the nation and the 'other', here expressed in terms of the relationships established between Portuguese and foreign characters. The issue of language becomes prominent as, for instance, Rufino speaks '*Portuñol*' (a mixture of Portuguese and Spanish) to Spanish clients in his hostel, and Evaristo tries to teach his employees, João Magrinho and Alfredo, French, so they are able to communicate with tourists entering the shop. At the same time, however, Evaristo keeps

Fig. 12.3 Rosa as seen by the narrator in *O Pátio das Cantigas*

mispronouncing the name of the Indian neighbour in his building (a character the 2015 version adds to the original plot, perhaps in an attempt to show a more cosmopolitan side to contemporary Lisbon). He also complains about the smell of curry (this neighbour runs a family restaurant nearby), and the film is not clear on whether the sought reaction is laughter, and indeed if the viewer is being prompted to laugh with him or laugh at his racism.[6]

O Pátio das Cantigas expresses a tension between an economic openness towards the foreign and a clear stance against the erosion of Portuguese culture. In another scene, characters come together to approve the potential hiring of a foreign DJ for the neighbourhood's traditional, annual street party. This scene predicts a real-life situation, since, in 2017, the organising commission of *Santos Populares*[7] in Alfama (one of the most

---

[6] A vivid debate developed in Portugal in September 2017 as new research presented the nation as one of the most racist countries in Europe. According to data published by the European Social Survey, over 52% of people in Portugal believe people from different ethnic groups are born with less intelligence; 54% see specific ethnic groups and cultures as intrinsically better than others. As argued above, in relation to the need to de-colonize the country (Câncio 2017), this is a pressing issue, which stems in part from the inability of successive Portuguese governments to promote a serious and wide discussion about the nation's colonial history. For more on this, see for instance Gorjão Henriques 2017.

[7] Santos Populares are annual street parties taking place in several locations across Lisbon in June, in honour of Saint Anthony, the city's patron.

252   M. LIZ

depicted neighbourhoods in the films of the *comédia à portuguesa*) prohibited foreign music, and only Portuguese songs could be heard. Similarly, in a completely different way from the original film, the 2015 version of *O Pátio das Cantigas* frames its final sequence around a Bollywood dance number performed by the film's protagonists, although this sequence is never justified in terms of plot or narrative. There is a referencing of 'other' cultures in the film, unlike in the *comédia à portuguesa*, but in *O Pátio das Cantigas* this appears as not more than a vague nod to a dense and complex issue.

Shaw (2003) argues the *comédia à portuguesa* films were de-historicised and de-politicised. To an extent, the remake too seems as if it could take place in any time period, ignoring pressing issues in contemporary society. As an exercise in cinematic remaking, *O Pátio das Cantigas* could be seen as a fantasy. If *Saint George* was a reality about (the European) fantasy, *O Pátio das Cantigas* is a fantasy about (Portuguese) reality. The film is grounded in the present, but its narrative relates something that does not exist. As is commonly accepted (Shaw 2003; Baptista 2010), the Lisbon and the nation constructed in the *comédia à portuguesa* was one essentially built for the censored cinema permitted during the dictatorship. As such, this new version of *O Pátio das Cantigas* presents not just an imagined contemporary Portugal, but also significantly, one based on an imagined past nation.

Although perhaps not as explicitly as in *Saint George*, the crisis is also present in *O Pátio das Cantigas*. For instance, Rosa complains about low sales in the shoe shop where she works. However, unlike in *Saint George*, the crisis appears here as a motor for change, rather than immobility: the film presents a number of opportunities arising from variations in the economy, namely in the tourism sector. As mentioned, Narciso is a *tuk tuk* driver; his brother Rufino runs a hostel (where Rosa also works part time); Evaristo's old grocery (in the 1942 film) is transformed, in 2015, into a gourmet grocery, where 'typical' produce is sold to tourists. Tradition is here re-branded as heritage for consumption, as tourism appears as an alternative form of globalisation—one that these characters can control—that projects a positive view of their city and their country on international media.

This issue is all the more pressing as Lisbon is increasingly becoming an international mass tourism destination. Trendy magazine *Monocle* suggested in 2015 that nostalgia saved Lisbon (Tuck 2015). However, the jury is still out on whether nostalgia is in fact saving or destroying the city, as we witness a simultaneous devaluation of cultural heritage and the growing value of material heritage, with housing prices sky-rocketing in the city's historical centre. The risks associated with gentrification are all the more worrying in the case of Lisbon as, since Sandra Marques Pereira argued at a conference on the future of the city in April 2017, Lisbon is actually unable to compete in the housing and tourism global market due to the structural poverty of country. For instance, in the past few years, even though Lisbon developed steadily, the middle classes never made it to the city centre, which was instead immediately taken over by foreign investors (Marques Pereira 2017).

To an extent, *O Pátio das Cantigas* is part of this gentrification process. It attempts to bank on the commercial value of heritage (namely the memory people had, not of actually watching these films, now too old, but of hearing comments about these films as 'good' examples of Portuguese cinema), while ignoring the symbolic value of the original examples of *comédia à portuguesa*: not only were these films not very good, but they were also complicit with the New State dictatorial regime. The idea of nationhood expressed in *O Pátio das Cantigas* ignores the dictatorial and colonialist past, even if it insists on a global positioning for the nation that draws on a vision of a supposed valuable past. In doing so, the film projects a homogenising notion of nationhood, which problematically ignores difference at many levels.

Conclusion

The two films examined here allow us to think about twenty-first century Portugal through the 2007–2017 crisis and its history. They have austerity as a referent, but point to a longer history of Portugal and its cinema, highlighting as key themes associated with visions of Portuguese nationhood exclusion and periphery, tourism and nostalgia. Austerity and gentrification become two sides of the same coin. The first shows just how much the crisis hurt people in Portugal, not so much because it was a moment of exception, but because it highlighted what many had noticed before, particularly in terms of growing inequality. The second seems to suggest a new beginning is possible, but while referencing the past and tradition as positive indicators, also seems to bypass this more recent history, that actually is not as nice as it appears to be. The Europe that emerges in these films is unstable because built on weak bases. It is a Europe of inequality, unjustified and uncontrolled speed, as well as shallow progress. Globalisation too,

254   M. LIZ

often ignoring Portugal's previous role in the world, and the historical responsibility the nation should carry forward because of it, is built on glossy and superficial visions of what an engagement with the other might be. Thinking about Portuguese nationhood in the twenty-first century in relation to the crisis proves particularly fruitful. This crisis, however, has a history, and this history is not yet over. Beyond the weak models these films seem to highlight (a Europe of inequality through speedy development and then austerity, or a Europe of inequality through speedy development based on tourism and nostalgia), alternative visions of nationhood in Portugal will hopefully develop in coming years of the twenty-first century.

Acknowledgement This research was kindly supported by FCT grant SFRH/BPD/115319/2016.

BIBLIOGRAPHY

Baptista, Tiago. 2010. Nationally Correct: The Invention of Portuguese Cinema *P: Portuguese Cultural Studies* 3: 3–18.
Bauman, Zygmunt and Carlo Bordoni. 2014. *State of Crisis*. Cambridge: Polity.
Câmara, Vasco. 2017. Portugal troika: uma violenta fábrica de histórias. *Público*, 16 March. Online. https://www.publico.pt/2017/03/16/culturaipsilon/noticia/sao-jorge-1765263. Accessed 6 July 2017.
Câncio, Fernanda. 2017. É preciso descolonizar Portugal! *DN*, 13 June. Online. http://www.dn.pt/portugal/interior/racismo-e-preciso-descolonizar-portugal-8558961.html. Accessed 2 October 2017.
Faulkner, Sally. 2015. Cinephilia and the Unrepresentable in Miguel Gomes "Tabu (2012)". *Bulletin of Spanish Studies* 92 (3): 341–360.
Faulkner, Sally Ed. 2016. *Middlebrow Cinema*. London and New York: Routledge.
Faulkner, Sally and Mariana Liz. 2016. Introduction – Portuguese Film: Colony, Postcolony, Memory. *Journal of Romance Studies* 16 (2): 1–11.
Finn, Daniel. 2017. Luso-Anomalies (Editorial). *New Left Review* 106: 5–32. https://newleftreview.org/II/106/daniel-finn-luso-anomalies. Accessed 2 October 2017.
Freire, André and José Santana-Pereira. 2016. The Portuguese National Election of 2015: From Austerity to the Fall of the Portuguese "Berlin Wall". *Pôle Sud* 44 (1): 143–152.
Freire, André, Marco Lisi and José Manuel Leite Viegas. Ed. 2015. *Crise Económica, Políticas de Austeridade e Representação Política*, Lisbon: Assembleia da República – Divisão de edições.
Garcia, José Luís, João Teixeira Lopes, Teresa Duarte Martinho, José Soares Neves, Rui Telmo Gomes and Vera Borges. 2016. Mapping Cultural Policy in

AFTER THE CRISIS: EUROPE AND NATIONHOOD... 255

Portugal: From Incentives to Crisis. *International Journal of Cultural Policy.* DOI: https://doi.org/10.1080/10286632.2016.1248950.

Gomes, Miguel e Luís Urbano. 2013. Cinema português: o alarme soa. *Público*, 31 August. http://publico.pt/opiniao/jornal/cinema-portugues-o-alarme-soa-27028888 Accessed 20 November 2014.

Gorjão Henriques, Joana. 2017. Portugal é dos países da Europa que mais manifestam racismo. *Público*, 2 September. Online https://www.publico. pt/2017/09/02/sociedade/entrevista/portugal-e-dos-paises-da-europa-que-mais-manifesta-racismo-1783934. Accessed 2 October 2017.

Grilo, João Mário. 2006. *O Cinema da Não-Ilusão.* Lisbon: Livros Horizonte.

Habermas, Jürgen. 2012. *The Crisis of the European Union: A Response.* Trans. Cronin, Ciaran. Cambridge: Polity.

Harvey, David. 2010. *The Enigma of Capital and the Crises of Capitalism.* Oxford: Oxford University Press.

Holton, Kimberly da Costa. 2006. Fado Historiography: Old Myths and New Frontiers. *P: Portuguese Cultural Studies* 0: 1–17.

Kourelou, Olga, Mariana Liz and Belén Vidal. 2014. Crisis and Creativity: The New Cinemas of Portugal, Greece and Spain. *New Cinemas* 12 (1 and 2): 133–151.

Leone, Carlos. 2016. *Crise e Crises em Portugal.* Lisbon: Fundação Francisco Manuel dos Santos.

Liz, Mariana. 2017. Introduction: Framing the Global Appeal of Contemporary Portuguese Cinema. In *Portugal's Global Cinema: Industry, History and Culture.* Ed. Mariana Liz, London: I.B. Tauris: 1–14.

Lobo, Marina Costa. 2003. Portuguese Attitudes Towards EU Membership: Social and Political Perspectives. *South European Society and Politics.* 8 (1–2): 97–118.

Magalhães, Pedro. 2013. A política – nem Portugal nem Europa. *20 Anos de Opinião Pública em Portugal e na Europa*, Lisbon: Fundação Francisco Manuel dos Santos: 47–52.

Marques Pereira, Sandra. 2017. Lisboom: a cidade renascida no contexto da globalização, paper presented at the 'Lisboa: Que Futuro?' Conference, ISCTE-IUL, Lisbon, Portugal, 18/04/2017. https://www.youtube.com/watch?v=EZLeIZ-AoV0. Accessed 27 July 2017.

Medeiros, Paulo de. 2015. Prefácio: No fio da navalha. In *Portugal a lápis de cor – A Sul de uma pós-colonialidade.* Ed. Khan, Sheila. Coimbra: Almedina: 7–13.

Medeiros, Paulo de. 2016. Post-imperial Nostalgia and Miguel Gomes's *Tabu. Interventions* 18 (2): 203–216.

Nagib, Lúcia. 2017. Colonialism as Fantastic Realism in *Tabu.* In *Portugal's Global Cinema: Industry, History and Culture.* Ed. Mariana Liz. London: I.B. Tauris: 223–238.

OECD. 2017. Portugal: Successful Reforms have Underpinned Economic Recovery. http://www.oecd.org/portugal/portugal-successful-reforms-have-underpinned-economic-recovery.htm. Accessed 2 June 2017.

Oliveira, Luís Miguel. 2015. Não temos cá disto. *Público*. 29 July. https://www.publico.pt/2015/07/29/culturaipsilon/noticia/nao-temos-ca-disto-1703564. Accessed 2 August 2017.

Owen, Hilary. 2016. Filming Ethnographic Portugal: Miguel Gomes and the Last Taboo. *Journal of Romance Studies* 16(2): 58-75.

Owen, Hilary and Anna Klobucka. Ed. 2014. *Gender, Empire, and Postcolony: Luso-Afro-Brazilian Intersections*. Basingstoke: Palgrave Macmillan.

Pinazza, Natália. 2017. Luso-Brazilian Co-Productions: Rescue and Expansion. In *Portugal's Global Cinema: Industry, History and Culture*. Ed. Mariana Liz. London: I.B. Tauris: 239–255.

Sabine, Mark. 2009. Killing (and) Nostalgia: Testimony and the Image of Empire in Margarida Cardoso's A Costa dos Murmúrios. In *The Genres of Post-conflict Testimonies*. Ed. Cristina Demaria and Macdonald Daly. Nottingham: Critical, Cultural and Communications Press: 249–276.

Samuel, Raphael. 1994. *Theatres of Memory: Past and Present in Contemporary Culture*, London: Verso.

Shaw, Lisa. 2003. Portuguese Musical Comedies from the 1940s and 1950s and the Transatlantic Connection. *International Journal of Iberian Studies* 15 (3): 153–166.

Soares, António Goucha. 2007. Portugal and the European Union: The Ups and Downs in 20 Years of Membership. *Perspectives on European Politics and Society* 8 (4): 460–475.

Sousa Santos, Boaventura de. 2011. Tales of Being and Not Being. In *Portuguese Literary and Cultural Studies* 19 and 20: 399–444.

Sousa Santos, Boaventura de. 2012. *Portugal: Ensaio contra a Autoflagelação*. Coimbra: Almedina.

Tuck, Andrew. 2015. How Nostalgia Saved Lisbon. *Monocle, The Urbanist*. https://monocle.com/radio/shows/the-urbanist/185/. Accessed 2 August 2017.

Vale de Almeida, Miguel. 2016. Multicultural: Stories of Political and Cultural (Mis)understandings. In *Transcultural Identity Constructions in a Changing World*. Ed. Irene Gilsenan Nordin, Chatarina Edefeldt, Lung-Lung Hu, Herbert Johnson and André Blanc. Frankfurt: Peter Lang: 23–32.

Vieira, Patrícia. 2015. Imperial Remains: Post-colonialism in Portuguese Literature and Cinema. *Portuguese Journal of Social Science* 14 (3): 275–286.

Villarmea Álvarez, Iván. 2017. Rostros y Espacios de la Austeridad en los Cines Ibéricos (2007–2016). *Iberoamericana. América Latina – España – Portugal* 17 (66). Forthcoming.

Vincendeau, Ginette. 1995. Cinéma du look. In *Encyclopedia of European Cinema*. Ed. Ginette Vincendeau. London: BFI: 82–83.

INDEX[1]

A

Accented cinema, 99, 148
Austerity, 3, 235, 236, 236n1, 238, 240–248, 253, 254

B

Beckett, Samuel, 28
Beur, 64n3, 65n4, 71–73, 71n10, 72n11, 72n15, 77, 77n18, 100
Border politics, 2, 3
Branding, 215–233
Brexit, 4, 13, 31, 45, 59–60
Buñuel, Luis, 27

C

Charlie Hebdo, 13, 63, 85–94
Class and architecture/built environment, 24, 47, 53, 182, 223
Class and cultural identity, 21–30
Class and landscape, 31–34

Colonialism, 68, 71, 74, 104, 108, 110, 237, 239, 240, 251n6
Contemporaneity, 2–5, 8, 10–14, 18n1, 20, 22, 34, 44, 45, 58, 65, 81, 85, 87, 90, 92–94, 105, 109, 118, 119, 126, 147, 152, 170, 173, 175, 186, 195n7, 196, 198, 204, 205, 209, 216, 233, 236, 239–241, 246, 248, 250–252
Crisis, 3, 14, 17, 32, 63, 64n2, 64n3, 65, 81, 87, 88, 92, 126, 145, 146, 151, 169, 173, 175–178, 180, 182, 183, 225, 235–254

D

Diaspora, 101, 106, 108, 112, 113, 116
Documentary, 13, 35, 44, 65, 73, 86–91, 93, 94, 98, 99, 114, 195, 196, 196n8, 199, 204n15, 205, 239

---

[1] Note: Page numbers followed by 'n' refer to notes.

© The Author(s) 2018
J. Harvey (ed.), *Nationalism in Contemporary Western European Cinema*, Palgrave European Film and Media Studies,
https://doi.org/10.1007/978-3-319-73667-9

258 INDEX

E
European Union (EU), 1, 4, 31, 59, 103, 145, 148, 162, 169, 192, 193, 198, 206, 237–239

F
Far-right, 1, 4, 69, 103, 191–211, 216
Fascism, 5, 6, 171

G
Genre, 11, 25, 101, 108, 113, 135, 147, 220n2, 230–232, 245, 247
Gentrification, 44, 253
Globalisation, 20, 21, 32, 38n20, 147, 149–151, 157, 176, 236, 238, 249, 252, 253
Godard, Jean-Luc, 26, 27
Grenfell Tower, 32, 43, 45, 59

H
Heritage, 2, 11, 68, 70, 71, 100, 108, 113, 147, 204, 239, 252, 253
Heterotopia, 156
Hip-hop, 100–106, 109–111, 113, 116, 119
Humour, 27, 86, 89, 90, 133, 135–137, 135n7, 136n8, 142, 217, 219, 220, 229, 230, 231n10
Hybridity, 2, 5, 111, 115, 153, 164

I
Integration, 17, 31n13, 66, 67, 77n18, 78, 79, 101, 118, 119, 130, 138, 149, 158, 195, 237, 238, 247

Interculturalism, 149–151, 155, 159, 161, 166
Irony, 27, 93, 142, 249
Islamophobia, 3, 64, 78, 194

L
Liberalism, 12, 18–20, 22, 31n13, 33, 34, 36, 38, 103, 139, 224

M
Multiculturalism, 136, 142, 150

N
National identity, 6–11, 13, 14, 38, 70, 105, 146, 170, 172–174, 185, 186, 192, 241
National image, 224
Nazism, 85, 94, 192, 193, 206
Neoliberalism, 4, 194, 224, 228, 236
Nostalgia, 1, 11–13, 22n5, 170, 172, 173, 236, 241, 247–254

P
Pastiche, 101, 110–112
Patriotism, 2, 171
Populism, 1, 3, 5, 8, 137, 192, 194, 216, 233
Propaganda, 12, 88, 228

R
Racism, 3, 13, 79, 103, 106, 108, 127, 128n4, 131, 135–138, 142, 166, 195, 198, 240, 251
Realism, 23, 35–37, 107, 109, 194

Refugees, 4, 17, 74, 145, 151, 169, 170, 173, 193, 195, 204
Religion, 66, 67, 76, 90, 102
Riots, 65, 68, 69, 99, 166
Rural, the, 11, 50, 179, 204, 220, 221, 223, 239

S
Satire, 86, 93, 125–143, 206n18, 209, 210, 230
Socialism, 12, 18–22, 33, 34, 181, 192, 193, 206
Social realism, 36, 108, 195

T
Temporality, 58, 88, 90, 109, 173, 175, 182, 186, 230
Territorialisation, 14, 20, 183
Terrorism, 17, 63, 65, 81, 88, 90, 97, 103, 230

Tourism, 222–224, 222n4, 226, 252–254
Transnationalism, 99–101, 147–149, 151

U
Urban, the, 24, 64n3, 105, 115–117, 141, 220, 239

V
Violence, 11, 45, 48, 54, 65n4, 67, 69, 72–77, 81, 104, 108, 109, 111, 112, 118, 141, 146, 165, 166, 195, 195n7, 201, 204n14, 205, 208, 210, 242, 243

X
Xenophobia, 3, 8, 146, 149, 194, 200, 204, 206

CPSIA information can be obtained
at www.ICGtesting.com
Printed in the USA
LVHW07*1938230618
581693LV00008B/27/P